INNOVATION IN
ORGANIZATIONS

INNOVATION IN ORGANIZATIONS

Innovation Adoption in School Organizations

Richard L. Daft &
Selwyn W. Becker

Elsevier · New York

NEW YORK · OXFORD

Elsevier North-Holland, Inc.
52 Vanderbilt Avenue, New York, New York 10017

Distributors outside the United States and Canada:

Thomond Books
(A Division of Elsevier/North-Holland Scientific Publishers, Ltd)
P.O. Box 85
Limerick, Ireland

©1978 by Elsevier North-Holland, Inc.

Library of Congress Cataloging in Publication Data

Daft, Richard L
    Innovation in organizations: Innovation adoption in school organizations

    First published under title: The innovative organization.
    Bibliography: p.
    Includes Index.
    1. High schools — United States — Administration.   I. Becker, Selwyn William,
    1929- joint author. II. Title.
LB2822.D3 1978b   373.1'2'00973   78-15711
ISBN 0-444-00286-3

Manufactured in the United States

To Kathy

—R.L.D.

To two superb teachers: JB and SS

—S.W.B.

Contents

Preface

It is our hope that this book will be useful to a diverse set of readers, from basic organization researchers to anyone who has felt frustration because of an organization's inability or unwillingness to innovate. We will first elaborate a relatively traditional view of how organizations innovate, and then we will present data from a longitudinal study of 13 high school districts to support that view. Our data reveal that the process of innovation is much more complex and multifaceted than we originally hypothesized, so we use the "garbage can model" of decision making as a vehicle to develop a new (and perhaps innovative) model of organizational innovation.

The data, data analysis, and new model of organizational innovation should primarily interest researchers and teachers of organization theory and organizational behavior. It should be of particular interest to those researchers and teachers who focus on the educational organization.

If the data analysis is taken more or less for granted, the remaining material can provide many insights into organizational functioning and should interest all who desire to create or be part of an innovative organization. This material should be of special interest to educational administrators, school board members, superintendents and principals, and to the people they administer—teachers and other support staff. The summaries of chapters 3, 4, and 5, and the final chapter in the book, on how to build a innovative educational organization, are directed to them.

Thanks are due to many people and organizations who aided us in our work. First, of course, we thank the many school board members, high school superintendents, principals, and curriculum coordinators for their cooperation and time. We also thank the Graduate School of Business, University of Chicago, and NASA for financial support, NASA for the 1965 portion of the study with grant NSG-730. Many of our colleagues gave freely of their advice and insights and we thank them. In particular, Gordon Antelman helped with the statistical analysis and Edward Petersen with the garbage can model. We are also indebted, beyond our citations, to *Innovations and Organizations*, by Gerald Zaltman, Robert Duncan and Jonny Holbek, wherein a great deal of recent literature on innovation has been consolidated.

THE
Innovative
Organization

1

Organizational Innovation

Bureaucracies are not innovative. At least, that's what almost everyone seems to think. Bureaucracy, as described by Weber, has functional specialization, rules and procedures, and hierarchy of authority. And as pointed out by many, it also has dysfunctions, conformity, and little or no room for personal growth.[1] The adoption of an innovation by an organization frequently results from a rethinking of old ways of doing things, a process that might require nonconformity in thinking and perhaps skepticism or disregard for existing rules and procedures. Nonconformity and disregard for rules are anathema to the bureaucracy; hence bureaucracies are supposedly not receptive to innovations. And performance supposedly suffers. Zaltman, Duncan, and Holbek recently reviewed much of the literature on innovations and organizations and cited at least eight works in which it was either predicted or empirically observed that bureaucracy (or bureaucratic variables) and innovation were negatively related.[2] A similar position was taken by Bennis: "Organizations are complex goal seeking units. . . . They must also accomplish the secondary tasks of (1) maintaining the internal system and coordinating the 'human side of enterprise' . . . and (2) adapting to and shaping the external environment—here called 'adaptability.' It is the requirement of adaptability to the environment which leads to the predicted demise of bureaucracy and the collapse of management as we know it now."[3]

Bennis's argument assumes rapidly changing environments, including the introduction of new tools and technologies. Organizational adaptation includes the adoption of the newer tools and technologies, a process we might consider organizational innovation. To Bennis and others the bureaucratic organization is much less likely to be innovative than some other, typically "looser," form of organization. Organization theorists are nearly unanimous in the view that bureaucracy means no innovation despite the fact that the empirical data are quite equivocal. As recently as 1966 Wilson was able to conclude that no organizational characteristics are consistently related either to innovation or lack of innovation.[4] Perhaps it might be relevant to ask the questions: *Are there conditions under which a bureaucracy innovates? Must a bureaucratic mechanism undergo change before innovations can be adopted? If so, how does one change a bureaucracy?* These are the most important of the questions to which this book is addressed. Before addressing the questions, however, we shall make more explicit what kind of organizational behavior we are investigating and why it is important to investigate that behavior.

ORGANIZATIONAL INNOVATIVENESS

Organizational innovation is usually defined as the adoption of a new idea or behavior by an organization. Innovation is very similar to change but is distinguishable by the criterion of newness. Innovation is the adoption of something new; change is the adoption of something different. Unfortunately, this simple distinction does not resolve the issue. There is considerable disagreement in the literature about what constitutes something new and thus, where to draw the line that separates innovation from change.

Becker and Whisler defined innovation as something new in relation to the organization's technological environment. They suggested that innovation is "the first or early use of an idea

4

by one of a set of organizations with similar goals."[5] Under this definition the adoption of an idea after it has been well established in other organizations would be considered change behavior rather than innovation.

Innovation has also been defined as the adoption of an idea or behavior that is new to the organization adopting it.[6] The idea can be either new or old with regard to other organizations so long as the idea has not previously been used by the adopting organization. The criterion of newness in this definition of innovation concerns the adopting organization's past experience rather than other organizations in the environment.

The competing definitions of innovation are actually related subsets of organizational change. Organizational change is the introduction into the organization of ideas or behavior that are different from those currently in use. Within this total set of change behaviors are those that have not previously been used by the organization and are thus considered new to it. Finally, within the set of behaviors new to the organization are those that can also be considered new to the group of organizations that share the same goals and technology.

This latter subset of organizational change, which is the behavior defined as innovation by Becker and Whisler, is the organizational behavior in which we are interested.[7] Adopted changes considered new to the organization's environment are innovations. Behavior that is new only to the adopting organization is organizational change.

Organizational change is an important area of study, but our interests are narrower. We want to identify the organizations that regularly risk early adoption of new ideas from the developing pool of these ideas and to identify some of the environmental and organizational conditions that underlie early adoption. The organizational attribute of frequent early adoption we will call *innovativeness*.

The distinction of innovation from change permits us to differentiate innovation from two other closely realted variables. Creativity, or organizational creativity, refers to the generation of new ideas, products, or technology. For us an innovative organization may be either creative or noncreative. The ideas that an innovative organization adopts can arise either inside or outside the adopting organization. The process of creation is conceptually independent of the process of organizational innovativeness.

The process of innovation is also independent of the implementation process, another important kind of organizational behavior. Once the decision is made to adopt an innovation, various strategies can be followed to induce organizational elements to accept and adapt to it. The process of implementation sequentially follows the decision to adopt and in that sense is not independent of the process of innovation adoption. However, the processes of adoption and implementation can be studied separately. Again, we are interested solely in the adoption of innovations.

Now that we have identified precisely what it is we are studying, the question of why to study it naturally arises. Can any meaningful contribution be made from studying the process of innovation? Wouldn't it make more sense to study how innovations affect production so that organization decision makers could use the findings? We don't deny that the effectiveness of innovations is another important area of study. But we feel that probing the process of innovation has equal benefit for decision makers. If we can unravel some of the cause-effect relationships that lead to innovation adoption, then organization administrators can use the findings to influence innovation. Whether an innovation enhances productivity is a separate problem. We will have achieved our goal if we can suggest how organizations should be designed and run in order to increase or decrease innovativeness. Decision makers can use our findings to include or exclude new developments depending upon the potential these developments have for performance.

At least since 1958, when March and Simon published their book on organization theory, the problem of organizational innovativeness has been prominent in the literature.[8] It has been prominent partly because of the view that rapidly changing environments require innovativeness by organizations if these organizations are to survive. Organizational survival seems to be one of the main reasons for the importance given to organizational innovativeness. This seems to be the case despite the fact that for March and Simon organizations are purposeful, decision-making mechanisms. When they and others write about what affects the innovation process, they consider the effects of slack resources (which seem relatively unrelated to goals) and distress situations where innovation is necessary for survival.[9]

We say survival is given major emphasis if we restrict our literature to that produced by psychologists, sociologists, and political scientists. If we include the literature of economists and economic historians, we find another important reason for studying innovativeness. The economists' sometimes implicit and sometimes explicit hypothesis is that an innovative firm gains a competitive advantage.[10]

The difference between innovating to survive and innovating to gain a competitive advantage may seem trivial in that survival in a competitive environment can imply gaining and maintaining a competitive advantage. However, we feel that there is a real and distinguishable difference between the two kinds of behavior. Innovating for purposes of survival implies innovating only in times of crisis or if other organizations functioning in the environment already have innovated or are about to innovate.[11] But it is clear that organizations in monopoly positions also innovate. The New York Port Authority has been characterized as innovative, and such a description could also have been applied to IBM over its history. In other words, organizations may innovate to survive, but they may also innovate as part of their strategy to gain a competitive advantage vis-à-vis their own goals. Even without competing organizations, that is, even without other organizations trying to achieve the same goal(s) in the same environment, organizations may innovate to make more money, to reduce ignorance, to increase knowledge, or to eradicate disease.

For-profit organizations have innovated in order to survive as well as to gain a competitive advantage. Manufacturers of steel adopting the oxygen furnace exemplify innovating in order to survive, while numerous examples of innovating to gain a competitive advantage could be drawn from the plastics or electronics industries. A not-for-profit hospital might adopt innovations in order to attract more physicians to its staff because its occupancy rate is so low it is in danger of closing, while another hospital might innovate merely because one of its physicians has built a new instrument to fight disease more efficiently. Similarly a high school may innovate because its students are in near revolt and teachers cannot be hired, while another high school may innovate in an attempt to decrease its dropout rate from 0.5 percent to 0 percent or to increase its graduates' college acceptance rate from 90 percent to 95 percent.

Organizations are complex goal-seeking units, and in the pursuit of those goals some firms may be innovative and others may not. And, we maintain, while some organizations may innovate merely in order to survive, most innovate in order to gain a comparative advantage, not just vis-à-vis other organizations but also to improve performance compared with their own previous success in goal achievement. In other words, innovativeness can be a rational strategy some organizations follow as a means of achieving their goals.

When we say organizations adopt innovations as a rational strategy to achieve organizational goals, we mean that the principal motive behind adoption is the desire to achieve goals. *We do not mean the innovation actually leads to goal achievement.* Innovation decisions are made under uncertainty, and some innovations may not work out. Neither does our use of rationality mean that organization decision makers use the rational decisionmaking approach taught in many management programs, that is, defining the problem, developing decision criteria, generating alternatives, assessing outcomes, and then making the decision using all the rational-analytic tools at the organization's disposal. A decision to innovate may be made on the basis of past experience or intuition, or simply to try it and see if it helps solve a problem. Consequently, the notion of rationality as we use it does not indicate how organizations go about making decisions or determine whether innovation decisions actually improve performance. Organizations are goal-seeking organisms, and they respond to events in the environment

8

in order to achieve goals. When an innovation is perceived to be the best alternative, the rational response would be to adopt it.

While this view is held primarily by economists, some other behavioral scientists also see innovation as part of a rational organizational strategy.[12] On the other hand, there are many other behavioral scientists who believe just the opposite.[13] Individuals and organizations are believed to resist change. People prefer the familiar, and stable behavior in organizations is a function of past experience, norms, and established interpersonal relationships. A desire for stability is believed to inhibit innovation and change, and intervention by an outside agent is often necessary to accomplish change.

Neither group's view is fully substantiated by empirical results. The problem, then, is to explain why, under norms of rationality, the few in a group of organizations that share a common technology adopt more quickly and more often the new ideas that are available to all. It is to be argued here that these differences can be explained along three dimensions: (1) the needs, or incentives, for innovation; (2) the mechanisms for bringing innovative alternatives into the decision-making process; and (3) the absence of organizational barriers to implementation.

NEED FOR INNOVATION

A need for change occurs when decisionmakers perceive that an existing procedure is inadequate and that a new procedure is desirable. It is the gap between actual performance and desired performance, or between actual procedures and desired procedures, that activates decision makers to consider adopting a new technique.

March and Simon stated that aspiration level tends to adjust to the level of achievement, and that in a steady state situation aspirations tend to rise slowly.[14] A similar point for the behavior of organizations was made by Thompson: "Under norms of rationality, organizations facing relatively stable task environments seek to demonstrate fitness for future action by demonstrating historical improvement."[15] Thus, unless turbulent conditions make the past meaningless, relatively successful as well as relatively unsuccessful organizations upgrade their aspirations and attempt to improve on past performance.

Gaps between aspiration and achievement arise as procedures become inadequate. Frequently, conditions that tend to make procedures obsolete and create needs for innovation stem from the organization's environment. For example, changes in the organization's technological environment, changing tastes for its output, increasingly high quality standards for its output, or information about new and better techniques developed elsewhere could create needs for new procedures. In such situations if organizations experience a gap between current and desired behavior they will attempt to eliminate or reduce the gap by adopting innovations.

It also seems reasonable that the persistence as well as frequency of needs will be related to the frequency of innovation adoption. A need that continues unsatisfied after new procedures are tried will continue to orient the organization toward new alternatives. Some organizations, for example, may experience unrelenting high uncertainty. A highly competitive environment, or a poor competitive position, or a very poor understanding of the cause-effect relationships in the production process are examples of needs that, under norms of rationality, should make organizations willing to innovate frequently.

Rational organizations do not act only in response to differences between achievement and aspiration. The serendipitous learning of new and better techniques will lead to their adoption as surely as their discovery through search. To improve performance, rational organizations will monitor their environments in order to anticipate new demands and to learn of new developments rather than just wait for a problem to hit. Thompson called this "opportunistic surveillance."[16]

Perhaps the word *incentive* describes better than *need* the reason organizations innovate. When there is promise of a better way to do things, the reward of improved efficiency is an incentive that is available to all organizations.

PROPOSITION 1: *Organizational innovativeness increases as the incentives for innovation increase.*

The incentives have to be identified, of course, before organizational innovativeness can be predicted. For one organization demands for increased output quality may provide the incentive to innovate; for another organization the incentive may arise from changing consumer tastes.

Assuming incentives are a motivating factor in innovation, proposition 1 may even help explain differences in the rates of technological development among industries. One might hypothesize that the average rate of innovation activity in an industry is a function of the incentives for innovation facing the individual organizations. Competitive organizations, on the average, would be hypothesized to be more innovative than non-competitive organizations because of greater needs, or incentives, for innovation as a way to survive and prosper.

If true, the proposition should be valid in for-profit as well as not-for-profit industries. It has been said there is more innovation in medicine than in education.[17] The value of medical advances to the society, or the believed uncertainty regarding the cause-effect relationships in medical treatment, or the difference between treatment outcomes and desires for treatment outcomes may be the incentives that help explain this difference.

Incentives alone are not enough to make an organization innovative. If they were, failing organizations would perhaps be the most innovative organizations. Needs or incentives for innovation must be accompanied by knowledge of the innovative alternatives and the ability to implement them.

INNOVATION ALTERNATIVES

The process of innovation is generally described as consisting of three essential steps, starting with the conception of an idea, which is then proposed and is finally adopted. It may seem trivial and obvious that failure at the early stages of the process guarantees failure to adopt. But the current rational models, except for Wilson, do not stress the steps prior to adoption. The knowledge of innovations is assumed to be equal for organizations, or else search behavior is expected to turn up the innovative alternatives.[18]

There is evidence to support the conclusion that although many innovations originate in the environment, search procedures are not the only mechanism through which organizations learn of new ideas. Myers and Marquis interviewed executives in 121 manufacturing firms about their organizations' most important innovations in recent years.[19] This produced detailed information on 567 product or process innovations. It was found that 77 percent of the innovations originated within the adopting firm. The remaining 23 percent were borrowed. Myers and Marquis concluded that a significant portion of the technological progress experienced by these manufacturing firms came from within the organization in the form of small, incremental innovations. They also concluded that these innovations contributed significantly to organizational success. Carter and Williams, and Utterback, supported the general direction of the Myers and Marquis findings.[20]

Whether from within or without, idea conception and proposal are necessary antecedents to adoption. To be an innovation leader, an organization is going to have to know about and consider ideas sooner than other organizations.

Rational organizational structures and processes that facilitate idea conception and proposal include the existence of boundary-spanning units charged with scanning the environment for new ideas; the existence of problem-solving units in the organization; the exposure of organization members to the technological environment via publications, personal exchanges, or information exchanges; the existence of procedures for proposing innovations; and rewards for proposing innovations. On the average, organizations geared toward creative activity and/or interaction activity with the technological environment can be expected to have more ideas in the system and more innovative alternatives to choose from. The increased awareness of new ideas may even increase the incentives to adopt these ideas by frequently making current procedures obsolete.

PROPOSITION 2: *Organizational innovativeness increases as the efficiency of the organizational mechanisms for developing innovative alternatives increases.*

It is difficult to say precisely how any given organization can most advantageously structure itself to develop innovative alternatives. There is no single process of innovation. Organizations sometimes create solutions to problems, or they search outside the organization, or a new idea may create the need for its adoption. Technological interdependence is probably great enough for all organizations that they must be in touch with developments in the environment in order to be an adoption leader. The specific mechanisms that will effectively generate innovation ideas and translate them into proposals will depend on the kind of organization, the division of labor, the goal orientations of its people, and its technological environment. It seems reasonable that those people charged with efficient functioning of the organization will more likely propose administrative innovations; those concerned with the organization's central function (the technical core) will propose technical innovations; and affecting both orientations are demands (incentives to innovate) from the client system and other environmental factors.

Thus we can see that various sorts of innovation proposals can be introduced into an organization. Some involve change of the organization itself, others in the way it achieves its goals. Further, any of these proposals can be more or less costly, more or less risky, or can represent relatively more or less organizational change. Whether these proposals are translated into adoptions depends partly on some intraorganizational characteristics we call enabler variables.

ENABLER VARIABLES

If the organization has incentives to innovate and has mechanisms through which innovation ideas are regularly available in the form of proposals, all that remains for an organization to be innovative are decisions in favor of adoption. A genuinely new innovation may entail certain risks or the outlay of certain expenditures. Appropriate facilities or special skills may be required. Even under norms of rationality an innovation has to "fit" the organization's ability to adopt it. The ability of the organization to afford the risk of early adoption and the cost of implementation, the existence of diverse facilities and personnel who can accommodate innovations, organizational growth, a favorable attitude on the part of administrators, and perhaps even the existence of special implementation procedures will all aid decisions in favor of adoption.

Those characteristics of the organization that tend to permit or facilitate the decision to adopt innovations are called enabler variables. Unlike incentives, which stem from the environment, and innovation ideas, which frequently originate in the environment, enabler variables are characteristics of the organization itself.

The notion of enabler variables helps explain why large, prosperous organizations are so often innovative. Large organizations have more complex and diverse facilities that will be compatible with a wide range of innovations. Innovations frequently cost money. Large organizations and organizations with surplus resources can better afford the risk and expense of trying new developments. Growth represents expansion; adding new parts to the organization offers an opportunity for the incorporation of the latest technological developments. A preference by decision makers for the innovative alternatives will also tend to increase the probability of a decision in favor of adoption.

PROPOSITION 3: *Organizational innovativeness increases as the presence of organizational characteristics enabling adoption increases.*

Important considerations for the enabling effect are the cost and risk of innovations proposed for adoption. The enabling function will be most crucial for innovations that are difficult to adopt. Most organizations that have incentives to innovate and have information-processing mechanisms can adopt innovations that are small and inexpensive. So if the concept of an enabling effect is valid, the presence of enabler variables should be most significant for the adoption of large, costly, relatively unproven ideas.

A study of hospitals by Kaluzny, Veney, and Gentry, and Myers and Marquis's study of for-profit organizations both support the important role of enabler variables.[21] Kaluzny, Veney, and Gentry found that the cosmopolitanism of administrators and the training of staff were very important to the adoption of low-risk innovations in hospitals. These variables represent the degree of professionalism and exposure of personnel to ideas. But for high-risk innovations structural variables, especially size, were important. Infusion of ideas was not enough. The structural characteristics became necessary to enable the adoption of risky innovations. Myers and Marquis found a similar effect for costly innovations. In three separate industries large firms adopted a greater proportion of expensive innovations than did small firms.

In sum, many of the organizational correlates of innovation discussed in the literature are believed to serve an enabling function (including lack of barriers) for innovation. Even with incentives and ideas for innovation the organization must be able to meet the requirements of implementation in order to complete adoption. This enabling function provides an additional explanation for why distressed or failing organizations are less likely to be innovative than successful ones. They are less likely to meet the requirements of adoption despite their pressing need for new procedures.

SUMMARY

It has been argued here that innovativeness is a patterned, predictable phenomenon that is governed by norms of rationality. The adoption of ideas new to the technological environment is hypothesized to be a consequence of three distinct influences—the incentives to innovate, the presence of innovative ideas as decision alternatives, and the ability of the organization to implement innovations. Most of the diverse findings in the innovation literature can be explained by the existence of one or more of these three factors.

The role of the environment is important. Both incentives and innovation ideas can emerge from the environment. Organizational structure is important insofar as it is designed to detect new ideas, translate them into decision alternatives, and enable their adoption.

The concepts of incentives, alternatives, and enabler variables have been discussed as three separate and distinct processes. In ongoing organizations the processes will tend to be highly interdependent and mutually reinforcing. Organizations that have high incentives to innovate will probably develop procedures to learn of and propose new ideas. If proposals tend to be rejected because of organizational barriers to implementation, the frequency of proposals will probably decline. But despite the interdependencies, the three processes will be treated separately in the research design. This will provide a more complete explanation for the innovation phenomenon and will allow the role of each part to be assessed separately. The overall theory can then be updated based on the research outcomes.

A general schema of the factors affecting decisions to innovate follows.

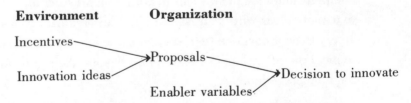

Environment   **Organization**

FIGURE 1.1 **Factors Affecting Decisions to Innovate**

Our model of the innovativeness of organizations is not especially innovative in the sense that brand new insights are presented. The environment as an inducer of change (the "incentive" in our terms) has been discussed by Terreberry; the necessity for innovative ideas as discussed by many has been summarized by Zaltman, Duncan, and Holbek; and the enabler variables of organizational complexity, stratification, centralization, etc., have been summarized and tested by Paulson.[22]

Although various parts of the model have been elsewhere discussed, nowhere have they all been brought together in a single theory and been subjected to empirical test.

HYPOTHESES FOR TEST

Our model of organizational innovativeness has the virtue of great generality; it is applicable to all organizations. Such generality is achieved at the cost of specificity; the particular incentives and enabler variables associated with a type of organization cannot be named, for they may differ from one type of organization to another. We want to test these ideas on a sample of high school districts. By identifying the incentives, the ways innovation alternatives become available, and the enabler variables that exist in the high school and in the community, we will develop hypotheses to test the theoretical model.

Incentives

Incentives to innovate are a function of the frequency with which existing techniques are perceived to be unsatisfactory. In communities where there are very high or increasingly high standards for the school's output new techniques will frequently be seen as attractive and will be preferred over current ones.

High standards for output quality will originate with consumers but will also be reflected in the product quality goals of top managers. High schools that face the highest standards for output quality will be in communities where parents have high aspirations for their children's educational success after high school. These high expectations will tend to occur when the parents themselves are highly educated. Student acceptance into and success in post-high-school education is very visible to parents. High schools, under norms of rationality, can be expected to try and score well on those measures of success that are visible to relevant environments.[23] One source of incentives for the adoption of new techniques will thus be high community expectations for quality education. New techniques offer the means to reach high standards. Conversely, those schools in communities with low standards have little incentive to try innovations.

HYPOTHESIS 1A: *High school innovativeness increases as the educational level of the community increases.*

This hypothesis is consistent with others' writings and findings. Pierce has written that "community good will toward education, then, may be said to be related to three factors: (1) the educational level of the community; (2) the occupational level of the community; and (3) social factors working to broaden the public mind with reference to education."[24] Arthur D. Little Inc., after interviewing teachers and principals in eight districts, found that community interest in education was most strongly related to innovation adoption.[25] However, Carlson stated that "domestication" of public schools is a barrier to change. To Carlson, domestication meant that the school is protected by the society it serves because it is seen as necessary.[26] A different outcome is derived from our model. Although system existence might be guaranteed because of domestication, lack of response to environmental pressure to adopt innovations that would better achieve desired outputs will increase pressure to elect school board members or acquire superintendents with favorable attitudes toward innovation adoption.

The quality standards of the community will affect innovation adoption only insofar as this influence is felt in the high school. One source through which this influence will be felt is the school board and superintendent. The board is typically elected by the community, and the superintendent is hired by the board. The aspirations for educational quality of the superintendent and board will tend to reflect the community's wishes. Thus, quality goals of the superintendent and school board are hypothesized to influence innovativeness.

HYPOTHESIS 1B: *High school innovativeness increases as superintendent and school board goals for educational quality increases.*

Again, the hypothesis is consistent with other findings. Arthur D. Little Inc. found that interest in innovation on the part of superintendents and board members was related to innovation adoption.[27] Carlson found that superintendents coming into a system from outside adopt more innovations than those promoted from within.[28] A contrary finding was reported by Mort and Cornell, who after surveying 48 communities found typical school boards ignorant of potential innovations.[29] They did not control for community educational level, however. In communities whose citizens had low levels of education, if our model is correct, we would not expect the board to be oriented toward innovations in education. However, even when the board is favorably disposed to adoption of innovation, the board member need not be the one to bring the idea into the system. He or she only has to be sympathetic toward its adoption.

All organizations, no matter how similar, differ as to the precise nature of their task and goals. Organizations will tend to adopt innovations that enable them to better accomplish their goals. For high schools the major task is educating students, and the task-relevant domain is the community. The community provides raw material and resources, and it is also the consumer of educational services. Thus the needs of the community, which is the major consumer, should be reflected in the kinds of innovations adopted. The major educational needs can be dichotomized as college preparation or terminal education. Most schools serve both kinds of students, but the mix varies. The rational high school will be expected to adopt more innovations that benefit the major consuming segment, whether it is college preparation or terminal education. Schools that serve equal groups will be expected to adopt innovations that benefit each group about equally. The hypotheses can be tested for the adoption of innovations that benefit each consuming group.

Innovation Alternatives

Individual high schools are very small in relation to their technological environment. Thousands of organizations share in and contribute to the development of educational techniques. Consequently nearly all educational innovations applicable to any given high school will originate in the environment. The successful innovation process for high schools, then, will entail their learning of new developments in the environment, bringing the ideas into the organization, preparing innovation proposals, and adopting them. High schools that have the highest probability of regularly adopting new ideas will be those that have the most efficient mechanisms for this process.

Each part of the proposal generation process can be evaluated separately. The first step is exposure to the environment. High schools can maximize the size of the interface between themselves and the technological environment through exposure of the teaching staff. Teachers have technical expertise, and they constitute the largest component in the organization. Relying on administrators, or even on a special staff department, as the input for new ideas would probably bring in fewer new ideas than harnessing the teaching group for this purpose. High exposure to new developments in the technological environment will tend to be through professional activities, such as journal reading and attendance at educational conferences.

HYPOTHESIS 2A: *The number of innovation ideas in high schools increases as teacher professionalism increases.*
HYPOTHESIS 2B: *The number of innovation ideas in high schools increases as teacher travel increases.*

With teachers as the major source of innovation ideas, the ideas will tend to "trickle up" from teachers to the top administrators for approval.[30] The trickle-up process will be facilitated if there is enough slack in the system to allow time for developing and processing proposals. Free time at the teacher level will facilitate the upward flow of ideas. The availability of administrators and other support staff personnel to assist in proposal preparation will also help this process.

HYPOTHESIS 2C: *The number of innovation proposals increases as nonteaching time for teachers increases.*
HYPOTHESIS 2D: *The number of innovation proposals increases as the administrative ratio increases.*

HYPOTHESIS 2E: *The number of innovation proposals increases as the availability of certified nonteaching staff increases.*

In brief, the function of the alternative–generating mechanisms is to sense the environment and translate ideas into proposals for inclusion in the decision process. As high school organizations do this process more efficiently, they will tend to have more ideas available for consideration, and they will have them sooner than other organizations in the same technological environment.

Enabler Variables

Once an organization has the need for an innovation and has the idea in the form of a proposed decision alternative, the enabler variables will tend to increase or decrease the probability that the decision will be made in favor of adoption. Being high on enabling characteristics means the organization can probably afford the cost, or it has the necessary facilities, or the decision makers tend to be predisposed toward innovation as a way to increase efficiency. There are fewer constraints or barriers to innovation implementation.

Slack resources and large size are the most obvious characteristics that increase the probability of decisions in favor of adoption. Slack is defined as the disparity between the resources available to the organization and the payments required to maintain it.[31] The rationale for the association of slack resources with the frequent adoption of innovations is straightforward. Most innovations will involve some financial cost. Without available resources the cost would be a barrier to adoption.

Similar reasoning explains why organizations with slack resources will also tend to be persistent adoption leaders. Adopting an innovation only after other organizations have used it successfully means less chance of failure. The innovation has had a chance to prove itself in other organizations. The decision makers that choose to adopt first do not have this assurance of success. Innovative organizations will probably have to absorb some failures because the new ideas are not yet proven. The existence of slack resources enables the top administrator to take the risk of early adoption; the organization is in a position to afford a possible loss.

HYPOTHESIS 3A: *High school innovativeness increases as the amount of organizational slack resources increases.*

HYPOTHESIS 3B: *High school innovativeness increases as the perceptions of school financial well-being by the superintendent and school board increase.*

Mansfield argued that size is important because of the amount of absolute resources in large organizations.[32] With greater resources the act of pioneering requires a smaller proportion of the organization's resources. The decision maker is more likely to decide in favor of an innovation because he or she will perceive less risk in terms of potential loss of the organization's absolute resources. Thus the existence of large size, like the existence of slack resources, makes possible both the frequent and early adoption of innovations.

HYPOTHESIS 3C: *High school innovativeness increases as high school size increases.*

Organizational complexity is also expected to increase the frequency of innovation adoption. Organizations are considered more complex as the number of different kinds of jobs and facilities in the organization increases. Complex organizations will thus be able to incorporate a wider range of innovations. Complexity is frequently associated with organizational size, but complexity is expected to have a separate influence on innovation adoption.

HYPOTHESIS 3D: *High school innovativeness increases as high school complexity increases.*

The growth rate of organizations is also expected to affect decisions to adopt. But the enabling effect is less clear cut than for slack resources, size, and complexity. On the one hand, rapid growth represents expansion, which affords the opportunity to incorporate the latest technical developments. This assumes that success and financial well-being are associated with rapid growth, thus enabling these purchases. Rapid growth is probably a sign of success in for-profit organizations. But rapid growth in not-for-profit government organizations will probably not be associated with financial well-being. Government funding tends to lag behind the rapidly increasing demands for the organization's services. If funding increases too slowly, the organization may be hard pressed just to offer essential services. Thus, by severely curtailing slack resources, rapid growth in tax-supported organizations can have a negative effect on decisions to innovate.

It is not possible in this study to test the effects of growth on innovation in for-profit versus not-for-profit organizations. But for high schools it is predicted that growth rate will have a negative enabling effect on innovation. The adverse influence of growth on slack resources places additional constraints on decisions to innovate.

HYPOTHESIS 3E: *High school innovativeness decreases as the rate of growth increases.*

The final two enabler variables concern the decision makers in the organization. The decision to innovate is usually passed up the hierarchy and approved by several people. As more people in the organizational hierarchy are required to approve the proposed innovation, the idea takes longer to process and the probability of someone disliking it increases. Hence, when decisions to innovate are decentralized, the probability of a favorable decision increases.

HYPOTHESIS 3F: *High school innovativeness increases as decentralized decision making increases.*

The school board, with the assistance of the superintendent, sets the policies and direction of the school. Under norms of rationality, these top decision makers are expected to make innovation decisions in the best interests of the organization.

23

But top administrators may disagree as to the perceived efficacy of early adoption. Thus, the favorable attitude or predisposition toward new ideas as ways to increase efficiency will increase the probability of decisions in favor of adoption. Even when decisions for innovation are decentralized, the attitude of the superintendent and school board is still expected to have an effect on the direction of decision making.

HYPOTHESIS 3G: *High school innovativeness increases as the favorable attitude of the superintendent and school board toward innovation increases.*

In summary, several organizational variables have been identified that are hypothesized to increase the probability of innovation adoption. Thus, among organizations that are equally aware of innovation ideas and that have equal incentives to adopt, those organizations that have characteristics that enable adoption are hypothesized to be most innovative. At this point we are unable to state which of the enabler variables are more important or if they are additive, although we do state that without incentives and innovation alternatives there will be no adoption. The model proposed by Arthur D. Little Inc. also requires a combination of initiating mechanisms (any factors that bring information into the system) and sustaining mechanisms (characteristics of the school districts that act primarily to create a climate within which initiating mechanisms can be effective). Their use of initiating mechanisms is like our use of innovation alternatives, and their sustaining mechanisms like our incentives. However, they ignored most of our enabler variables and hence were only able to support their model weakly with the perceptual data they collected. Our data, both "hard" and "soft" measures collected longitudinally, should provide us with a fairly strong test of our model.

NOTES

1. Max Weber, "The Essentials of Bureaucratic Organization: An Ideal-Type Construction," in *Reader in Bureaucracy*, ed. Robert K. Merton, Alisa P. Gray, Barbara Hockey, Hanan C. Selvin (Glencoe, Ill.: Free Press, 1952); cf., for example, James G. March and Herbert A. Simon, *Organizations* (New York: John Wiley & Sons, 1958).
2. Gerald Zaltman, Robert Duncan, and Jonny Holbek, *Innovations and Organizations* (New York: John Wiley & Sons, 1973).
3. Warren Bennis, *Changing Organizations* (New York.: McGraw-Hill, 1966).
4. James Q. Wilson, "Innovation in Organizations: Notes toward a Theory," in *Approaches to Organizational Design*, ed. James D. Thompson (Pittsburgh: University of Pittsburgh Press, 1966), pp. 193–218.
5. Selwyn W. Becker and Thomas L. Whisler, "The Innovative Organization: A Selective View of Current Theory and Research," *Journal of Business* 40 (October 1967): 463.
6. Lawrence Mohr, "Determinants of Innovation in Organizations," *American Political Science Review* 63: 111–26; and Jerald Hage and Michael Aiken, *Social Change in Complex Organizations* (New York: Random House, 1970).
7. Becker and Whisler, "The Innovative Organization."
8. March and Simon, *Organizations*.
9. Richard M. Cyert and James G. March, *A Behavioral Theory of the Firm* (Englewood Cliffs, N.J.: Prentice-Hall, 1963); Kenneth E. Knight, "A Descriptive Model of the Intra-Firm Innovation Process," *Journal of Business* 40 (October 1967): 478–96; and March and Simon, *Organizations*.
10. G. M. Walton, "Obstacles to Technical Diffusion in Ocean Shipping," *Explorations in Economic History* 8: 123–40; Y. Hayami, "Elements of Induced Innovation," *Explorations in Economic History* 8:445–72; and Edwin Mansfield, "Size of Firm, Market Structure, and Innovation," *Journal of Political Economy* 41 (December 1963): 556–76.
11. Herbert A. Shepard, "Innovation-Resisting and Innovation-Producing Organizations," *Journal of Business* 40 (October 1967): 470–77; and Wilson, "Innovation in Organizations."
12. March and Simon, *Organizations*; Wilson, "Innovation in Organizations"; Knight, "A Descriptive Model of the Intra-Firm Innovation Process"; and Edward Harvey and Russell Mills, "Patterns of Organizational Adaptation: A Political Perspective," in *Power in Organizations*, ed. Mayer N. Zald (Nashville, Tenn.: Vanderbilt University Press, 1970).
13. Paul R. Lawrence, "How to Deal with Resistance to Change," *Harvard Business Review* 32 (May-June): 49–57; Shepard, "Innovation-Resisting and Innovation-Producing Organizations"; Daniel Katz and Robert Kahn, *The Social Psychology of Organizations* (New York: John Wiley & Sons, 1966); and Goodwin Watson, "Resistance to Change," in *Processes and Phenomena of Social Change*, ed. Gerald Zaltman (New York: Wiley Interscience, 1973).
14. March and Simon, *Organizations*, pp. 182–83.
15. James D. Thompson, *Organizations in Action* (New York: McGraw-Hill, 1967), p. 89.
16. Ibid., p. 51.

17. Paul R. Mort, *Principles of School Administration* (New York: McGraw-Hill, 1946); Everett M. Rogers, "What Are Innovators Like?" in *Change Process in Public Schools* (Eugene, Oreg.: Center for Advanced Study of Educational Administration, University of Oregon, 1965); and Richard O. Carlson, "Barriers to Change in Public Schools," in *Change Process in Public Schools*.

18. Everett M. Rogers, *Diffusion of Innovations* (New York: Free Press, 1962); and Wilson, "Innovation in Organizations."

19. Sumner Myers and Donald G. Marquis, *Successful Industrial Innovations* (Washington, D.C.: National Science Foundation, NSF 69-17, 1969).

20. C. F. Carter and B. R. Williams, *Industry and Technical Progress: Factors Governing the Speed of Application of Science* (London: Oxford University Press, 1957); and James M. Utterback, "The Process of Technological Innovation within the Firm," *Academy of Management Journal* 14 (March 1971): 75–88.

21. Arnold D. Kaluzny, James E. Veney, and John T. Gentry, "Innovation of Health Services: A Comparative Study of Hospitals and Health Departments" (Paper presented at the University of North Carolina Health Services Research Symposium on Innovation in Health Care Organizations, Chapel Hill, N.C., 18–19 May 1972); and Myers and Marquis, *Successful Industrial Innovations*.

22. Shirley Terreberry, "The Evolution of Organizational Environments," *Administrative Science Quarterly* 12 (March 1968); Zaltman, Duncan, and Holbek, *Innovations and Organizations*; and Steven K. Paulson, "Causal Analysis of Interorganizational Relations: An Axiomatic Theory Revised," *Administrative Science Quarterly* 19 (September 1974): 319–37. It is interesting to note that Paulson found innovative organizations characterized by both looseness (low formalization) and rigidity (low complexity, high stratification, and high centralization). Our model suggests that such apparently contradictory findings in the enabler variables can be explained by reference to incentives for adoption and innovation alternatives.

23. Thompson, *Organizations in Action*, p. 90.

24. T. M. Pierce, *Controllable Community Characteristics Related to the Quality of Education*, New York: Bureau of Publications, Teachers College, Columbia University, 1947, pp. 6–7, cited by Donald H. Ross, *Administration for Adaptability* (New York: Metropolitan School Study Council, 1958), p. 235.

25. Arthur D. Little Inc., *A Model for Innovation Adoption in Public School Districts* (Boston: Arthur D. Little, 1968).

26. Carlson, "Barriers to Change in Public Schools."

27. Arthur D. Little Inc., *Model for Innovation Adoption*.

28. Carlson, "Barriers to Change in Public Schools."

29. P. R. Mort and Francis G. Cornell, *American Schools in Transition*, (New York: Bureau of Publications, Teachers College, Columbia University, 1941), p. 227, cited by Ross, *Administration for Adaptability*, p. 509.

30. William M. Evan, "Organization Lag," *Human Organization* 25 (Spring 1966): 53.

31. Cyert and March, *Behavioral Theory of the Firm*.

32. Mansfield, "Size of Firm, Market Structure, and Innovation."

Design and Methods

Data on innovation adoption in 13 suburban Cook County, (Illinois) high school districts were collected during the mid-1960s. Due to delays of various sorts the data were not completely analyzed until 1970. At that time we decided that the data could be used as part of a longitudinal study, so additional data were collected from the same organizations for the period 1968–72.

Studying only 13 organizations presents some problems, namely, statistical analysis with a small sample size and the potentially limited generalizability of the results. But several studies using small samples of organizations have made distinct contributions to our understanding of organizational functioning: Hall, and Lawrence and Lorsch, for instance, each reported studies of 10 organizations; Hage and Aiken studied 16 welfare agencies.[1] A methodologist might argue that large sample size is a major consideration. However, despite the small sample size we sensed the opportunity to develop new insights into the process of organizational innovation, and this seemed of primary importance. This feeling was based on our ability to achieve four methodological criteria.

Foremost was the longitudinal design. The number of cross-sectional studies of organizations had been increasing. Data from most of these studies concerned a single time period. There is little evidence that single time period, cross-sectional findings accurately represent the internal processes that occur in ongoing, changing organizations. The longitudinal design permitted us to collect data in the 1970s relevant to variables for which we had observations from the early 1960s. Because of the elapsed time the variables associated with innovation in one period could be used to predict the adoption of a different set of innovations in the other period. This is a rigorous test of the observed relationships because the high school districts changed considerably between the two periods. If the same variables predict innovation in both sets of observations, the likelihood that the observed relationships are spurious is reduced considerably.

Second, we were able to obtain information on the adoption of a relatively large number of innovations. This is not a minor consideration. The circumstances surrounding the adoption of a single innovation or a very small number of innovations may not represent the general patterns of adoption behavior occurring within the organizations. By observing organizations' responses to a relatively large number of innovations, we felt that we would be observing typical rather than idiosyncratic behavior vis-à-vis adoption of innovations. Changes occur rapidly in high school education. In the 1965 study over 100 innovations were reported by the districts as having been adopted from about 1958 to 1964. Only about 38 of these innovations were really new[2] to the high school industry at that time, but 38 was a large number compared to other studies of organizational innovation.

Third, we obtained and used as many *hard* measures of organizational variables as possible. We define hard measures as ones not based on the subjective opinions or perceptions of organization members or others. This kind of data enabled us to reduce perceptual biases and eliminate spuriously high correlations that can arise when the same respondents provide the data for different structural variables. Data on the teaching staff, administrative arrangements, size, and financial arrangements of the districts were stored in state and regional educational agencies. The schools had to file annual reports with these agencies. From these sources we were able to obtain data consistent for both time periods for most variables. We did use questionnaire responses to measure attitudes, opinions, and aspirations, as well as decentralization.

Fourth, we wanted to gather data about the innovation process that would enable us to corroborate conclusions based on the two cross-sectional analyses. Innovations have to be conceived, proposed, and then adopted. The conception and proposal steps are essential to adoption. Organizational characteristics that facilitate or inhibit the earlier steps may be as important to innovation adoption as is the final decision to adopt. Research to date has concentrated on the adoption stage of the process. Data relevant to conception and proposal were not collected in the 1965 study, but they were for the period 1968–72. We attempted to document where the ideas came from, who proposed them, and how this process was affected by type of innovation. Acquiring these data couldn't tell us everything about process, but it might answer some of our questions.

In sum, a study of the 13 suburban Cook County high school districts appeared to be methodologically sound. We could obtain data that were reasonably error-free, would enable a vigorous cross-validation of the findings, and might provide some insight into the process underlying the correlates of innovation.

THE SAMPLE

The 13 high school districts are all located in suburban Cook County, Illinois. The original selection of the districts took place in 1964. Fourteen districts were chosen at that time as being representative of the 28 suburban Cook County high school districts on the basis of size. One district did not participate fully, leaving 13 districts for the study.

Each high school district has a seven-member school board elected by the district residents. The school board is the top policy and decision-making body in the district. The superintendent is the top operating manager in the district, reporting directly to the school board. The major subunit of the district is the school. Most schools have approximately 2,000 students. A principal is assigned to each school, and he or she is the line officer. The usual line of authority extends from the school board to the superintendent to the principal and then to the teachers.

Superintendents and principals also have assistants, department heads, clerical staffs, and other specialists reporting to them. These other groups are usually not in the direct line of authority from teacher to school board.

It should be emphasized that the unit of analysis is the school district, not the individual high school. The district is the legal organizational entity in Illinois. Most of the data stored in educational agencies are for the district and cannot be obtained for individual high schools. The variables involving the school board and superintendent are district level variables. The high school districts in the sample are composed of from one to seven high schools.

TIME PERIODS

The data for the analysis cover these 13 districts for two separate time periods. The first period includes the five school years, 1959/60 to 1963/64. The second period includes data for four school years, 1968/69 to 1971/72. Data across multiple years are used for each period to smooth out year-to-year fluctuations in the data and to allow time for the adoption of many innovations by the districts.

The average size of the districts in the first period was approximately 3,300 students, with a range of approximately 1,900–5,100 students. For the latter period the average size was almost 6,100 students, with a range of approximately 4,000–15,000 students.

INDEPENDENT VARIABLES

As detailed in chapter 1, several variables have an impact on the innovativeness of organizations. During the major fieldwork portion of the study in 1973 we were fortunate to be able to gather a large part of the data on these variables from three agencies that collect and record annual reports from the high school districts in Illinois. The cooperating agencies that provided the centralized pool of data are: the Office of the Cook County Superintendent of Schools, the Office of the Illinois State Superintendent of Public Instruction, and the North Central Association of Colleges and Secondary Schools.

The use of these centralized sources proved to be very beneficial. The data were uniform both across districts and over time. The school districts were familiar with the reporting procedures and the information contained in each category on a given form represented the same information for each district. The year-to-year records were also used to check that each measure was consistent from 1959 to 1972. New categories were occasionally added to the reporting forms, but we were able to obtain comparable data items for each school and year in the study. Obviously, if observations of the school districts change from year to year because of reporting procedures, the valid interpretation of the results becomes very difficult. Great emphasis was given to collecting data so it would be uniform for all years in the study.

The data were obtained by visits to and correspondence with the respective offices. The historical records from these agencies also enabled us to recover measures of a few variables important to the theory but which hadn't been collected during 1965.

The value for each variable obtained from these agencies is an average for the years in the respective time periods. The measure of organizational size, for instance, is student enrollment in the district. The student enrollment figure was recorded for each of the school years, 1959/60–1963/64, and the average for the five years computed. The average value is the measure used for the 1959–64 period. An average value for the student enrollment was computed the same way for the measure of organizational size in the second period, 1968/69–1971/72.

The variables in the following list are the ones obtained from the three educational agencies. There are a few variables that were not measured in the 1965 data collection that we simply could not recover because records on the variables were not kept. The variables that are measured for the second period only are

indicated.

1. *Organizational size.* Average daily student enrollment. From a report compiled and furnished by the Cook County Superintendent's Office.

2. *Organizational growth rate.* Average annual percentage increase in organization size during the time period.

3. *Organizational complexity.* Number of professional occupational categories employed in the district. From "Teacher Service Record," State Superintendent's Office. Measured for 1968–72 only.

4. *Administrative ratio.* Number of administrators divided by number of teachers. From "Annual Report," North Central Association of Colleges and Secondary Schools.

5. *Support staff ratio.* Number of certified nonteaching, nonadministrative staff divided by the number of teaching staff. From "Annual Report," North Central Association of Colleges and Secondary Schools.

6. *Affluence.* Total educational expenditures per pupil. From "Annual Financial Report," State Superintendent's Office.

7. *Slack resources.* Percentage increase in educational expenditures per pupil during the time period.

8. *Teacher professionalism.* Percentage of district teaching staff who have completed a master's degree. From "Teacher Service Record," State Superintendent's Office.

9. *Teacher free time.* Percentage of teaching staff teaching four or fewer courses. From "Annual Report and Application for Recognition," State Superintendent's Office. Measured for 1968–72 only.

10. *Teacher exposure.* Travel expenditures per teacher. From "Annual Financial Report," State Superintendent's Office. Measured for 1968–72 only.

11. *District emphasis on terminal education.* Percentage teaching staff with vocational teaching assignment. From individual school district directories for 1959–64 period; from "Teacher Service Records," State Superintendent's Office, for 1969–72 period.

Another source of data was the *U.S. Census of Population and Housing*. Census data for the 13 districts were compiled by overlaying school district boundaries on census maps. The values for the census tracts lying within each school district were recorded and summed. There were an average of 15 census tracts per school district. Frequently school district boundaries and census tract boundaries were not coterminous. When a partial tract lay within the district, the proportion of tract residents living within the district was estimated on the basis of land area within the district.

Data from the 1960 census are assumed to be representative of the communities for the 1959–64 period. Data from the 1970 census are assumed to be representative of the 1968–72 period. The following variable was operationalized for this study from census data.

12. *Community educational level.* The percentage of community residents over 25 years of age who have completed a high school education.

The remaining independent variables were measured with questionnaire responses from the district superintendents and school board members who are the "elite" in these organizations. These responses were collected during the last year of the respective time periods. Thus, the data may not perfectly represent the attitudes held by superintendents and board members throughout the respective periods. We feel justified in using these measures because superintendent and school board positions are not transitory. Most of the superintendents and board members responding were in their positions throughout the time period under study. The responses from these individuals provide a useful measure of the differences in elite attitudes that existed across these districts.

Questionnaire data for the 1959–64 period were collected in one-and-one-half hour interviews held individually with the superintendent and each board member. For the 1968–72 period self-administered questionnaires were mailed to superintendents and board members. The questionnaires were pretested in a high school district not in the sample.

In both periods all superintendents participated. Follow-up contacts were continued with school board members until at least 5 of the 7 members in each district participated. For the 1959–64 period an average of 6.6 board members per district completed interviews. For the 1968–72 period an average of 6.1 board members per district returned usable questionnaires.

A list of four variables that were operationalized from the superintendent and board member questionnaires follows. Superintendent and school board responses in each district are combined to yield the elite score. Each respondent is weighted equally to form the composite variable.[3]

13. *Elite attitude toward innovation adoption.* Coded on a three-point scale from 0, if respondent preferred less innovation in district, to 2, if respondent preferred more innovation. Measured for both time periods.

14. *Elite goals for quality of school district.* Coded on a four-point scale from 1, if below-average quality was okay with respondents, to 4, if respondent wanted one of the best schools in the country. Measured for 1968–72 period only.

15. *Elite perception of slack resources.* Coded on a five-point scale from 1, if respondent felt district was severely short of money, to 5, if respondent felt district had more than enough money. Measured for 1968–72 period only.

16. *Decentralization of decision making.* The superintendents reported whether school principals were free to act without superintendent or board approval on 16 potential decisions. Eight of these potential decisions form a Guttman scale. A high score on the scale means greater decentralization of decision making. The coefficient of reproducibility for the Guttman scale is .94. The coefficient of scalability is .68. Both coefficients are above the minimum Guttman scale requirements.[4] Measured for 1968–72 period only.

Our operationalizations separated measures of variables that are sometimes confounded in the literature. Mohr, for example, measured organizational size as total expenditures.[5] Total expenditures confound organizational size, affluence, and slack resources, each of which may have a separate impact on innovation. We separated these concepts by using number of students as the measure of organizational size, dollar expenditures per student as the measure of affluence, and the increase in expenditures per student as the measure of experienced slack resources in the system. We even measured perceived slack resources to learn whether actual slack or perceived slack is important to innovation. We also made a distinction between the concepts of organizational complexity and employee professionalism.[6] Operationally separating these concepts should help us gain insight into the processes underlying organizational innovation.

THE DEPENDENT VARIABLE: ORGANIZATIONAL INNOVATIVENESS

The dependent variable presents several problems. First, we must operationalize it so that it represents overall organizational innovativeness for the organizations under study. Second, to test some of the incentives and enabler variables, we should be capable of discriminating between administrative and technical innovations, and we should be able to categorize innovations relative to the client population served, costliness, and the amount of organizational change necessitated by adoption.

We have defined innovation as a technique that is new to the group of organizations using the same technology. An innovation, operationally, is an educational technique that is new to our sample of high school organizations. Innovations can include new courses, new curricula, new teaching techniques, and new freedom and responsibility for students.

There are several techniques for combining innovation adoptions into an innovation score. Perhaps the most rigorous measure of organizational innovation in the literature is the technique used by Gordon et al. for a study of hospitals. [7] From 200 reported innovations they extracted 10 that formed a Guttman scale for the hospitals in the sample. The Guttman scale criterion means that the innovations are arranged along a single continuum, presumably from most to least innovative. A disadvantage of this technique is the loss of information on the other 190 innovations. If the 10 innovations are representative of the 200 innovations, then this technique is excellent. If the 10 represent a unique dimension of innovation, such as riskiness, then conclusions about all innovations are likely to be erroneous.

A technique commonly used to measure innovation is to ask informants from each organization in the sample about recent innovation adoptions. The reported innovations are then tallied into an innovation score for that organization. Usually one point is given for each adoption. This technique is probably the easiest way to arrive at an innovation score, but a couple of drawbacks are evident.

First, what organizations report as new may be old hat to the technological environment. Another organization in the sample may have adopted the innovation 10 to 15 years earlier; that organization wouldn't even get credit, whereas the recently adopting organization would. The technique of counting currently reported innovations measures current organizational change, not innovation defined as being new to all organizations in the environment with similar goals.

Another problem with this method of counting innovations is the criterion problem. Each organization receives credit for innovations that are unlike innovations adopted by other organizations in the study. The net effect of this strategy is that the innovation score (the dependent variable) measures different innovations for each organization. This is similar to giving students intelligence tests that do not contain the same test items. Although each test item might measure some aspect of intelligence, one student would be solving math problems, another would be solving verbal problems, another puzzles, and so on. If one student scored higher than the others, it wouldn't necessarily mean he or she had greater intelligence because each student would have taken a different test. If all items are combined into a single list, however, and each student completes all items, a common criterion is established. The investigator can conclude that a high score probably represents greater ability insofar as that test is concerned. The same is true for a study of organizational innovation. A high score by an organization on a common list of innovations probably indicates greater innovativeness insofar as those innovations are concerned.

Occasionally an investigator may try to compare organizations that use different technologies. In this instance the criterion problem can't be solved because the organizations are not eligible to adopt the same innovations. The investigator will have to settle for a count of current changes as the dependent variable.

For this study we have a sample of similar organizations. Establishing a common criterion of innovation is important, so a single list of innovations that are adoptable by each organization was developed. The innovations were new to the set of organizations and conformed to our definition of innovation.

In order to learn what was new to the high school districts in our sample, similar data collection procedures were used for each time period. The school districts in the sample were surveyed to learn what new techniques each had adopted during the prior four to five years. Professional educators outside the districts and books on education were also consulted, but the majority of information on what constituted educational innovations came from personnel in each school district.

The reported innovations from all districts were assembled into a master innovation checklist. This list was returned to each district, and with the help of key people in the district it was determined which of the innovations were in use and the year adopted. These key people were usually senior teachers or administrators. We frequently had to talk to several key people in a district to learn about all the innovations. For the 1968–72 time period information was also gathered on who proposed the innovation (e.g., teacher, principal, board member). Many of the innovations reported by individual school districts did not turn out to be new to all districts in the study. A comparison of dates of adoption across districts revealed that most reported innovations had been adopted by one or more districts some time prior to the period under consideration. We eliminated these innovations from the innovation checklist. By using only innovations that had not been adopted by any district prior to the appropriate time period, we narrowed the master checklist to 38 innovations for the 1959–64 period and 40 innovations for the 1968–72 period. The innovations thus met the criterion of being new to the districts in the sample. The innovations also formed a list from which all districts were eligible to adopt. The organizations are thus compared according to the same criterion of innovativeness.

> 17. *School district innovativeness*. A count of the number of innovations from the narrowed down master list adopted during the time period.

Our definition of innovation implies that early adoption is more innovative than late adoption. We did try to develop an index based on the relative speed of adoption. We gave the most weight to the first organization to adopt an innovation, less weight to the second adoptor, and so on, with the least weight given to the last adoptor. Weighting the innovativeness scores for speed of adoption made almost no difference. The weighted score was almost perfectly correlated with the simple number of adoptions. Since we have restricted the definition of innovation to techniques that are new to the technological environment, the discriminating factor for these organizations is the number of innovations they adopt rather than the speed with which they adopt them. Innovative organizations simply adopt a lot more innovations than noninnovative ones.

We were able to obtain an independent measure of innovativeness in these schools against which we could validate our methodology for measuring innovativeness. A survey of new programs in Cook County high schools was conducted in 1965 by the Office of the Cook County Superintendent of Schools. An innovativeness score was developed for each of the 13 districts in our sample by counting the number of innovations reported in the superintendent's survey. The correlation coefficient between the score from that survey and the measure of innovativeness for our study for the 1959–64 period is .87. The high correlation coefficient with an independent measure of innovativeness indicates that both scores are measuring the same thing and gives us some confidence that our scale is a valid measure of the construct, organizational innovativeness.[8] Having solved to our satisfaction the problem of measuring overall organizational innovativeness, we can turn to the other problems mentioned: proposal costliness, client orientation, and amount of organization change involved in the adoption. Our attempts to measure these attributes led to some unexpected findings and some revisions in our operationalization of high school district innovativeness.

UNEXPECTED FINDINGS

We were simply not able to measure and test some of our hypotheses about the innovation process. As we puzzled over these failures, we began to realize that we had learned something about organizational innovation by our inability to measure certain things. These early glimmerings of insight were later clarified and confirmed by the analyses reported in chapters 3 and 4.

One of our strongest beliefs as we began this study was that organizational variables that generate innovation proposals are different from the variables that prompt a decision to adopt.[9] We assumed we could construct a separate dependent variable that would represent innovation proposals. The correlates of innovation proposals were to be evaluated separately from innovation adoptions.

For the 1968–72 period the school districts were asked if and when innovations had been considered or proposed for adoption even if they had never been adopted. While coding these data we discovered that for the hundreds of innovation adoptions reported by these 13 school districts, only about half a dozen instances occurred where the innovation was proposed but not adopted. What did this mean? It could mean that the organizational memory trace for unadopted proposals is short; the informants simply forgot about the proposals that were not adopted. However, the informants usually seemed certain that a given innovation had never been considered for adoption. Perhaps some informal processes are at work whereby innovations that have a high probability of adoption are the ones that tend to be proposed. It could also mean that most innovation proposals are adopted. It might be rare indeed for proposed innovations to be rejected. This could mean that getting the innovation proposed is the most important step in the innovation process. We will consider that possibility when we discuss the findings in the next chapter.

The sameness of proposals and adoptions has consequences for the data analysis. Only one dependent variable—number of adoptions—will be used in the analysis. We will not be able to discriminate between number of proposals and number of adoptions.

We also collected data on the attributes of the innovations adopted in the districts. There hadn't been much research reported in the organizational innovation literature that considered how innovation characteristics influenced adoption frequency.[10] It seemed possible to elaborate the innovation process by bringing innovation characteristics into the analysis. For example, if slack resources is an important variable in the process, it will probably be more influential for expensive than for inexpensive innovations. Likewise, if structural variables such as size or complexity remove barriers to the decision to adopt, the removal of these barriers will probably have the greatest impact on innovations of large magnitude.

A relatively easy characteristic to identify is whether innovations are technical or administrative.[11] Technical innovations are innovations in curricula and teaching techniques. These innovations represent changes in the content and process of educating students. Administrative innovations relate to the social structure of the organization and do not directly affect classroom method or content.

As we developed our index of innovation, we found that by defining innovations as techniques new to the technological environment, we were excluding the reported administrative changes. There apparently were administrative changes taking place in these organizations, but not many were really considered new to the technological environment. Only educational innovations seemed continuously to be hitting the technological environment and then diffusing through the districts in the sample. This finding makes sense after the fact. Innovation action is apparently in the technical core, which is directly involved in organizational goal attainment. Technological innovations occur more frequently than administrative ones.[12]

The other innovation attributes of interest to us are the cost of innovations, the amount of change involved in adoption, and whether the innovations tend to benefit collegebound or terminal students. It was virtually impossible to secure data on the actual cost, change, and benefit of each innovation, so we asked experts to rate each innovation on a five-point Likert scale. A separate scale was developed for each of the three innovation characteristics. Twenty-eight superintendents, assistant superintendents, principals, curriculum directors, and other experts from the school districts in the sample rated the innovations, each completing one scale. Ten experts completed the cost scale, and 9 experts completed the change and benefit scales. The final value given to each innovation is the average score assigned by the experts.

As we compiled these data, we received more surprises. We experimented with different ways of combining innovations to reflect innovation attributes, and we found the cost and change involved in adoption didn't seem to make much difference. But whether collegebound or terminal students were the beneficiaries did make a difference. As we examined the data further, we found that the identity of the beneficiaries was having a completely unexpected impact on our analysis.

We hadn't considered the possibility that the kind of innovations adopted in the second period might differ from those adopted in the first period. Nearly all of the innovations adopted from 1959 to 1964 tended to be of primary benefit to collegebound students. From 1968 to 1972, however, there was a big increase in the number of innovations adopted to benefit terminal

41

students. What could this mean? One possibility was that the kinds of innovations adopted during each period were actually the same but that our samples of innovations were badly drawn and did not reflect this similarity. We consulted with educational authorities, and they advised us that our finding was probably not a sampling problem. The early 1960s was a time when nearly all parents wanted their children to go on to college. It was also the Sputnik era. Most educational developments were oriented toward college preparation, especially toward preparation in math and science. By 1968 the emphasis on college preparation had diminished. Parents were more tolerant of noncollege careers. The schools felt obligated to offer programs for noncollegebound students as well. The content of our dependent variables changed due to these changing social forces. College preparatory innovations were clearly in the majority in each period, but from 1968 to 1972 they were not adopted to the exclusion of innovations for terminal students.

This presented a unique problem for our longitudinal analysis. The content of the dependent variable had changed over time because the kind of innovations adopted shifted toward those that benefited terminal students. This change is illustrated in table 2.1. The average cost of adoption was pretty much the same for both periods. The shift from 3.62 to 3.15 for whether in-

TABLE 2.1
Means and Standard Deviations of Selected Innovation Variables

VARIABLE	1959-64		1968-72	
	MEAN	(S.D.)	MEAN	(S.D.)
Cost of adoption[a]	2.44	(.84)	2.32	(.93)
Change involved in adoption[a]	2.13	(.59)	2.49	(.86)
Benefit from adoption[a]	3.62	(.55)	3.15	(.71)
Change involved in adoption— college-oriented innovations[b]	2.11	(.61)	2.06	(.69)
Change involved in adoption— terminal-oriented innovations[b]	2.32	(.60)	2.64	(.82)

[a]For cost and change ratings, 1 = very low; 5 = very high. For benefit rating, 1 = benefit terminal only; 5 = benefit collegebound only.

[b]College-oriented innovations are considered to be those that received a score of 3.13 or greater on the benefit scale; terminal-oriented innovations are considered to be those that received a score of 2.87 or less.

novations benefit collegebound or terminal students is a large shift in favor of terminal students. The difference between 3.62 and 3.15 is statistically significant at the .01 level. (Throughout the text significance levels are based on one-tailed tests.)

There is also a small increase from 2.13 to 2.49 in the amount of change involved in adoption. This increase is explained by the added emphasis given terminal-oriented innovation in the second period. In the last two rows in table 2.1. we can see that terminal oriented innovations involve more change than college-oriented innovations. Terminal-oriented innovations frequently require change in facilities or equipment that are not required in college-oriented innovations. The amount of change associated with terminal-oriented innovations was greater in 1968–72 than it was in 1959–64. This was probably a result of the increased activity involving programs that benefited terminal students.

The problem facing us was whether to develop a single index of educational innovations for each time period or whether to work with separate indices of college-oriented and terminal-oriented innovations. If different factors influenced the adoption of each kind of innovation and we developed a single innovation index for each period, the findings from both periods wouldn't be comparable because the second period contained more terminal-oriented innovations. By separating the two types of innovations we would be certain that our dependent variables were measuring the same thing in each time period. We decided to divide the innovations into separate groups. The innovations that received a score of 3.13 or higher on the benefit scale completed by the experts were considered to be of benefit to college-oriented students. Innovations receiving a score of 2.87 or less were considered to be of benefit to terminal-oriented students. Innovations receiving scores from 2.88–3.12 were ignored. Separate innovation scores were calculated by counting the number of each kind of innovation adopted by the districts.

We have already indicated that there was not very much innovation activity for terminal-oriented students from 1959 to 1964. The innovations in that period were so skewed in favor of college-oriented students that only four innovations received a score of 2.87 or less. None of the four innovations received a score of 2.00 or less. A score below 2.00 would mean the innovation was of major benefit to terminal students. Of the four innovations only one was adopted by ten of the districts, and none were adopted by the other three districts. The result for an innovation index is that we have a dichotomous measure of terminal-oriented innovations for the first period, and the measure is not very representative of terminal-oriented innovations. For this reason we will not use terminal-oriented innovations as a dependent variable when we consider the 1968–72 period.

The model can thus be tested in both time periods for innovations that benefit college-oriented students. The majority of the technical innovations in high school education throughout the years 1959 to 1972 were of primary benefit to college-oriented students. Having a separate measure for these innovations enables us to deal accurately with this major component of innovation activity in these organizations. We can also test the model using innovations that benefited terminal students for the 1968–72 period. That part of the analysis will not be subject to cross-validation.

Separating the innovations into two homogenous subgroups gave us easier, clearer, and more believable interpretations. Interpreting the adoption of innovations that have a common function has much more meaning than simply explaining the adoption of "new" techniques.

By separating innovations into separate groups we reduced the number of innovations in our analysis. For the 1959–64 period there were 31 innovations that benefited college-oriented students. For the 1968–72 period there were 18 innovations that benefited college-oriented students and 11 innovations that benefited terminal-oriented students. A few innovations didn't fit into either category and were dropped from the analysis. The number of innovations in each dependent variable category is smaller than originally planned. The number of innovations is still greater than most other studies of innovations, however, and is apparently large enough to give us useful and reliable results.

44   We were still interested in the effects of innovation cost and change. After we had divided the innovations into the categories of college and terminal orientation, it still seemed possible to consider the cost and change involved in adoption. We didn't want to subdivide the innovations into still smaller groups, so we weighted each innovation according to cost and change. Each innovation adoption was weighted from 1 to 5 depending on the cost rating assigned by the experts, and the sum of the weighted adoptions was the "cost" score for the district. Each innovation adoption was also weighted from 1 to 5 depending on the change involved in adoption, and the sum of the weighted adoptions was the "change" score for the district.

This weighting procedure had absolutely no impact. Each weighted index was correlated with the simple number of adoptions of college-oriented or terminal-oriented innovation by .95 or higher. The obvious interpretation is that the school districts were adopting innovations without regard to cost or change. Each district was adopting college-oriented innovations, for instance, that involved about the same cost or change as the college-oriented innovations adopted by the other districts. If the cost or change involved in adoption made a difference, this weighting scheme doesn't reveal it.

We decided to go ahead and subdivide the college-oriented and terminal-oriented innovations into subgroups of high versus low cost and large versus small change to see what would happen. The innovations were assigned to the respective groups depending on whether they were above or below the mean rating of cost and change given by the experts. At this point the number of adoptions by the districts in each subgroup of innovations was getting precariously small. The noninnovative districts were not seen to adopt many innovations when the pool of innovations was large. As we shrank the pool by dividing it into subpools, we were losing the wide range of adoptions across districts.

Despite the possible unreliability because of the small number of adoptions involved in each category, our results were similar. The high and low cost and large and small change categories of college-oriented innovations for 1959–64, for instance, were intercorrelated from .65 to .97. For 1968–72 these categories were intercorrelated from .65 to .91. By comparison, the number of college-oriented innovations was correlated with terminal-oriented innovations in 1968–72 only by .2. Our conclusion is that the cost or change involved in adoption doesn't have much impact on whether a district will adopt an innovation. The innovative districts are simply adopting more of each kind of innovation than the noninnovative districts. But it does make a difference whether innovations benefit collegebound or terminal students. For the major part of our analysis in the next two chapters we will deal separately with the college and terminal orientations. Further subcategorization will not be used.

We come away from the innovation index-constructing phase of our research with a few tentative facts about innovation adoption in our sample.

1. Innovations that are proposed tend to be approved.
2. Current developments diffusing through the organizations tend to apply to the technical core rather than to administration.
3. Most technical innovations in these high school districts are of benefit to college-oriented students.
4. From the early 1960s to the early 1970s increasing emphasis was given to innovations that benefited terminal students. This emphasis is reflected in the increasing number and proportion of innovations adopted to benefit terminal-oriented students.
5. Whether an innovation benefits collegebound or terminal-oriented students affects whether an organization adopts it.
6. The cost or change involved in adoption does not seem to affect whether an innovation is adopted.

Some of these preliminary findings will help explain later findings. We are also hopeful that the careful construction and evaluation of the innovation indices will contribute to the soundness of our later conclusions.

ANALYSIS PROCEDURE

The limiting factor in our analysis is the small number of organizations. Tests of statistical significance do consider sample size, but many researchers are critical of conclusions derived on the basis of small samples, even when the findings are statistically significant.

Each independent variable can be tested by correlating it with the dependent variable. The advantage of this type of analysis is that degrees of freedom are maximized by evaluating only one independent variable at a time. But some sort of multivariate analysis provides stronger evidence than simple correlations from which to support or refute hypothesized causal relationships. Observed simple correlations between independent and dependent variables can misrepresent the true relationships.[13] Multivariate analysis is not a panacea for isolating true causal effects. But it does offer a means statistically to control extraneous variables that may confound a given relationship. When outside variables are controlled, the computed relationship between an independent and a dependent variable is more likely to represent the true relationship.

Research is clearly a series of hard choices. The argument for using multivariate analysis is a strong one. But there are more variables to be tested than there are cases. We decided upon the following strategy: We will report the simple correlations between the independent variables and innovation adoption. We will offer an interpretation of these correlations. Then we will use multiple regression to test whether any of the observed simple correlations are spurious. To maintain confidence in the findings, we will limit the number of independent variables evaluated simultaneously. Up to three or four variable will be identified and used in a regression equation that predicts innovation adoption.

The actual mechanics of the regression analysis will consist of fitting the independent variables to the dependent variable observations. This means literally sorting through the independent variables to find the three or four that best predict innovation. After the best-fit equation has been identified, other variables that are hypothesized to be associated with innovations can be brought into the equation and taken out one at a time to test whether they have any additional effect on innovation adoption.

The curve-fitting procedure is resisted by some investigators, who consider it theoryless and a fishing trip. However, the procedure has its advantages. First, it is not theoryless; theory does its job by telling us where to look and by directing us to a limited set of variables. Second, some elements of a fishing trip make good research. Most research on organizations is still exploratory. We are still trying to learn which variables are associated with innovation. The curve-fitting process involves our ransacking the data to learn which variables are strongly and genuinely related to innovation. We can use these findings to revise and improve our theory of organizational innovation.

Our procedure is similar to a laboratory experiment in the biological sciences—theory is used to set up the experiment. Then the investigator watches the experiment develop. A good investigator will want to observe and record everything that happens. Unexpected findings may be more valuable than expected ones. Data analysis is the social scientist's opportunity to observe the relationships that exist in his natural experiment. We don't want to miss anything by observing only the predicted zero-order associations.

The most serious difficulty in using regression procedures to identify the best predictors of innovation adoption is the selectivity problem. With 10 or 15 variables under consideration and only 13 cases some variables may be associated with innovativeness on the basis of random error alone. A way to test whether the findings in either time period are due to chance is cross-validation.[14] If the regression equation that predicts innovation in one period can also predict innovation in the other period, then the findings are unlikely to be due to chance. Successful cross-validation will validate our conclusions despite the small sample size.

The analysis in chapter 5 will consist of cross-tabulations of the variables that are not amenable to correlation and multiple regression techniques. Who proposed the innovations, innovation type, and other variables that can elaborate the findings of chapters 3 and 4 will be included.

NOTES

1. Richard H. Hall, "Intraorganizational Structure Variation," *Administrative Science Quarterly* 7 (December 1962): 295–308; Paul R. Lawrence and Jay W. Lorsch, *Organization and Environment* (Homewood, Ill.: Richard D. Irwin, 1969); and Jerald Hage and Michael Aiken, "Program Change and Organizational Properties," *American Journal of Sociology* 72 (March 1967): 503–19.
2. "New" means the innovations had not been adopted by any of the districts in the sample prior to the 1959–64 period.
3. Hillel J. Einhorn and Robin M. Hogarth, "Unit Weighting Schemes for Decision Making," *Organizational Behavior and Human Performance* 13 (1975): 171–92.
4. Norman H. Nie, Dale H. Bent, and Hadlai D. Hull, *SPSS: Statistical Package for the Social Sciences* (New York: McGraw-Hill, 1970).
5. Lawrence B. Mohr, "Determinants of Innovation in Organizations," *American Political Science Review* 63 (March 1969): 111–26.
6. Hage and Aiken, "Program Change and Organizational Properties."
7. Gerald Gordon, E. V. Morse, S. M. Gordon, J. deKervasoone, J. Kimberly, M. Moch, and D. G. Schwartz, "Organizational Structure and Hospital Adaptation to Environmental Demands" (Paper presented at the University of North Carolina Health Services Research Center Symposium on Innovation in Health Care Organizations, Chapel Hill, N.C., 18–19 May 1972).
8. It should be emphasized that the innovativeness score does not reflect the extent of implementation of the innovations in the school district or the quality of the innovation. This study is a test of the process leading to an adoption decision, and the initial implementation, regardless of extent, is considered to be evidence of a decision to adopt.
9. James Q. Wilson, "Innovation in Organizations: Notes toward a Theory," in *Approaches to Organizational Design*, ed. James D. Thompson (Pittsburgh: University of Pittsburgh Press, 1966).
10. Arnold D. Kaluzny, James E. Veney and John T. Gentry, "Innovation of Health Services: A Comparative Study of Hospitals and Health Departments" (Paper presented at the University of North Carolina Health Services Research Center Symposium on Innovation in Health Care Organizations, Chapel Hill, N.C., 18–19 May 1972) is an exception.
11. William M. Evan, "Organizational Lag," *Human Organization* 25 (Spring 1966): 51–53.
12. We will relax our assumptions about novelty and consider administrative innovations somewhat in chapter 5, but the major correlation analysis excludes administrative innovations because there were not enough innovations to constitute a dependent variable.

13. James A. Davis, *Elementary Survey Analysis* (Englewood Cliffs, N.J.: Prentice-Hall, 1971); and Morris Rosenberg, *The Logic of Survey Analysis* (New York: Basic Books, 1968).
14. Hillel J. Einhorn, "Alchemy in the Behavioral Sciences," *The Public Opinion Quarterly* 36 (Fall 1972): 367–78.

3

Adoption of Innovations for the Collegebound Student

Having constructed two dependent variables, adoption of innovations benefiting collegebound students and adoption of those benefiting terminal students, we can test our hypotheses twice, once with each of the two dependent variables. The data regarding collegebound students are richer, that is there are more such innovations and they were adopted in both time periods. It seems that the major focus of high school districts, at least in our sample, is on the collegebound student. Since this is the case, it is appropriate to test first our hypotheses using adoption of innovations to benefit collegebound students as the dependent variable.

Our model of organizational innovation was only partly elaborated prior to the 1965 portion of the study, so data pertinent to some of the hypotheses were collected only during the 1972 portion of the study. For that reason we begin our analysis with the data from the 1968–72 period; then we will look at as many of the same relationships as possible for the 1958–64 period. Finally we will examine the changes that occurred over time in both the independent and dependent variables and in their relationships to one another. Having data from two time periods permits us to cross-validate our findings, that is, to use the relationships in one time period to predict effects in the other.

THE ANALYSIS

The 1968–72 Period

Let us first look at the zero-order correlations for the 1968–72 time period. In our model of organizational adoption of innovation we posit a process. The process begins with incentives from the environment and, in the case of high schools, the existence of innovation alternatives in the environment. Then organizations will be able to innovate if they are properly structured and contain the proper human talent and attitudes. Many of these factors may be interrelated, and we try to untangle those relationships when we look at the regression analyses; but in order to see if our description of the process is valid, at the very least we ought to be able to specify the correlates of adoption of innovation.

In the first chapter we argued that incentives for innovation would arise from highly educated consumers and from school board members who held goals for high-quality education. From table 3.1 we see that both factors, community education ($r = .62$) and elite goals for quality education ($r = .67$), are positively correlated with adoption of innovations. We also see that as the proportion of teachers assigned to vocational education decreases, the adoption of innovations for collegebound students increases ($r = -.73$). This is compatible with the position that innovations are adopted congruent with the goals of the district and the needs of consumers.

We also argued in chapter 1 that teacher professionalism and travel to meetings and conventions brings knowledge of innovations into the organization and that when teachers know about possible innovations, those possibilities become proposals if the teachers have help in preparing the proposals. That help can come in the form of free time, more administrators, and more certified nonteaching support staff. From table 3.1 we can see that one of the two factors supposedly associated with getting knowledge of innovation alternatives into the organization is positively correlated with adoption of innovations; teacher

TABLE 3.1
Zero-Order Correlations of Independent Variables with the Adoption of Innovations for Collegebound Students, 1968–72

INDEPENDENT VARIABLE	CORRELATION WITH INNOVATIONS
Community education	.62[b]
Elite quality goals	.67[a]
Vocational teacher ratio	−.73[a]
Teacher professionalism	.65[a]
Travel expenditures per teacher	−.30
Teacher free time	.23
Administrative ratio	−.13
Support staff ratio	.54[b]
Affluence (expenditures per pupil)	.55[b]
Slack resources	−.18
Elite perception of slack resources	.07
District size	.41
Complexity	.24
Growth rate	−.15
Decentralization	.11
Elite attitude toward innovation	.47[b]

[a]Significant at .01 level
[b]Significant at .05 level

professionalism ($r = .65$). Of the three factors that help in the development of proposals, only one, availability of certified nonteaching support staff, is positively correlated with adoption of innovations ($r = .54$). The enabler variables: affluence, slack, perceived slack, size, complexity, growth rate, decentralization, and a favorable attitude from the elite are all supposed to be positively related to innovation adoption, except growth rate, which is supposed to be negatively related. Again, from table 3.1, two of these variables, affluence (expenditure per pupil) ($r = .55$) and elite attitude toward innovation ($r = .47$), are significantly related to adoption of innovations.

Now for the difficult question: What do these correlations mean? Obviously, one can't make inferences about causal relationships based on zero-order correlations observed in one time segment; however, given the hypothesized model and the correlational relationships, we can make some judgments. We have hypothesized: (1) the need for incentives to innovate; (2a) the ability to get knowledge of possible innovations into the organization, and (b) the wherewithal to turn them into proposals; and, finally, (3) enabler variables like people's attitudes, slack resources, and certain structural characteristics that permit or facilitate adoption of innovations. We had two or more measures for each of the four major categories, and we found at least one measure from each of the four categories significantly related to adoption of innovations. At this point the incentives to innovate seem to be the best predictors of innovation.

What of the variables that were posited to be, but weren't, significantly related to adoption of innovations? The bulk of them, five of eight measures, were in the enabler variable category. It is possible that what we considered enabler variables really weren't, or that some enabler variables are more important than others, or that our measures of the enabler variables were too crude. In any case, the fact that at least one measure from each category was significant gives us hope that our proposed process is a good description of how and why organizations adopt innovations. Pending further analyses, we will, therefore, tentatively cling to that judgment.

We say "tentatively" because we know just from looking at the correlation matrix (see appendix D) that many of our independent variables are associated with each other in a tangle of positive and negative relationships. Regression analysis is one way to partially untangle these relationships. First, we used multiple regression procedures to determine which of our hypothesized independent variables were most important for predicting adoption of innovations. We decided to limit the equation that best predicts adoption of innovations to about four independent variables because of the small sample size. The contribution of a variable to the predictive power of the regression equation was judged by its t-value, the adjusted R^2, and the standard error of residuals. The t-value measures the statistical significance of the association between the independent variable and the dependent variable. The R^2 is the percentage of variance in the dependent variable explained by all independent variables in the regression equation. The standard error of residuals is the standard deviation of the dependent variable about the regression plane. If the regression equation is to be effective for predicting innovation, the standard error of the residuals should be considerably smaller than the original standard deviation of innovation.

The computations for both adjusted R^2 and the standard error of residuals take sample size into consideration. Adding variables to the regression equation that do not make a substantive contribution toward explaining innovation will actually decrease the values for adjusted R^2 and the standard error of residuals by reducing the degrees of freedom upon which these values are based.

Using these guidelines, we reduced the hypothesized variables to the four shown in table 3.2. Ninety-six percent of the variance in the adoption of college-oriented innovations is explained, and the standard deviation of innovation is reduced from 3.35 to 0.79. Quite clearly, a high level of community education, a large certified support staff component, a favorable attitude toward innovation by the superintendent and school board, and decentralized decision making are very positively associated with adoption of innovations.

TABLE 3.2
Multiple Regression of College-Oriented Innovativeness on Its Best Predictors, 1968–72

INDEPENDENT VARIABLE	REGRESSION COEFFICIENT	STANDARDIZED REGRESSION COEFFICIENT	t-VALUE	ONE-TAIL p-VALUE
Community education	18.20	.69	9.70	$<.001$
Elite attitude toward innovation	11.79	.63	8.67	$<.001$
Decentalization	0.77	.40	5.28	$<.001$
Support staff ratio	36.75	.35	4.93	$<.001$

$R^2 = .96$, adjusted R^2; standard error of residuals $= 0.79$, $n = 13$

These four variables do not fully explain school district innovativeness, however. In tables 3.3 and 3.4 are summaries of regression equations in which different variables are brought into the equation that best predicts adoption of innovations. The t-values in each column identify the independent variables used in each regression equation. At least two additional variables are worthy of serious consideration.

The t-values in columns 2 and 3 of table 3.3 show that perceived slack resources ($t = -2.30$) and growth rate ($t = 1.86$) each have a fairly substantial association with college-oriented innovativeness. The addition of either of these variables improves the overall predictability of the regression equation. Adjusted R^2 increases from .95 to .96 in each case, and the standard error of residuals decreases to .63 when perceived slack is used and to .69 when growth rate is used. The size of the t-values and the improvement in the prediction of innovativeness suggest that either or both of these two variables could be added to the best-fit regression equation.

The t-value for perceived financial well-being in column 2 of table 3.3 ($t = -2.30$) can be interpreted to mean that perceived financial well-being is negatively related to innovativeness. The relationship is opposite the direction hypothesized. The importance of growth rate is not indicated by the simple correlation ($r = -.15$). Growth is negatively associated with the other predictors of innovation. When the other variables are controlled, the positive effect of the infusion of new personnel and facilities can be observed. We will explain these findings in more detail—especially the puzzling negative relationship between perceived slack and innovation—after we see how the remaining independent variables affect the best-fit equation. What follows is somewhat complicated and tedious but necessary for a fuller understanding of the process of adopting innovations.

Leaving growth in the analysis temporarily, we can see that the t-values in columns 4 through 7 of table 3.3 indicate that the independent variables involved are interrelated and that they are associated with innovation in a complex fashion. In column 4 teacher professionalism is simply added to the equation, and it appears unimportant with a t-value of 0.39. But notice the large drop in the t-values for community education and decentralization and the somewhat smaller drop for growth rate from

TABLE 3.3

t-Values for Multiple Regressions of College-Oriented Innovativeness on Selected Sets of Independent Variables, 1968–72[a]

INDEPENDENT VARIABLE	1 t-VALUE	2 t-VALUE	3 t-VALUE	4 t-VALUE	5 t-VALUE	6 t-VALUE	7 t-VALUE
Community education	9.70	11.71	10.64	1.49			4.88
Elite attitude toward innovation	8.67	10.98	10.05	9.40	8.47	5.60	5.40
Decentralization	5.28	6.68	4.94	1.95		2.55	
Support staff ratio	4.93	4.48	5.84	5.39	5.28		4.79
Elite perception of slack resources		−2.30					
Growth rate			1.86	0.88	7.62	4.16	2.70
Teacher professionalism				0.39	8.84		
Affluence (expenditures per pupil)						6.28	
Administrative ratio							−1.68
R^2	.96	.98	.98	.98	.96	.88	.92
Adjusted R^2	.95	.96	.96	.95	.94	.82	.87
Standard error of residuals	0.79	0.63	0.69	0.73	0.82	1.23	1.23

[a]With 8 d.f., when $t = 1.1$, one tail $p = .15$; when $t = 1.4$ one-tail $p = .10$; when $t = 1.8$, one-tail $p = .05$; when $t = 2.9$, one-tail $p = .01$.

column 3 to column 4. Teacher professionalism is intercorrelated with these other variables and explains some of the same variance in innovativeness. In column 5 teacher professionalism is used to predict innovativeness in place of community education and decentralization. Teacher professionalism becomes very important ($t = 8.84$), and the overall prediction equation is a good one. Growth also becomes more important in column 5.

The data in columns 4 and 5 of table 3.3 indicate multicollinearity. Multicollinearity occurs when independent variables are substantially correlated. Collinear variables can replace one another in the regression equation without making a large difference in the ability to predict the dependent variable. In this case teacher professionalism combined with growth explains almost the same variance in innovation as community education and decentralization.

In terms of inference it would be spurious to conclude either that none of the collinear variables is important or that one variable is important and the others are not. The most accurate conclusion is that the variables move together and each is important. It is difficult, however, to gauge their relative importance. The conclusion based on the data in columns 4 and 5 of table 3.3, then, is that the highly educated communities have the highly educated teachers and decentralization is high where the teachers are best educated and organizational growth is rapid. Innovation appears to be a function of all four variables.

There are two additional variables in this cluster of collinear variables. Affluence overlaps community education and the amount of certified support staff. In column 6 of table 3.3 the effect of substituting affluence ($t = 6.28$) for these other two variables can be seen. The overall equation loses some of its predictive power, but affluence appears to be closely related to community education and the support staff ratio.

The last variable in the cluster of variables is administrative ratio. According to the t-values in column 7 of table 3.3, administrative ratio has a negative relationship with innovativeness ($t = -1.68$) when decentralization is not in the equation. The importance of administrative ratio is not great. But the t-values do imply that administrative ratio is inversely associated with decentralization and explains roughly the same variance in college-oriented innovativeness as does decentralization.

If we consider the cluster of variables that overlap in the explanation of college-oriented innovativeness, it would have been spurious to impute singular causal influences to the four variables in the best-fit equation in table 3.2. The attitude of the superintendent and school board toward innovation does have a separate and distinct association with district innovativeness. This attitude probably has such a strong influence because it creates a climate favorable to innovation and encourages and reinforces the teachers by approving proposed new ideas.

The other three of the best-fit variables, however, are part of a tangle of seven variables that are all associated with the adoption of college-oriented innovations. In retrospect this cluster of variables makes intuitive sense. Affluence and teacher professionalism reflect community demand for, and ability to pay for, quality education. Certified support staff and teacher professionalism reflect the level of expenditures per pupil (affluence) in the district. Decentralization reflects the teacher professionalism (educational level), the smallness of the administrative component, and to some extent the growth rate of the district.

There seem to be two overlapping and complementary dimensions in this cluster of variables. On the one hand are community education, affluence, teacher professionalism, and certified support staff, which seem to represent an educational quality dimension. On the other hand is a complementary structural dimension of decentralization, administrative ratio, and growth. The quality-oriented community can afford to pay for highly professional teachers and a large auxiliary staff to support the teachers. More ideas enter the system, are translated into proposals, and are adopted under these conditions. The professional teachers and the certified nonteaching staff apparently have more freedom to innovate in search of quality education because of decentralization and the small administrative ratio.

It is interesting to note that the districts that seem to be striving to produce a quality product, and that are also adopting the most college-oriented innovations, tend to spend their money to obtain highly educated teachers and a large certified non-teaching support staff. These districts also settle for a smaller administrative component. Rather than just spending more money, the innovative districts seem to be spending it in a different way from the noninnovative districts. This brings us back to the negative relationship between perceived slack and innovation. Innovative districts spend more money than non-innovative districts for things *conducive* to innovation. The superintendent and school board members in these high-expenditure districts report being short of money, of being overextended financially. The net effect apparently benefits innovation. The things and people acquired with the money generate innovations, and feeling short of money is not a barrier to implementation. The hypothesis that slack resources are a necessary antecedent to favorable adoption decisions is clearly rejected.

The remaining variables in the analysis of college-oriented innovativeness apparently do not have an important independent relationship to frequency of adoption. Hence, organizational complexity, elite quality goals for the district, the emphasis given to terminal education, district size, slack resources, teacher free time, and travel expenditures per teacher can be ruled out as dominant factors in the innovation process. The t-statistics shown in table 3.4 for these variables are not large enough to conclude support for them.

Two of the variables that appear unimportant in Table 3.4 do seem to have some role in the innovation process, despite their small t-values. Both elite quality goals and vocational teacher ratio have strong zero-order correlations with college-oriented innovativeness ($r = .67$ and $-.73$, respectively). These two correlations literally mean that college-oriented innovations tend to be adopted in districts where the superintendent and board express a desire for educational quality and where the proportion of vocational teachers is small.

The reason these two variables do not show up as significant in the regression equation, despite their large zero-order correlations, is that they overlap several of the variables already

TABLE 3.4

Additional t-Values for Multiple Regressions of College-Oriented Innovativeness on Selected Sets of Independent Variables; 1968–72[a]

INDEPENDENT VARIABLES	1 t-VALUE	2 t-VALUE	3 t-VALUE	4 t-VALUE	5 t-VALUE	6 t-VALUE	7 t-VALUE	8 t-VALUE
Community education	9.70	9.95	8.62	6.13	7.98	8.71	8.80	9.17
Elite attitude toward innovation	8.67	8.47	6.54	7.83	7.49	6.04	8.42	8.50
Decentralization	5.28	5.50	5.01	4.81	4.11	4.18	4.24	4.56
Support staff ratio	4.93	4.60	4.13	4.31	4.56	4.68	4.72	4.95
Number of occupations		−1.19						
Elite quality goals			−0.41					
Vocational teacher ratio				1.00				
District size					0.20			
Slack resources						−0.52		
Teacher free time							−0.88	
Travel expenditures per teacher								−1.00
R^2	.96	.97	.96	.97	.96	.96	.97	.97
Adjusted R^2	.95	.95	.94	.95	.94	.94	.94	.95
Standard error of residuals	0.79	0.77	0.83	0.79	0.84	0.83	0.80	0.79

[a]With 8 d.f., when $t = 1.1$, one-tail $p = .15$; when $t = 1.4$, one-tail $p = .10$; when $t = 1.8$, one-tail $p = .05$; when $t = 2.9$, one-tail $p = .01$.

represented in the regression equation. The other variables already explain the variance in innovativeness that is due to elite quality goals and vocational teacher ratio. Elite quality goals, for instance, are positively associated with elite attitude toward innovation, teacher professionalism, certified support staff ratio, and affluence and are negatively associated with administrative ratio. A possible explanation for these associations is that elite quality goals have an indirect effect on college-oriented innovativeness. Elite quality goals may have a direct effect on affluence, teacher professionalism, and certified support staff ratio, and these variables in turn affect innovation. Elite quality goals may thus have an indirect effect on innovativeness through their positive influence in shaping these other important associates of innovativeness.

Similar reasoning seems to also explain the strong zero-order association between vocational teacher ratio and innovativeness. Vocational teacher ratio measures the goal or task of the district with regard to educating collegebound or terminal students. Vocational teacher ratio is negatively associated with community education, affluence, teacher professionalism, and elite attitude toward innovation. This suggests that the educational quality dimension of the school district tends to be associated with the college preparatory function of the district. A high-quality education seems to mean a college-preparatory education. If this interpretation is true, the educational quality dimension of the district should not be an important explanation for the adoption of innovations that benefit terminal students.

There is one last bit of evidence that helps clarify the process of adopting innovations that benefit collegebound students. The presence of highly professional teachers is believed to be important because innovation ideas will flow upward from them to the administration for approval. Evidence for this upward flow is illustrated in table 3.5. Sixty-nine percent of all educational innovations in the 13 districts originated with teachers. This increases to 83 percent when only college-oriented innovations are counted.

The last item in table 3.5 compares what might be called technical innovations to all others. Curriculum and teaching

TABLE 3.5
**Percentage Innovations Proposed by Teachers,
All School Districts, 1968–72**

VARIABLE	PERCENTAGE
All innovations	69
Innovations that benefit collegebound students	83
Innovations that benefit terminal students	55
Curriculum and teaching techniques only	87
All other innovations	26

techniques are in the teacher's area of technical expertise. Teachers are the source for 87 percent of these innovations, compared with only 26 percent for other kinds of innovations. Administrators proposed those innovations that were not proposed by teachers. Teachers apparently propose most of the innovations that affect the classroom. Administrators tend to propose other innovations. College-oriented innovations are mostly classroom innovations, so the innovative districts will tend to be those that utilize professional teachers to propose the new ideas.

To briefly summarize this section of the analysis, high school districts with a high level of adoption of college-oriented innovations are characterized by four factors:

1. The high school district functions in the context of a community that expects a high-quality, college preparatory education for its young people, and the community provides the resources to pay for it.
2. The elite in the school organization direct the school district toward quality and innovativeness, and they support and approve behavior that furthers these ends.
3. The larger amount of money spent in innovative districts does not directly buy innovations. Rather, this money finances highly professional teachers and a large support staff; with the assistance of the support staff the teachers generate and propose new ideas within their area of expertise.
4. The decentralized structure and small administrative com-

ponent complement the above activities by giving teaching personnel the freedom and decision-making authority to try new ideas that will help meet the quality and innovation goals of the school district.

These findings permit us to conclude that our general model of the innovation process seems to be a reasonably good description of what actually occurs. Where there are environmental incentives to innovate, innovative alternatives are sought and proposed, and if appropriate enabling factors exist in the organization, proposals are adopted. We can also claim fairly good support for our hypotheses specific to school districts. Those concerning the educational level of the community and the goals for quality education held by elites were shown to be necessary to explain the innovation process. We also demonstrated that more professional teaching staff and certified support staff lead to innovation. Our original hypothesis about the administrative ratio was not supported, and in fact the data are opposite to what we predicted: Innovations increase as the administrative ratio decreases. Our hypotheses involving enabler variables fared least well. Of the seven only two were confirmed. In those we predicted that decentralization and elite attitude toward innovation would each have a positive relationship with innovation adoption. Our hypotheses regarding perceived slack resources and growth rate were reversed. Perceived slack resources were negatively related to innovation, and growth rate was positively related. To this point in the analysis, then, we can claim reasonably good support for the general model and more modest support for our operationalization of this model for high school districts. Our ideas on what constituted intraorganizational enabler variables were not completely accurate.

The 1959–64 Period

Data from the 1959–64 period enable us to perform a second test of our model of organizational innovation. The characteristics of school districts in the sample in the 1959-64 period were different from those in the 1968–72 period.[1] The districts were only half as large in the earlier period and were experiencing a much more rapid growth rate. Nearly all superintendents and school board members were different in the earlier period also.

The organizations were different enough so that the relationships among the independent variables were not exactly the same in each period. Moreover, data are available on fewer variables from the 1959–64 period. Nevertheless, the variables and their relationships provide additional evidence from which inferences can be made about the underlying process of innovation adoption. If the findings permit us to say that the same process occurred despite differences in the organizations and their circumstances, then the evidence for our theory is strong.

In table 3.6 are the correlations between adoption of innovations that benefitted collegebound students and the independent variables that were measured in that period.[2] From this table we can see that of the seven relationships that were significant in 1968–72, six of the seven were also significant and in the predicted direction for the 1959–64 period. The one that doesn't reach significance, support staff ratio, comes close ($p < .10$). Further, we again have at least one significant relationship in each of the four categories; incentives from the

TABLE 3.6
Zero-Order Correlations of Independent Variables with the Adoption of Innovations for Collegebound Students, 1959–64 and 1968–72

INDEPENDENT VARIABLE	INNOVATION	
	1959–64	1968–72
Community education	.77[a]	.62
Vocational teacher ratio	−.74[a]	−.73
Teacher professionalism	.63[a]	.65
Administrative ratio	−.48[b]	−.13
Support staff ratio	.37	.54
Affluence (expenditures per pupil)	.72[a]	.55
Slack resources	.05	−.18
District size	.28	.41
Growth rate	−.26	−.15
Elite attitude toward innovation	.60[b]	.47

[a]Significant at .01 level
[b]Significant at .05 level

environment, ability to get knowledge of alternatives into the organization, the wherewithal to turn them into proposals, and the enabler variables within the organization. So far, our hypothesized process seems to be a highly accurate description of the actual process of the adoption of innovations. However, as we have already seen, zero-order correlations can be misleading. Let us turn to the regression analysis.

Regression procedures were used to identify the four variables that best predict college-oriented innovativeness. These four variables—community education, affluence, administrative ratio, and certified support staff ratio—are shown in table 3.7. The R^2 is .89, and the standard deviation of college-oriented innovations was reduced from 4.83 to 1.98.

TABLE 3.7
Multiple Regression of College-Oriented Innovativeness on Its Best Predictors, 1959–64

INDEPENDENT VARIABLE	REGRESSION COEFFICIENT	STANDARDIZED REGRESSION COEFFICIENT	t-VALUE	ONE-TAIL p-VALUE
Community education	16.28	.47	3.27	< .006
Affluence (expenditures per pupil)	0.013	.36	2.48	< .02
Administrative ratio	− 82.92	− .40	− 3.32	< .005
Support Staff ratio	20.07	.22	1.72	< .06

$R^2 =$ .89, adjusted $R^2 =$ .83; standard
error of residuals = 1.98, $n =$ 13

Our interpretation of this analysis is very similar to that of the 1968–72 findings for college-oriented innovativeness. Community education and affluence represent the demand for school quality and the ability to pay for it. The certified support staff are facilitators of the idea development and proposal process. The small administrative ratio represents the decentralized structural arrangement that gives the professional teachers and the support staff the freedom to innovate in search of better educational techniques.

A problem with multicollinearity is also present in these data. In column 2 of table 3.8, teacher professionalism is added to the equation and has a t-value of only 0.25. In column 3 teacher professionalism replaces affluence and appears to be fairly important, with a t-value of 1.62. Teacher professionalism does not replace affluence perfectly in terms of the overall equation. But the findings do support the interpretation that one reason affluence is important is that it finances the hiring of highly professional teachers.

The effect of vocational teacher ratio is shown in column 4 of table 3.8. Collinearity exists between community education and vocational teacher ratio. Vocational teacher ratio is significant in a negative direction without dropping community education from the equation ($t = -1.90$). The emphasis given to college preparation closely reflects the educational level of the community. Moreover, the districts that display the characteristics associated with school quality tend to consider college preparation their major task. None of the remaining variables in table 3.8 have quite large enough t-values to be considered important.

The overall findings are quite similar to those of the 1968–72 period. Two variables, community education and certified support staff ratio, are among the best predictors in both periods, and if a small administrative ratio can be taken as a proxy for decentralization, then we can say that three of the four best predictors are the same in both periods.

The variables not in the best-predictor equations also functioned in similar fashion in both periods. Growth rate was an important factor in the adoption of college-oriented innovations in 1968–72 but was not quite important enough to conclude it was a factor in the 1959–64 period. Growth rate from 1959 to 1964 was almost three times as great as from 1968 to 1972. Perhaps growth was too fast in the first period to be as beneficial to innovation adoption. Organizational size was not an important factor in either period, nor was slack resources. Excess resources apparently are not a necessary condition to adoption of innovations.

The single variable that seems to have a different association

TABLE 3.8

t-Values for Multiple Regressions of College-Oriented Innovativeness on Selected Sets of Independent Variables, 1959–64[a]

INDEPENDENT VARIABLE	1 t-VALUE	2 t-VALUE	3 t-VALUE	4 t-VALUE	5 t-VALUE	6 t-VALUE	7 t-VALUE	8 t-VALUE
Community education	3.27	3.08	3.88	0.73	1.95	3.36	2.98	2.88
Affluence (expenditures per pupil)	2.47	1.53		2.55	2.46	2.38	1.52	2.23
Administrative ratio	−3.32	−2.92	−2.51	−1.17	−3.49	−3.24	−3.25	−2.79
Support staff ratio	1.72	1.41	1.21	2.09	2.01	1.54	1.46	1.53
Teacher Professionalism		0.25	1.62					
Vocational teacher ratio				−1.90				
Growth rate					1.03			
District size						1.10		
Slack resources							−0.76	
Elite attitude toward innovation								0.21
R^2	.89	.89	.85	.92	.90	.90	.90	.89
Adjusted R^2	.83	.81	.78	.86	.83	.84	.82	.81
Standard error of residuals	1.98	2.10	2.28	1.78	1.97	1.95	2.03	2.11

[a]With 8 d.f., when $t = 1.1$, one-tail $p = .15$; when $t = 1.4$, one-tail $p = .10$; when $t = 1.8$, one-tail $p = .05$; when $t = 2.9$, one-tail $p = .01$.

with innovation in the two periods is superintendent and board attitude toward innovation. The t-value of 0.21 in column 8 of table 3.8 is very small. In 1968–72, however, elite attitude toward innovation was a major factor in college-oriented innovativeness (table 3.2). The simple correlation between elite attitude and innovativeness for the 1959–64 period is .60. This is actually stronger than the simple correlation of .47 between the same two variables in 1968–72.

The fact that elite attitude had a larger simple correlation with innovation in 1959–64 yet was found to be less important in the regression analysis compared with 1968–72 illustrates one problem in trying to make causal inferences from intercorrelated variables. The reason elite attitude does not appear important in the 1959–64 regression analysis is that it is intercorrelated with the best predictors of innovation. A favorable attitude toward innovation in 1959–64 tended to exist in those districts that were in highly educated communities, that had high expenditures per pupil (affluence) and a large certified support staff ratio, and so on. Thus elite attitude did not appear to have a separate and important effect on college-oriented innovativeness.

In the 1968–72 period, however, the attitudes of the organizational elite were relatively orthogonal to the other best-predictor variables. Thus, when elite attitude is found associated with innovativeness, it is probably because elite attitude directly affected the frequency of adoption.

Both periods taken together suggest that elite attitude is an important factor in innovativeness. In both periods innovativeness had a substantial simple association with elite attitude. In 1959–64 elite attitude was intercorrelated with the important variables and could only be said to affect innovativeness through its association with these other variables. In 1968–72, however, elite attitude existed in school districts without these other factors present and was still associated with innovativeness. Thus an important association with innovativeness was found.

In sum, then, the findings from the 1959–64 period are compatible with the 1968–72 findings for college-oriented innovativeness. Community education and affluence represent the demand for school quality and the ability to pay for it. The certified support staff are facilitators of the idea development and proposal process. The small administrative ratio represents the decentralized structural arrangement that gives the professional teachers and the support staff the freedom to innovate in search of better educational techniques.

Looking at both periods, we can say that several factors are associated with the adoption of innovations for collegebound students. Innovative districts are oriented toward a quality, college-preparatory education and can afford to finance it. The innovative districts have highly professional teachers and the support of a large, certified nonteaching support staff. A small administrative ratio, or the presumed decentralization it implies, enables the professional teachers and the nonteaching support staff to try innovative ideas for future adoption. A favorable attitude toward innovation by the superintendent and school board was found to exist in the innovative districts, but at this point we are unable to say whether it affects adoption of innovations directly or through its effect on other variables.

THE CROSS-VALIDATION

We argue that the data from both time periods support our conclusion that the process of adopting innovations for collegebound students is similar in both periods. The combination of variables that best predicts college-oriented innovation, however, is not exactly the same in the two periods. One reason for the difference in predictor variables is that we did not obtain measures of all the variables in the earlier period. Decentralization, for instance, had a strong relationship with innovativeness in 1968–72 but was not measured in 1959–64. Despite these differences we still maintain the underlying process is the same.

With longitudinal data such as ours there are at least two ways to draw out additional evidence concerning the relationships among variables. One technique is to assess the lag effects among the variables.[3] If independent variables are theorized to influence a dependent variable over some finite time period, then the dependent variable from the second period can be regressed on itself and other variables in the first period to see if this is the case. This procedure has a couple of important advantages: First, it controls for the prior influence of the dependent variable (autocorrelation), and consequently the causal influence is assessed only on the change that takes place in the dependent variable. Second, by regressing each variable in period 2 on the period 1 variables, it is possible to identify causal direction.

Unfortunately, we cannot justify the use of the lag technique with our data. Too much time has elapsed between the two periods of data collection. The lag model requires that the time lag between periods approximate the true causal lag among variables. The observations of our high school districts occurred an average of eight years apart (the midpoints of the time periods are 1962 and 1970). This is far longer (we think) than necessary for most independent variables to influence innovation. Most school innovations can be adopted fairly quickly. We anticipate that variables such as teacher professionalism, nonteaching support staff, and elite attitude toward innovation will effect innovation within a year or two. Since each period of data collection is an average of several years (1959–64 and 1968–72), the actual causal effects would be felt within each period, not across them. When the true causal lag among variables is not similar to the measured time lag, the findings can be seriously distorted.[4] Consequently, we used a different technique to take advantage of our longitudinal data.

Another analysis technique that is appropriate to our data is cross-validation.[5] Typically in cross-validation one finds the regression equation that predicts a dependent variable in one sample from a population of organizations (or people, or whatever is being studied). Then the same regression equation is used with data from an entirely different sample of organizations to predict what the dependent variable will be. If the predicted values of the dependent variable are highly correlated with the actual values in the second sample, then the cross-validation is a success. The investigator can conclude that his findings from the original sample are probably not idiosyncratic. The cross-validation strengthens the investigator's inference that the observed relationships really do exist in nature and that they have some generalizability.

Cross-validation is essentially a replication of a very rigorous nature; the investigator has to predict outcomes in a new sample. If successful, the original equation can be characterized as having predictive validity. This kind of rigorous test is not often done in the social sciences and is very infrequent in studies of organizations.

Our use of cross-validation is different. We do not have two separate samples of organizations on which to test the relationships, but we do have a single sample of organizations with observations taken an average of eight years apart. A successful cross-validation will have a somewhat different interpretation than when separate samples of organizations are used. Failure to cross-validate, however, means the same thing no matter how it is done—the findings cannot be substantiated, and the investigator's original findings are probably not valid.

One consequence of using one rather than two populations is that the reliability and generalizability of the results are weakened because there is no increase in the number of organizations for which the relationships are valid.[6] However, if the organizations in the sample undergo substantial change so that characteristics of the organizations in the second period are different from those in the first period, the investigator can generalize to some degree. For example, if the organizations increase in size to the point that they represent a different range of organizational size, and if the same predictive relationships exist in each period, then the relationships are apparently valid across the whole span of organizational sizes included in the two tests.

Indeed, cross-validation across separate observations from the same set of organizations has considerable value. One valuable aspect concerns internal validity.[7] If the relationships are found to hold up despite the passage of time, it increases our confidence that the observed relationships really do exist in these organizations. This is important because we are dealing with a small sample, and some of our observed relationships could have occurred by chance alone.

Our organizations did not change dramatically, but there were sufficient changes so that successful cross-validation will increase our confidence in the validity of our findings. First, an entirely different set of innovations was used in the second period. Second, the average size of the high school districts increased from 3,332 to 6,076 students, which is almost double. This not only means more personnel, but also an influx of new personnel. Moreover, only one superintendent was the same in both periods. Third, the percentage of teachers assigned to teach vocational courses increased from 10 to 15 percent of the teacher population. This is congruent with our earlier conclusion that the goals of the districts changed, with increasing emphasis given to vocational education (chapter 2). Fourth, expenditures per pupil affluence also increased substantially—from $745 per pupil to $1,369—but some of this was undoubtedly due to inflation. Finally, the educational level in the communities increased. In 1960 an average of 55 percent of the population had a high school education or more. In 1970 67 percent had completed high school. (The means and standard deviations for each variable are in appendix D.) These changes suggest that in the second time period the school districts in our sample were operating in somewhat different community environments, they were larger and had many new personnel, and the goals of some districts were no longer totally focused on college preparation.

Another value of cross-validation with the same sample is the opportunity it affords to assess changes over time. If the independent variables and innovation change in the same direction as time passes, this is stronger evidence for causality than cross-sectional findings, even if such findings are cross-validated on a separate sample. Data over time can be used for something like a natural experiment. In those instances where the school districts change with respect to an independent variable, we would expect the dependent variable to follow. For instance, some districts may have added certified nonteaching support staff over the interval between 1962 and 1970, while other districts may have reduced support staff. These additions and reductions should have been associated with similar additions and reductions in innovation. If not, a causal relationship does not exist. If the school districts did not change over the two time periods, then we would expect the same districts to have adopted innovations in each period.

From the correlation coefficients in table 3.9 we can judge the stability of the major variables in our sample of school districts. A large correlation coefficient, say greater than .9, indicates little change in the districts relative to each other. We emphasize *little change relative to each other*. A large serial correlation coefficient could mean either the observed values are the same for each period or that all values changed by about the same amount. The districts must change in varying amounts—be somewhat unstable—in order for us to assess the effect of change on innovation using correlation analysis. We can see that community education ($r = .93$), teacher professionalism ($r = .81$), and affluence ($r = .86$) are fairly stable over time. Schools may gradually change on these characteristics, but all schools appear to change at about the same rate. Since these variables are relatively stable, it is not possible to test whether major changes in these variables covary with changes in the number of innovations adopted by the school districts.

Three variables show instability over time: the proportion of

TABLE 3.9
Serial Correlations of Selected Variables over the Two Waves

VARIABLE	CORRELATION COEFFICIENT
Community education	.93[a]
Vocational teacher ratio	.45
Teacher professionalism	.81[a]
Administrative ratio	.79[a]
Support staff ratio	.70[a]
Affluence (expenditures per pupil)	.86[a]
District size	.73[a]
Elite attitude toward innovation	.14
Innovations for collegebound students	.45

[a]Significant at .01 level

teachers assigned to vocational teaching ($r = .45$), the elite attitude toward innovation ($r = .14$), and the number of innovations adopted for collegebound students ($r = .45$). We have already discussed the finding that these school districts are increasing the proportion of vocational teachers, but apparently they are doing so at different rates. This means that the districts differ in the new emphasis given to vocational education. The elite attitude toward innovation is practically uncorrelated over time. This finding suggests that attitudes are relatively independent of the other independent variables. Finally, there is instability in the rate of innovation itself, which indicates that innovation is not simply a characteristic that persists in the same district over time. Other factors affect the relative rate of innovation in these districts. There is some correlation over time ($r = .45$), but we need to know more than the prior innovation rate in order to predict innovation accurately.

In table 3.10 we test whether the three independent variables that experienced considerable change are associated with changes in the rate of innovation. We have computed the first difference (time 2 value minus time 1 value) for each independent variable and have correlated that change with the first difference in innovativeness. The findings lend moderate support to the idea that the independent variables affect innovation over time. An increase in vocational teachers, which indicates increasing emphasis on vocational education, is associated with a decrease in innovation for collegebound students ($r = -.42$). This is not highly significant, but it is clearly in the right direction.

The change in elite attitude is likewise associated with a change in innovation ($r = .53$). These districts have undergone

TABLE 3.10
Zero-Order Correlations of Changes in Selected Independent Variables with Changes in Innovation for Collegebound Students

INDEPENDENT VARIABLE	Δ INNOVATION
Δ Vocational teacher ratio	−.42
Δ Elite attitude toward innovation	.53[a]
Δ Support staff ratio	.45

[a]Significant at .05 level

substantial reshuffling with regard to the attitudes expressed by the elite, so this finding provides strong evidence that the attitude from the top of the organization has a major influence on innovation adoption within the organization.

The size of the support staff ratio is moderately stable over time ($r = .70$) Some change has taken place in this variable, and this variable is central to our explanation of innovation adoption, so we include it in table 3.10 also. Change in the support staff ratio is correlated with change in innovation in the predicted direction ($r = .45$). An increase over time in the support staff ratio is associated with an increase in the frequency of innovation adoption.

Combined with the earlier finding that these same variables are substantially correlated with innovation in each time period, table 3.10 data constitute modest support for saying that the three independent variables causally affect innovation adoption.

The final test is the cross-validation of the regression findings. We will cross-validate by using the best-fit regression equation from one time period to predict adoption of innovations in the other time period. A regression equation is designed to fit the idiosyncrasies of the data from which it arises. Hence, when it is used with other data, it loses some of its predictive power. As variables are added to the equation to achieve a better fit with the original data, the equation will fare less well in the cross-validation. Normally, a best-fit equation of two or three variables that successfully predicts the dependent variable in another set of data can be considered a successful test. As a fourth or fifth variable is added to the equation, the equation increases in its ability to predict the dependent variable in the original data but decreases in ability to predict the dependent variable in the second set of data.

The four variables that predicted innovation adoption in the 1968–72 period were community education, elite attitude toward innovation, support staff ratio, and decentralization. Decentralization was not measured in the 1959–64 period. The remaining three variables are central to the explanation of college-oriented innovativeness, however, and will be used to predict innovation in both periods.

The regression of innovativeness on community education, elite attitude, and support staff ratio for the 1968–72 period is shown in table 3.11. This equation has an R^2 of .84. A predicted innovation score for the 1959–64 period can then be computed using the same regression equation (the first equation in table 3.11). The correlation coefficient between predicted and actual 1959–64 innovation is .78. This coefficient is statistically significant at the .01 level using a one-tailed t-test. The variance explained in the 1959–64 innovation using the 1968–72 prediction equation is .60, a shrinkage of .24 from the R^2 of .84 for the 1968–72 period. Some shrinkage in explained variance is expected, of course. The observed 1968–72 relationsips can be used successfully to predict innovation in the 1959–64 period.

TABLE 3.11
Cross-Validation of Prediction Equations

BEST-FIT PERIOD	EQUATION	1968–72		1959–64	
		R	R^2	R	R^2
1968–72	15.57 COMMED + 9.233 ELITE + 45.31 SUPPST	.92[a]	.84	.78[a]	.60
1968–72	15.21 COMMED + 11.11 ELITE + 56.39 SUPPST + 7.68 GROWTH	.94[a]	.89	.68[a]	.46
1959–64	16.28 COMMED + .01335 EDEXP + 20.07 SUPPST − 82.92 ARATIO	.65[a]	.42	.94[a]	.89

[a]Significant at .01 level

The second equation in table 3.11 shows what happens when a fourth variable is added to the best-fit equation for 1968–72. Growth rate is the next best-fit variable that was measured in both time periods. The addition of the fourth variable improves the ability to predict innovation in the 1968–72 period compared to the first equation (R changes from .92 to .94). However, the addition of the fourth variable hurts the ability of the regression equation to predict innovation in the 1959–64 period (R changes from .78 to .68). Even with the four variables the cross-validation is successful. The correlation between predicted and actual innovation in the 1959–64 period is .68, which is significant at the .01 level. The innovation relationships observed in the 1968–72 period also existed in the 1959–64 period.

The third equation in table 3.11 uses the best-fit equation in the 1959–64 period to predict innovation adoption in the 1968–72 period. The variables of community education, affluence, support staff ratio, and administrative ratio predict innovation adoption in the 1959–64 period quite well. The R^2 for this equation is .89. When this equation is used with the 1968–72 data, the correlation between predicted and actual innovation is .65. Again, this represents shrinkage in the ability of the equation to predict innovation but does provide support for the inference that similar innovation relationships exist in both time periods.

We did a lot of experimentation with the cross-validation. We added variables, took out variables, and tried different combinations. When we used just two variables, we found that there was little shrinkage in the ability to predict data from one time period to the other. But every time we added a variable that made a substantial improvement in the ability to predict the original data, it also reduced our ability to predict innovation in the second set of data. We also double-cross-validated the findings. In this procedure we took the independent variables from one period and derived a best-fit equation for the innovation data in the other period. We then used that best-fit equation to predict innovation in the original period. In every case of cross-validation or double cross-validation the findings were the same: The correlation coefficient between predicted and actual rate of college-oriented innovation was significant at the .01 level. The lowest correlation coefficient observed between predicted and actual innovation was .65. There seems little doubt that our cross-validation is a success. Our findings are characterized by predictive validity and are apparently not due to chance.

There is one aspect of this cross-validation analysis that we feel is more important than any other: The independent variables in the prediction equations predict innovation adoption in the other period more successfully than does the known rate of innovation. The correlation coefficient of innovation across the two periods is .45. In no case was the coefficient between predicted and actual innovation that low when a prediction equation was used. Thus we conclude that our findings are not explained by the supposition that some school districts simply innovated more than other school districts through time.

Taken together, the findings in tables 3.9, 3.10, and 3.11 permit us to conclude that the independent variables push on innovation in different directions. The districts were quite stable along such dimensions as community education, expenditures per pupil (affluence), and teacher professionalism. This stability could have led to a stable rate of innovation in each district. Along other dimensions, such as elite attitude toward innovation, support staff ratio, and vocational teacher ratio, the districts were much less stable. These changes could have led to major changes in the rate of innovation across districts. The net effect of the stable and unstable independent variables is that innovation is only moderately correlated over time. The same organizations were not adopting innovations at the same rate, yet the independent variables successfully predict innovations in both periods. At any point in time, the districts that scored high on both stable and unstable independent variables were the most innovative. We conclude that the observed correlates of innovation for collegebound students are valid, and that the relationships between the independent variables and innovation adoption are not due to chance or small sample size.

SUMMARY OF EMPIRICAL FINDINGS

1. The educational level of community residents has a substantial positive association with the adoption of innovations for collegebound students. The requirements of highly educated residents are an incentive for the district to provide a quality, college preparatory education for the students (clients).

2. The superintendent and school board goals for district quality have a strong simple correlation with innovation for collegebound students, but are not significant in the

regression analysis. The aspirations of the district elite do not affect innovation directly; rather, aspirations tend to affect other variables associated with quality—e.g., teacher professionalism, expenditures per pupil—which in turn influence the adoption of college-oriented innovations.

3. The vocational teacher ratio has a strong negative correlation with innovation for collegebound students and is modestly significant in the regression analysis. The vocational teacher ratio reflects the goal of terminal education rather than college preparation of students. The vocational teacher ratio is negatively related to other variables that influence college-oriented innovation, such as community education and teacher professionalism.

4. Teacher professionalism (education) has a substantial positive association with the adoption of innovations for collegebound students. Highly educated teachers are knowledgeable about innovation and propose new ideas for adoption.

5. Innovations that benefit collegebound students tend to originate with teachers and "trickle up" to administrators for approval. Teachers span the boundary between the school district and the outside educational environment. The bottom-up flow of innovations from teachers to administrators is greatest for innovations that directly affect the classroom.

6. The support staff ratio has a substantial positive association with college-oriented innovativeness. Support staff are certified to teach, but work full time as support staff. They apparently facilitate innovation by exchanging ideas with teachers and preparing proposals for approval. These activities facilitate the upward flow of innovation proposals.

7. Educational expenditures per pupil (affluence) have a substantial positive association with innovation adoption for collegebound students. Affluence does not seem to affect the ability to purchase innovations directly (the chapter 2 findings suggest that districts adopt both ex-

pensive and inexpensive innovations). Affluence is highly related to teacher professionalism and the support staff ratio and thus influences innovation through the acquisition of personnel who generate innovation proposals.

8. Decentralization has a substantial positive association with innovation for collegebound students. Decentralization appears to provide teachers with freedom to experiment and propose innovations for approval.

9. The administrative ratio has a modest negative association with innovations for collegebound students. The administrative ratio appears to be negatively related to decentralization, and a small administrative ratio means greater freedom at the teacher level in the district.[8]

10. Superintendent and school board attitude toward innovation has a strong positive association with adoption of innovations for collegebound students. Elites with a positive attitude tend to approve innovation proposals and encourage the upward flow of innovation ideas.

11. Superintendent and school board perceptions of district financial well-being are negatively related to innovation for collegebound students. The negative relationship indicates that perceptions of free resources have little to do with approval of innovation proposals. Districts that are financially extended to acquire teachers and other staff tend to be the most innovative.

12. The growth rate of the district has a moderate positive association with college-oriented innovativeness. Growth rate has a negative relationship with variables such as expenditures per pupil, however. But when other variables are controlled, growth rate, which represents the infusion of new personnel and the expansion of facilities, is observed to have a positive impact on innovation.

13. Teacher free time (class load) and travel expenditures per teacher are not related to innovation for collegebound students. These variables were hypothesized to influence the availability of innovation ideas and the trickle-up process, but they apparently do not do so.

14. District size, district complexity, and the presence of

slack resources in the system are not related to college-oriented innovation. These variables were hypothesized to increase the probability of favorable adoption decisions, but they are apparently not needed because most innovation proposals are adopted (chapter 2).

Based on the empirical findings, we describe the innovation process as follows: Districts that adopt college-oriented innovations function in communities where residents expect high quality, college-preparatory education for their young people and where sufficient resources are available to pay for this type of program. The superintendent and school board obtain appropriate personnel, they direct the school district toward quality and innovativeness, and they support and approve behavior that furthers these ends. Most college-oriented innovations are proposed by teachers and trickle up in the organization. The larger amount of money spent in innovative districts does not directly buy innovations—rather, this money finances highly professional teachers and a large support staff. With the assistance of the support staff the teachers generate and propose new ideas within their area of expertise. A decentralized structure gives lower-level teaching personnel the freedom and decision-making authority to try new ideas that will help meet the quality and innovation goals of the school district.

NOTES

1. Means and standard deviations for the variables in both periods are in appendix D.
2. There is a correlation matrix for all 1959–64 variables in appendix D.
3. David R. Heise, "Causal Inference from Panel Data," in *Sociological Methodology 1970*, ed. Edgar F. Borgatta and George W. Bohrnstedt (San Francisco: Jossey-Bass, 1970), pp. 3–27.
4. Donald C. Pelz and Robert A. Lew, "Heise's Causal Model Applied," in *Sociological Methodology 1970*, pp. 28–37.
5. Hillel J. Einhorn, "Alchemy in the Behavioral Sciences," *The Public Opinion Quarterly* 36 (Fall 1972): 367–78.
6. Donald T. Campbell and Julian C. Stanley, *Experimental and Quasi-Experimental Designs for Research* (Chicago: Rand-McNally, 1963).

7. Ibid.

8. A similar relationship between decentralization and the administrative ratio is reported in Peter M. Blau, *The Organization of Academic Work* (New York: John Wiley & Sons, 1973), p. 165.

Adoption of
Innovations for
the Terminal Student

In chapter 2 we discussed why innovations that benefit terminal students were better treated separately from those designed to benefit collegebound students. Briefly, those reasons were:

1. The proposals originated from different sources and so could have been responding to different influences.
2. Very few innovations for the terminal student were adopted in the 1959–64 period, so an overall innovation index wouldn't permit comparison of adoption across the two time periods.

Keeping separate the two kinds of innovations was a fortunate choice because, as you shall see from our analysis, the process leading to adoption of innovations also differs.

THE ANALYSIS

Let us again start by examining the zero-order correlations shown in table 4.1. We have grouped the variables into the same categories as in table 3.1: variables related to incentives to innovate; knowledge of innovations; wherewithal to develop proposals; and enabler variables. The most striking feature of the table is the disappearance of relationships that are significant

TABLE 4.1
Zero-Order Correlations of Independent Variables with the Adoption of Innovations for Terminal Students, 1968–72

INDEPENDENT VARIABLES	CORRELATION WITH INNOVATIONS
Community education	.04
Elite quality goals	−.30
Vocational teacher ratio	.08
Teacher professionalism	−.31
Travel expenditures per teacher	−.12
Teacher free time	−.28
Administrative ratio	.43
Support staff ratio	.14
Affluence (expenditures per pupil)	.33
Slack	−.05
Elite perception of slack resources	−.05
District size	.54[a]
Complexity	.27
Growth rate	.64[b]
Decentralization	.33
Elite attitude toward innovation	−.10

[a]Significant at .05 level.
[b]Significant at .01 level.

when innovations benefiting collegebound students are the dependent variable. In table 3.1 community education, elite goals for quality education, teacher professionalism, certified staff ratio, affluence, and elite attitude toward innovation were all significantly related to the adoption of innovations. In table 4.1 none of these variables is related to innovativeness, but two others, district size and growth rate, are.

The most perplexing aspect of table 4.1 concerns the incentives to innovate. Community educational level is unrelated to innovativeness $(r = .04)$. We might expect that since community education is positively related to innovation adoption for collegebound students that it would be negatively related to innovation adoption for terminal students. The children of less well educated residents would be less likely to go on to college and would have greater needs for terminal and vocational programs. If that need exists, it is not reflected in the type of innovation adopted. Likewise, the presence of a large ratio of vocational teachers does not seem to stimulate terminal-oriented innovation ($r = .08$). The superintendent and school board goals for quality has a small negative correlation with innovation ($r = -.30$). Perhaps elite aspirations for quality education affects only adoption of college-oriented innovations. Does the presence of such goals mean that terminal students are ignored in favor of programs for the collegebound? Whatever the explanation, using our zero-order correlations, we haven't been able to identify the incentives that lead to innovations that benefit terminal students.

A clue that may help explain the table 4.1 correlations was in chapter 3 (table 3.5): Teachers propose a smaller share of terminal-oriented than college-oriented innovations. If administrators initiate a larger share of terminal-oriented innovations, then it makes sense that a large vocational teacher ratio would not necessarily be associated with innovativeness. We also notice in table 4.1 that administrative ratio has a mild positive relationship to innovation ($r = .43$), and teacher of professionalism a negative correlation ($r = -.31$). If terminal-oriented innovations are adopted in districts with less well educated teachers and large administrative ratios, it could be because administrators are more active in the innovation process.

Our first look at the correlations suggests to us that the process leading to innovation for terminal students may be substantially different from the process that leads to innovation for college-bound students. Even if the process is different, however, we still haven't identified the incentives for adoption of terminal-oriented innovations. Rather than try to interpret further the data in this table, which can be misleading because of inter-correlations among the independent variables, let us turn to the regression analysis, where we try to overcome the effects of these intercorrelations.

In table 4.2 we show the four variables—growth rate, certified support staff ratio, travel expenditures per teacher, and elite attitude toward innovation—that best fit the terminal-oriented innovation data. This equation does not predict terminal-oriented innovativeness as well as the best-fit equation in the previous chapter predicted college-oriented innovativeness, but the R^2

TABLE 4.2
**Multiple Regression of Terminal-Oriented Innovativeness on
Its Best Predictors, 1968–72**

INDEPENDENT VARIABLE	REGRESSION COEFFICIENT	STANDARDIZED REGRESSION COEFFICIENT	t-VALUE	ONE-TAIL p-VALUE
Growth rate	30.51	1.19	5.04	$<.001$
Support staff ratio	61.32	0.62	3.19	$<.006$
Travel expenditures per teacher	0.061	0.42	2.12	$<.03$
Elite attitude toward innovation	5.47	0.32	1.67	$<.07$

$R^2 = .77$, adjusted $R^2 = .66$; standard error of residuals $= 1.83$, $n = 13$

is a respectable .77, and the standard deviation of innovation
is reduced from 3.11 to 1.83.

These results are somewhat more encouraging than are the
zero-order correlations. We can see that two of the variables,
support staff ratio and elite attitude toward innovation, were also
in the best-fit equations predicting college-oriented innovations.
The best single predictor, however, is growth rate, although it
is not immediately clear why it is such an important factor in
adoption. Perhaps the explanation for the importance of growth
rate is due to the fact that adoption of educational techniques
to benefit terminal students seems to be a recent phenomenon
(chapter 2). There were few, if any, terminal-oriented innovations in the 1959–64 period. Their presence in the early 1970s
may mean the interest of educators has shifted toward terminal
students. However, innovations benefiting terminal students
require greater change in the organization than do those benefiting college-oriented students (see table 2.1). Then, growth,
which was not necessary to college-oriented innovativeness,
could provide districts the opportunity to incorporate programs
and facilities for vocational students. At least part of the incentive for adopting innovations for terminal students may have
been a general awakening to the needs of terminal students
rather than pressure from less well educated residents in the
immediate community. Growth is important because it provides
the opportunity for the adoption of these kinds of programs.
Rapid growth also brings recent graduates—administrators and

teachers—into the school system, who share the developing concern for terminal students.

As with college-oriented innovations, the certified support staff ratio also seems important for the adoption of terminal-oriented innovations. Certified nonteaching support staff bring new information to the relevant users, help prepare proposals, and act as facilitators and integrators within their individual areas of expertise. The presence of a large certified nonteaching support staff appears to assist the adoption of innovations of all kinds.

The association of teacher travel expenditures with terminal-oriented innovativeness was unexpected. Travel expenditures were hypothesized to affect innovativeness by exposing teachers to new ideas in the field. These ideas would subsequently be imported and proposed in the district. In table 3.5, however, we saw that teachers were the source of more college- than terminal-oriented innovations. Travel expenditures should have been more important for college-oriented innovations than for terminal-oriented ones. We found the opposite.

A telephone call to one of the district superintendents in the sample clarified the travel expense finding. There is a great deal of travel by teachers in support of cooperative terminal and vocatonal programs. Teachers transport themselves and students to and from off-campus sites where vocational training takes place. The cooperating organization might be a factory, a garage, a bank, or some other business in which students are participating. Sometimes they travel to and from a house that students are designing and/or constructing. Thus, travel expenditures per teacher are not simply a measure of teacher exposure to new ideas. They also measure expenses involved in carrying out programs for terminal students. Deployment of resources to travel represents the commitment of the district to vocational programs. Thus travel expenditures measure to some extent the district goals for terminal student education.

Elite attitude toward innovation is the fourth variable in the best-fit equation. The positive attitude of the organizational elite has a modest but positive association with the adoption of innovations to benefit terminal students ($t = 1.67$). It is reassuring to see that a positive superintendent and school board attitude toward innovation can have a positive impact on terminal- as well as college-oriented innovativeness. In table 4.2, elite quality goals are also shown to have a small positive influence on innovation for terminal students. Our speculation earlier in this chapter that elites might be oriented away from terminal preparation is apparently unjustified. When other variables are controlled, the effects of elite attitude and goals show through. The effect is not as strong as it was for college-oriented innovations, but it is present nonetheless.

Elite attitude toward innovation is the best fourth variable to use in the regression equation, but it seems to be somewhat collinear with four other variables. The data in columns 2 through 5 of table 4.3 reveal that district size, number of vocational teachers, elite quality aspirations, and slack resources each can be inserted as the fourth variable in the prediction equation. In each case the variable is mildly important and the regression equation does not lose much of its ability to predict innovation. If any two of these variables are used together, however, the t-values for both variables are quite small.

It is not at all obvious why these particular variables tend to coexist and explain the same variance in terminal-oriented innovativeness. In table 3.5 we saw that teachers are less often the source of terminal-oriented ideas than college-oriented ideas. Administrators are responsible for proposing relatively more terminal-oriented innovations. This suggests a somewhat different adoption process for innovations that benefit terminal students. Administrators supportive of innovation apparently play an active role in the conception and proposal stages of the terminal-oriented innovation process.

One reason administrators are more involved in the early stages of terminal-oriented innovations is probably that these innovations are sometimes special programs for slow or problem students. The more professional teachers seem to be less interested in these innovations than in what is new for their bright, collegebound students. The administrators are thus the people who must sense the needs for these special programs and be responsible for proposing them.

TABLE 4.3

t-Values for Multiple Regressions of Terminal-Oriented Innovativeness on Selected Sets of Independent Variables, 1968–72[a]

INDEPENDENT VARIABLE	1 t-VALUE	2 t-VALUE	3 t-VALUE	4 t-VALUE	5 t-VALUE
Growth rate	5.04	3.86	3.45	3.92	5.00
Support staff ratio	3.19	2.63	2.67	2.36	3.13
Travel expenditures per teacher	2.12	1.75	1.46	2.11	2.41
Elite attitude toward innovation	1.67				
District size		1.52			
Number of vocational teachers			1.22		
Elite quality goals				1.24	
Slack resources					−1.61
R^2	.77	.76	.74	.74	.77
Adjusted R^2	.66	.64	.61	.61	.65
Standard error of residuals	1.83	1.87	1.95	1.94	1.84

[a]With 8 d.f., when $t = 1.1$, one-tail $p = .15$; when $t = 1.4$, one-tail $p = .10$; when $t = 1.8$, one-tail $p = .05$; when $t = 2.9$, one-tail $p = .01$.

The need for terminal programs tends to increase as district size increases. District size ($t = 1.52$) seems to be part of this cluster because it provides an incentive to the administrators to adopt terminal-oriented innovations. The absolute number of vocational teachers was calculated, and it can replace district size in the best-fit equation ($t = 1.22$). This indicates a threshold effect for terminal-oriented innovations. When the absolute number of terminal-oriented students and teachers is large enough, the demand for terminal programs is sufficient to be recognized by administrators. Consequently the number of vocational teachers but not the percentage of vocational teachers is related to innovation for terminal students. District size may also play an enabling role because the larger terminal-oriented innovations are more likely to fit into large districts. Thus a large vocational group in the district, large district size, a positive elite attitude toward innovation, and the desire for a top quality district all exist together in explaining terminal-oriented innovativeness. Administrators who favor innovation and want a quality district propose innovations for terminal students when the need exists.

The last variable in table 4.3 is slack resources ($t = -1.61$). Their negative relationship with terminal-oriented innovation suggests that free resources are not a necessary antecedent to innovation adoption. This is similar to our finding for college-oriented innovation. Vocational innovations are adopted to meet the need for terminal programs, regardless of immediate school district financial circumstances.

The remaining variables in the analysis of terminal-oriented innovations appear to be unimportant. The cluster of variables that represent the educational quality of the district—community education, teacher professionalism, and affluence—are not at all significant in the adoption of innovations for terminal students. It is the orientation and attitude of the administrators that seems to count, and then only as the needs of the terminal group become fairly large. (See table 4.4.)

Because we have data for only one time period, cross-validation is not possible and conclusions are more difficult to sustain. However, despite differences in the content of the proc-

TABLE 4.4

Additional t-Values for Multiple Regressions of Terminal-Oriented Innovativeness on Selected Sets of Independent Variables, 1968–72[a]

INDEPENDENT VARIABLE	1 t-VALUE	2 t-VALUE	3 t-VALUE	4 t-VALUE	5 t-VALUE	6 t-VALUE	7 t-VALUE	8 t-VALUE	9 t-VALUE	10 t-VALUE
Growth rate	5.04	3.99	4.72	4.73	4.18	3.76	4.85	4.80	4.58	4.53
Support staff ratio	3.19	2.90	2.96	2.66	2.87	2.43	1.82	3.05	2.83	2.97
Travel expenditures per teacher	2.12	1.85	1.97	2.07	2.01	2.04	1.93	1.74	2.09	2.00
Elite attitude toward innovation	1.67	1.57	1.56	1.48	1.61	1.66	1.79	1.55	1.68	1.50
Administrative ratio		−0.29								
Community education			0.05							
Vocational teacher ratio				−0.49						
Teacher professionalism					0.31					
Affluence (Expenditures per pupil)						0.48				
Number of occupations							0.86			
Elite perception of slack resources								0.45		
Decentralization									0.55	
Teacher free time										0.28
R^2	.77	.77	.77	.78	.77	.78	.79	.78	.78	.77
Adjusted R^2	.66	.61	.61	.62	.61	.62	.64	.62	.62	.61
Standard error of residuals	1.83	1.94	1.95	1.92	1.94	1.92	1.86	1.92	1.91	1.94

[a]With 8 d.f., when $t = 1.1$, one-tail $p = .15$; when $t = 1.4$, one-tail $p = .10$; when $t = 1.8$, one-tail $p = .05$; when $t = 2.9$, one-tail $p = .01$.

ess of innovation when comparing innovations that benefit collegebound students with those that benefit terminal students, the general model seems to have been upheld. If you accept our explanation that in the 1968–72 period there was increasing emphasis on terminal education in the educational community; that teacher travel expenditures partially reflect district goals for terminal education; and that as the district increases in size, the *number* (not necessarily the proportion) of terminal students increases and provides an incentive to adopt innovations for their benefit, then the model of incentives, innovation ideas, and enabler variables seems to fit. The specific process, however, is quite different from college-oriented innovations. What constitutes a relevant incentive, or a relevant enabler variable, seems dependent on the kind of innovation involved.

SUMMARY OF EMPIRICAL FINDINGS

1. The growth rate of school districts has a strong positive association with the adoption of innovations for terminal students. Growth enables the adoption of terminal-oriented innovations because of expanding facilities and staff. Expanding districts seem to be able to respond to the increasing awareness and concern by educators for the needs of terminal students.

2. Travel expenditures per teacher have a substantial positive association with the adoption of innovations for terminal students. Local travel is required for many vocational programs. Consequently, travel expenditures partially represent the involvement of the district in terminal education. This involvement seems to indicate a goal emphasis toward education of terminal students.

3. The support staff ratio has a substantial association with terminal-oriented innovation. The support staff facilitates innovation by exchanging ideas with administrators and teachers and by assisting in proposal preparation. These activities apparently increase the flow of innovation ideas and proposals in the district.

4. Administrators are relatively active in the initiation of innovations for terminal students (chapter 3, table 3.5). Administrators as well as teachers respond to the needs of noncollegebound students. Consequently, innovations for terminal students both trickle up and trickle down in the districts.

5. Superintendent and school board attitude toward innovation has a mildly positive association with innovation for terminal students. This relationship is observable when other district variables are controlled. Elites with a positive attitude toward innovation initiate some terminal-oriented innovations themselves and apparently also encourage proposals from teachers.

6. The superintendent and school board goals for district quality are also mildly associated with innovations for terminal students. This relationship is similar to that for elite attitude toward innovation. Elites who desire educational quality may initiate innovations as well as encourage innovation proposals from teachers. However, the influence of elite attitudes and elite quality goals is considerably less for terminal-oriented than for college-oriented innovations.

7. District size has a mild positive association with innovations for terminal students. Large school districts have a larger absolute number of terminal-oriented teachers and students, which represents a greater need for terminal programs. The change involved with innovations for terminal students is also more likely to be compatible with the available facilities in large school districts.

8. Slack resources have a modest negative relationship with the adoption of terminal-oriented innovations. Thus, slack, or free, resources do not lead to innovation adoption. When the need for terminal innovation is felt and the innovation alternative is available, districts respond with appropriate innovations regardless of financial circumstances.

9. The vocational teacher ratio is not related to the adoption

of innovations for terminal students. It is apparently the absolute size rather than the proportional size of the vocational component that influences innovations for terminal students.

10. Community educational level is not associated with the adoption of innovations for terminal students. The presence of a large proportion of less well educated residents apparently does not translate into a felt need for terminal programs in the school districts.

11. Teacher professionalism and affluence (educational expenditures per pupil) are unrelated to the adoption of innovations for terminal students. These variables are important to the adoption of innovations for collegebound students, but the adoption of innovations for terminal students is the result of a different process.

12. Decentralization and the administrative ratio are unrelated to the adoption of innovations for terminal students. These variables are important to the adoption of innovations for collegebound students because teachers initiate most proposals (a trickle-up process). Terminal-oriented innovations, however, tend to be initiated by both teachers and administrators.

13. District complexity and teacher free time (class load) are unrelated to innovation for terminal students. These variables are also unrelated to innovation for collegebound students and apparently have little effect on innovation in high schools.

In summary, the process of adopting innovations that benefit terminal students is different from the process for innovations to benefit collegebound students. The nonteaching support staff seem to play a similar role in facilitating the adoption of both kinds of innovations. The incentives to adopt innovations for terminal students seem to be the existence of a large number of students in the district who can benefit from these innovations, an increasing concern for terminal students in the educational community, and district involvement in terminal education.

Growth rate is extremely important because it enables the implementation of these new programs. Many terminal-oriented ideas originate with administrators rather than with teachers. The attitude of administrators toward innovation is important because administrators as well as teachers seem to be aware of the needs of noncollegebound students, and they propose innovations to satisfy those needs.

5

The Internal
Innovation
Process*

Thus far our major findings have depended upon correlation and regression analyses. These types of analyses are efficient and enable us to identify the correlates of innovation adoption, but they do not yield specific evidence about internal organizational processes.[1] Researchers can make conjectures about internal organizational processes on the basis of correlations and regressions. We've done that in the preceding chapters in an attempt to weave the correlation findings into a coherent explanation about the innovation process. But these explanations remain conjectures unless we can verify them with data about what is happening inside the high school districts.

When this study was undertaken, we felt we could gain some understanding of the internal innovation process by tracing innovation adoption back to the point of initiation in the school district. There is very little data in the innovation literature on organizational activity prior to adoption. Little is known about where ideas enter the organization, who proposes them, or why. By tracing adoptions back to their beginnings, we hope to provide partial answers to these questions. We say partial because this procedure will not reveal anything about innovations that are never adopted but will only provide evidence about the process by which innovations are successfully proposed and adopted.

*Some data in this chapter were reported in R.L. Daft, "A Dual-Core Model of Organizational Innovation," *Academy of Management Journal*, 21 (June, 1978).

In chapters 3 and 4 we dealt exclusively with educational innovations. In this chapter we will introduce administrative innovations and compare the processes associated with adoption of administrative and educational innovations. After comparing administrative and educational innovation processes, we will subdivide educational innovations into those that benefit terminal students and those that benefit collegebound students, and we will compare the processes associated with those innovations. Then we will relate these findings to our earlier conjectures and conclude the chapter with a brief examination of the role of search activity in the innovation process.

In our earlier analyses the years between 1964 and 1968 were not included. In those years several administrative innovations began diffusing into these organizations. By incorporating these years into this part of the analysis, we not only add many additional innovation adoptions to our analysis, but we are also able to compare administrative and educational innovations. The larger number of innovations also increases the reliability of our findings with regard to the process we are identifying.

During the years 1964–72, 68 innovations became available to this set of organizations. Fifty of the innovations were educational innovations. Most of the educational innovations were innovations in curricula and teaching techniques. These innovations included new subject matter areas, the use of mini-courses, individually paced coursework, and dial-access retrieval systems. These innovations are classified as educational because they represent changes in the content and method of educating students. The other 18 innovations are administrative innovations. Administrative innovations represent developments in such things as the scheduling of students, the structure of high school organizations, the location of classes, and program budgeting. These innovations do not directly affect classroom method or content.

Our classification of innovations as administrative or educational is less than perfect. Some of the innovations put in the administrative category might well have been classed as educational because they do affect students. Block scheduling of students, for instance, does not affect classroom content, so we classified it as an administrative innovation, although it could benefit students who wish to take their courses in a compact time period. Block scheduling gives the student free time in the afternoon for other activities, such as a part-time job. We had to draw the line between educational and administrative somewhere, and our criterion for educational innovations was that they directly influence what happens inside the classroom.

During 1972, while we were collecting data on adoption of innovations, we also obtained data on the origin of each innovation. The origin was identified through interviews with people at various levels in the district. Superintendents, principals, department heads, and teachers were interviewed. Senior teachers and professional support staff, however, provided the bulk of the information. A knowledgeable person in the organization was sought until as many as possible of the origins were identified. Five hierarchical levels were coded as initiating innovation ideas: student, teacher, principal, superintendent, and school board. The teachers are the lower-level line workers in school organizations and are most directly involved in the production process. Principals are administrators at the middle management level. The superintendent is the top administrator.

For the analysis described in this chapter any adoption of the 68 innovations by any of the 13 districts is counted as a separate observation. This strategy of analyzing separate innovation decisions enables a clear test of the hypothesis that different types of innovations have their origins in different groups within the organization. A total of 414 adoptions occurred in these 13 districts from the pool of 68 innovations. It was not possible to trace 26 adoptions to the point of initiation. Thus the analysis is based on 388 innovation adoptions.

ADMINISTRATIVE VERSUS EDUCATIONAL INNOVATIONS

Where do innovation ideas enter the organization and who proposes them for adoption? We have argued that educational innovations tend to flow upward in the organization from teachers to administrators. Most new ideas probably originate with organization members who span the boundary between the organization and the technological environment, and teachers are the major boundary-spanning component for the educational environment.

William Evan has theorized that administrators and lower employees are both involved in initiating innovations, depending on the type of innovation to be proposed.[2] Evan argued that organizations can maximize adoptions by having innovation ideas originate at both ends of the organizational hierarchy: Administrative ideas would originate near the top of the hierarchy and trickle down, and technical innovations would originate near the bottom of the hierarchy and percolate upward. The different ideas follow different paths from conception to approval and implementation.

The notion of two distinct innovation flow patterns is intriguing. Innovation ideas may be moving through the hierarchy in different directions, and the direction taken may affect chances for adoption. We presume that origination of new ideas is related to task differentiation within the organization. Organization members who work within a functional area will tend to be the local experts in that area. They will be the most knowledgeable people in the organization regarding problems, new ideas, and the suitability of ideas for use in their task domain.

The technical experts in an organization will tend to be those people working on or near the core technology—in school districts, the teachers. Teachers are aware of educational problems, they can tell whether a new idea will fit into their current technology, and they have the expertise (but not necessarily the authority) to implement the innovation. Technical ideas proposed by administrators and others outside the educational domain will tend to be less synchronous with actual needs and are less likely to be acceptable. Hence, new ideas that relate to the production (educational) process will tend to originate below the administrative level.

Innovation initiation will also depend to a great extent on the professionalism of the teachers. The educational level and professionalism of teachers should be associated with their participation in professional activities, autonomy, internalized performance standards, and desire for recognition from peers rather than from the formal hierarchy. Professional teachers probably read publications and attend meetings where new developments are described. Innovation as an attempt to improve performance is congruent with professional standards and is a source of recognition for the innovator. The division of labor between administrators and teachers concerning technical innovations should be at its greatest when the teachers are highly professional. Highly professional teachers can be expected to learn about and propose nearly all educational innovations adopted in the organization. The administrative role in the initiation of educational innovations will be minimized.

When teacher professionalism is low, they will tend to be less active as innovation initiators. If the school district is to be innovative, administrators will have to initiate a larger percentage of the educational innovations. Division of labor will therefore be reduced. Administrator initiative will probably meet with some success because teachers with minimally acceptable levels of education and little professional orientation will be less autonomous and less resistant to influence from top administrators.

Another strategy available to administrators is collaboration with teachers on educational proposals. If an administrator and teacher work together on an innovation proposal, resistance to management's initiative will be reduced. The collaborative strategy will engage teachers in the innovation process. Administrator innovation initiative, either proposed by administrators alone or in collaboration with teachers, is a realistic innovation strategy. But this strategy is not expected to be needed or used when teachers are highly professional.

The initiation process for administrative innovations should differ. Top managers are the experts with regard to administrative arrangements. They are concerned with administrative problems and will be tuned to new developments that apply to these problems. Lower-level managers and workers (technical experts) are less likely to see the administrative picture as accurately, so their administrative proposals are not likely to be as appropriate. Ideas for administrative innovations will thus tend to originate from administrators. Board members may also propose administrative innovations. These innovations will tend to be proposed and approved near the top of the hierarchy and will be implemented downward. Thus administrators have a definite role in initiating innovations, but it is most frequently limited to administrative ideas.

Collaborative proposals can probably be a useful strategy for administrative innovations also. The administrator is the expert concerning administrative innovations, but implementation downward may be smoothed by having teachers participate in the early stages of the innovation process. Administrator initiative is expected to be paramount for administrative innovations. Teachers, if anything, will collaborate on administrative innovations rather than initiate them.

In sum, then, administrators and teachers are expected to play important but very different roles in the innovation process. Each group is expected to be the source for different kinds of innovations: Educational innovations will percolate up from teachers, and administrative innovations will trickle down from administrators. The percentage of innovations initiated by teachers is expected to be influenced by teacher professionalism. Teacher professionalism is also expected to influence the absolute number of innovations adopted.

The data in table 5.1 provide support for the hypothesis that different processes underly the different kinds of innovations. Teachers are by far the major source of educational ideas (70 percent). The principal and superintendent levels are about equally active as sources of educational ideas (8 percent and 9 percent, respectively), but both levels are much less active than teachers. For administrative ideas activity increases with hierarchical level. Teachers initiate only 13 percent of administrative innovations, principals initiate 22 percent, and superintendents initiate 45 percent. Collaborations between administrators and teachers account for a similar proportion of each innovation type.

Very few innovation ideas originate with students or school boards. There is little reason to expect students to be the source of innovations. Students are recipients of educational services. Students may occasionally appear to activate change, but they

TABLE 5.1
Innovation Type and Where Initiated

WHERE INITIATED	INNOVATION TYPE EDUCATIONAL		ADMINISTRATIVE	
	%	N	%	N
Students	1	(4)	4	(4)
Teachers	70	(210)	13	(11)
Principals	8	(24)	22	(19)
Superintendents	9	(26)	45	(40)
School board	.3	(1)	1	(1)
Collaborations	12	(35)	15	(13)
	100	(300)	100	(88)

$\chi^2 = 108.7$ with 5 d.f., $p < .001$

have little expertise and little exposure to new ideas. The paucity of ideas from the school board is a little bit surprising. One might expect the community's elected representatives to make more initiatives, especially in the area of administration. But board members are laymen and apparently leave the responsibility for initiating innovations to personnel within the organizations. If the board does influence innovation adoption, it is apparently by establishing a favorable climate for innovation, not by being the source of new ideas. This supports our earlier conclusion about the role of the organizational elites (chapters 3 and 4).

The relationship between innovation type and where the ideas originate is summarized in table 5.2. Students and school board members are dropped from the analysis at this point because they account for so few innovations. Principals and superintendents are combined into the administrator category. Table 5.2 highlights the very strong relationship between innovation type and where the innovation is initiated. Seventy-one percent of educational innovations originate with teachers alone, and the same percentage of administrative innovations originate with administrators.

Administrators initiate nearly as many educational as administrative innovations (50 versus 59), while teachers deal almost exclusively with educational innovations (210 versus 11). This may mean that administrators devote a fair amount of

TABLE 5.2
Summary of Innovation Type and Where Initiated

WHERE INITIATED	INNOVATION TYPE EDUCATIONAL %	N	ADMINISTRATIVE %	N
Teachers	71	(210)	13	(11)
Administrators	17	(50)	71	(59)
Collaborations	12	(35)	16	(13)
	100	(295)	100	(83)

$\chi^2 = 103.8$ with 2 d.f., $p < .001$

innovation time to educational innovations, unless educational innovations are much smaller in scope than administrative innovations. The total number of educational innovations is much larger than the number of administrative innovations, however, so the involvement of administrators in the teachers' innovation domain accounts for a relatively small proportion of educational innovations. There is definite support for Evan's hypothesis that technical ideas will tend to percolate up and that administrative ideas will tend to trickle down in organizations.

In table 5.3 the school districts are divided into categories according to the educational level (professionalism) of the teachers in the district. The average educational level of teachers was relatively stable over the 1964–72 period (serial correlation in table 3.9 is .81), so it is reasonable to compare districts with differing degrees of teacher professionalism for that time period.

TABLE 5.3
Teacher Professionalism and Where Initiated:
Educational Innovations

WHERE INITIATED	PROFESSIONALISM HIGH %	($\bar{x}$)	MEDIUM %	($\bar{x}$)	LOW %	($\bar{x}$)
Teachers	93	(24.0)	66	(14.8)	53	(11.0)
Administrators	7	(1.8)	15	(3.3)	29	(6.0)
Collaborations	0	(0.0)	19	(4.3)	18	(3.6)
	100	(25.8)	100	(22.3)	100	(20.6)
Number of adoptions	$N = 103$		$N = 89$		$N = 103$	

$\bar{x}$ = the average number of adoptions per district
$\chi^2 = 46.3$ with 4 d.f., $p < .001$

From table 5.3 we can see that teacher professionalism has considerable bearing on where educational ideas originate in the school district. In organizations with highly professional teachers the teachers propose 93 percent of the educational innovations. This drops off to 66 percent and 53 percent, respectively, in the districts with medium and low professional levels. The proportion of educational innovations initiated by administrators is reversed: Administrators propose only 7 percent of the educational innovations in the districts with a high professional level, whereas they propose 29 percent in the districts with a low professional level. Collaboration between administrators and teachers is also more important in the districts with medium and low professional levels.

There may be some question about who initiates collaborations. From discussions with the superintendents in the study we learned that nearly all collaborations are initiated by administrators. Teachers have little reason to seek a collaboration with an administrator. Teachers have to work with educational innovations, and when teachers really want an educational innovation, they can nearly always have it. But when administrators want the teachers to adopt an educational innovation, it is a different matter. If the teachers don't want an innovation, they can resist administrator influence. One way to combat this is for the administrator to collaborate with one or more teachers in proposing the innovation for adoption.

The average number of adoptions per school district ($\bar{x}$) is included in table 5.3 and subsequent tables to indicate the frequency of innovation adoptions. In the districts with a high professional level teachers account for more than twice as many educational innovation adoptions per district as in the districts with a low professional level (24 versus 11). The increased activity of administrators in the districts with a low professional level is partly successful in overcoming the lack of teacher activity, but the districts with a high professional level still adopt somewhat more innovations than the others (25.8 versus 20.6).

A similar pattern of activity is observable for administrative innovations in table 5.4. Teachers are proportionately more active in districts with a high professional level. Teachers propose nearly half (47 percent) of the administrative innovations in the districts with a high professional level and none in the districts with a low professional level. Highly educated teachers appear to generate an idea "push" from the bottom of the organization. The professional push even intrudes into what might be considered administrator territory—ideas for administrative innovations. When teachers are less professional and less active, administrators take on a larger share of the idea load. They initiate a significant portion of educational innovations and all administrative innovations. Administrator initiative also results in a somewhat larger absolute number of administrative innovations in the districts with a lower professional level.

TABLE 5.4
Teacher Professionalism and Where Initiated:
Administrative Innovations

| | PROFESSIONALISM | | | | | |
| | HIGH | | MEDIUM | | LOW | |
WHERE INITIATED	%	$(\bar{x})$	%	$(\bar{x})$	%	$(\bar{x})$
Teachers	47	(2.0)	10	(0.8)	0	(0.0)
Administrators	47	(2.0)	56	(4.5)	97	(6.6)
Collaborations	6	(0.3)	34	(2.8)	3	(0.2)
	100	(4.3)	100	(8.0)	100	(6.8)
Number of adoptions	$N = 17$		$N = 32$		$N = 34$	

$\chi^2 = 36.8$ with 4 d.f., $p < .001$

Tables 5.3 and 5.4 also provide evidence on the importance of division of labor in school organizations. The districts where teachers propose the largest percentage of educational innovations also adopt a greater absolute number of educational innovations (25.8 versus 20.6). And the districts where administrators propose the largest percentage of administrative ideas also tend to adopt a greater number of administrative innovations (6.8 versus 4.3). School districts appear only to adopt a large number of innovations of either type when individuals in the relevant task domain actively initiate them. The involvement of teachers in administrative innovations or administrators in educational innovations is associated with fewer total adoptions of each innovation type.

Thus the data in tables 5.3 and 5.4 suggest that school organizations are characterized by different innovation processes depending on teacher professionalism. In the districts with a high professional level the process tends to be bottom up. Teachers are active initiators and propose most innovations that are adopted in the district. The administrators can be involved in activities other than innovation initiation. The consequence of this bottom-up process is a large number of educational innovation adoptions. The districts with a low professional level are better characterized by a top-down innovation process. The administrators play a greater role in the initiation phase of innovation. Administrators initiate more educational innovations, which partly offsets the smaller number of innovations initiated by teachers. The top-down districts are also somewhat more innovative regarding administrative innovations.

In table 5.5 we compare districts that adopt many educational innovations with districts that adopt few educational innovations. It seems clear that districts that adopt many educational innovations do so because of teacher activity. Teachers alone propose 77 percent of the educational innovations in the highly innovative districts, for an average of 22.2 adoptions per district. In the least innovative districts teachers alone propose only 54 percent of educational innovations, which is 7.3 innovations per district. This pattern is similar to the one seen in table 5.3. From these data we can't say that teachers "cause" innovation adoption, but we can conclude that they are the means through

TABLE 5.5
Number of Adoptions and Where Initiated:
Educational Innovations

| | NUMBER OF ADOPTIONS | | | | | |
| | HIGH | | MEDIUM | | LOW | |
WHERE INITIATED	%	($\bar{x}$)	%	($\bar{x}$)	%	($\bar{x}$)
Teachers	77	(22.2)	71	(15.4)	54	(7.3)
Administrators	16	(4.6)	19	(4.2)	14	(2.0)
Collaborations	7	(2.2)	10	(2.2)	32	(4.3)
	100	(29.8)	100	(21.8)	100	(13.6)
Number of adoptions	$N = 145$		$N = 109$		$N = 41$	

$\chi^2 = 19.1$ with 4 d.f., $p < .001$

which most educational innovations are adopted in the highly innovative districts.

The proportion of educational innovations proposed by administrators is similar across districts, suggesting that administrator initiative is not a major factor in the explanation of educational innovation. The proportion of innovations initiated via collaboration increases as the frequency of educational innovation decreases (7 percent versus 32 percent). Collaboration is probably a response by administrators to low educational innovation activity. In the highly innovative districts there is little need for administrators to collaborate with teachers on educational proposals.

We can see a top-down innovation process in the data on frequency of administrative innovation adoption in table 5.6. Administrators alone do propose a larger proportion of administrative innovations in the districts with a high number of adoptions (75 percent versus 60 percent), and they initiate a larger absolute number of innovations in districts with a high number of adoptions (6.4 per district versus 1.0). The key to the adoption of administrative innovations clearly rests with administrators. They propose most administrative innovations in all districts. From these data we do not know exactly why administrators are more active in some districts, but it may be because of few professional teachers and a centralized, top-down administrative process.

TABLE 5.6
Number of Adoptions and Where Initiated:
Administrative Innovations

| | NUMBER OF ADOPTIONS | | | | | |
| | HIGH | | MEDIUM | | LOW | |
WHERE INITIATED	%	($\bar{x}$)	%	($\bar{x}$)	%	($\bar{x}$)
Teachers	16	(1.4)	6	(0.4)	40	(0.7)
Administrators	75	(6.4)	68	(4.8)	60	(1.0)
Collaborations	9	(0.8)	26	(1.8)	0	(0.0)
	100	(8.6)	100	(7.0)	100	(1.7)
Number of adoptions	$N = 43$		$N = 35$		$N = 5$	

$\chi^2 = 8.8$ with 4 d.f., $p < .10$

COLLEGE-ORIENTED VERSUS
TERMINAL-ORIENTED INNOVATIONS

To this point we would conclude that teacher professionalism is important for all educational innovations. However, such a conclusion would not be consistent with our findings in chapters 3 and 4. There we found a strong relationship between teacher professionalism and innovation for collegebound students but not with innovation for terminal students.

In tables 5.7, 5.8, and 5.9 we divide educational innovations into those that benefit collegebound students and those that benefit terminal students. From table 5.7 we can see that teachers propose most innovations for both terminal and collegebound students. Administrators are somewhat more likely to propose innovations for terminal than for collegebound students (21 per-

TABLE 5.7
Innovation Type and Where Initiated

WHERE INITIATED	INNOVATION TYPE COLLEGE-ORIENTED %	n	TERMINAL-ORIENTED %	n
Teachers	78	(104)	71	(58)
Administrators	10	(13)	21	(17)
Collaborations	12	(16)	8	(7)
	100	(133)	100	(82)

TABLE 5.8
Teacher Professionalism and Where Initiated:
College-oriented Innovations

WHERE INITIATED	PROFESSIONALISM HIGH %	$(\bar{x})$	MEDIUM %	$(\bar{x})$	LOW %	$(\bar{x})$
Teachers	94	(12.8)	75	(7.5)	58	(4.6)
Administrators	6	(0.8)	5	(0.5)	21	(1.6)
Collaborations	0	(0.0)	20	(2.0)	21	(1.6)
	100	(13.5)	100	(10.0)	100	(7.8)
Number of adoptions	$N = 54$		$N = 40$		$N = 39$	

TABLE 5.9
Teacher Professionalism and Where Initiated:
Terminal-oriented Innovations

| | PROFESSIONALISM | | | | | |
| | HIGH | | MEDIUM | | LOW | |
WHERE INITIATED	%	($\bar{x}$)	%	($\bar{x}$)	%	($\bar{x}$)
Teachers	95	(5.3)	75	(4.5)	53	(3.8)
Administrators	5	(0.3)	17	(1.0)	33	(2.4)
Collaborations	0	(0.0)	8	(0.5)	14	(1.0)
	100	(5.5)	100	(6.0)	100	(7.2)
Number of adoptions	$N = 22$		$N = 24$		$N = 36$	

cent versus 10 percent), but there is only a little difference in the process for the two types of innovations.

The impact of teacher professionalism on the source of initiation is shown in tables 5.8 and 5.9. For college-oriented innovations (table 5.8) the relationship between professionalism and where innovations are proposed is similar to that seen for all educational innovations (table 5.3). Teachers initiate 94 percent of innovations in districts with a high professional level but only 58 percent in districts with a low professional level. The proportion of innovations proposed by administrators alone and in collaboration with teachers increases as teacher professionalism decreases. There is one marked difference between the data in table 5.8 and those describing all educational innovations (table 5.3). In table 5.8 there is a much greater disparity in the total number of adoptions across districts. Districts with a high professional level adopt nearly twice as many college-oriented innovations as do districts with a low professional level (13.5 versus 7.8). In table 5.3 the total number of adoptions in both types of district was more nearly equal, 25.8 versus 20.6.

In table 5.9 a similar pattern is again observed in the source of innovations. Teachers propose nearly all innovations for terminal students in districts with a high professional level and only about half the innovations in districts with a low professional level (95 percent versus 53 percent). It seems clear that highly professional teachers have an exclusive domain on educational innovations whether the innovations benefit collegebound or terminal students.

However, when we consider average number of adoptions per district, the process has quite different results when the innovations benefit terminal students (table 5.9) rather than collegebound students (table 5.8). The presence of highly professional teachers does not result in greater numbers of innovation adoptions for terminal students. In fact, the districts with a low professional level, where administrators play a larger role in innovation, end up with slightly more adoptions per district (7.2 versus 5.5).

These data are congruent with our chapter 3 and 4 findings after all and tell us something about what happens within the school organizations. Teachers propose nearly all educational innovations in school districts characterized by a high level of teacher professionalism. They propose both terminal-oriented and college-oriented innovations. But the absolute number of college-oriented innovations initiated is much greater in the districts with a high professional level. Thus teacher professionalism is substantially correlated with the number of innovations for collegebound students, while there is no strong relationship between teacher professionalism and the number of terminal-oriented innovations. Administrator activity in the districts with a low professional level makes up for the small number of terminal-oriented innovations proposed by teachers.

In tables 5.10 and 5.11 we compare the innovation process in districts that adopt large and small numbers of terminal-oriented and college-oriented innovations, respectively. The process that results in large numbers of adoptions is significantly different for innovations that benefit terminal students from those that benefit collegebound students. In table 5.10, college-oriented innovations, we see a familiar pattern. Teachers propose most innovations in districts with a high number of adoptions. Administrators alone and in collaboration with teachers become more important in districts with a low number of adoptions. This relationship is very similar to what we found when we looked

11

TABLE 5.10
Number of Adoptions and Where Initiated:
College-oriented Innovations

| | NUMBER OF ADOPTIONS | | | | | |
| | HIGH | | MEDIUM | | LOW | |
WHERE INITIATED	%	$(\bar{x})$	%	$(\bar{x})$	%	$(\bar{x})$
Teachers	94	(15.7)	74	(7.6)	59	(3.8)
Administrators	4	(0.7)	14	(1.4)	13	(0.8)
Collaborations	2	(0.3)	12	(1.2)	28	(1.8)
	100	(16.7)	100	(10.2)	100	(6.4)
Number of adoptions	$N = 50$		$N = 51$		$N = 31$	

at the role of teacher professionalism in table 5.8. The professional level of teachers is probably a major reason for this bottom-up process and the large number of adoptions.

In table 5.11, however, an entirely different process is associated with frequent adoption of innovations for terminal students. The highly innovative districts have much greater involvement of administrators in innovation initiation. Teachers alone propose only 55 percent of the terminal-oriented innovations in the districts with a high number of adoptions. Administrators alone initiate 32 percent. Another 13 percent of the innovations are the result of administrator-teacher collaboration. The teacher role is important, of course. The average number of terminal-oriented innovations proposed by teachers alone is greater in the highly innovative districts (5.7 adoptions per district versus 3.5). But administrators make an important difference. Administrator involvement in addition to teacher activity is necessary if districts are to adopt large numbers of innovations that benefit terminal students.

These findings about terminal-oriented innovation adoption help explain the findings in chapter 4. The incentives for adoption of innovations for terminal students were found to be the existence of a large vocational teacher component in the district and what seemed to be a trend in education concerning non-collegebound students. More emphasis was given to preparing terminal students for life after graduation. Administrators seemed to be involved in this process. One reason administrators might have been involved is that these innovations are sometimes

TABLE 5.11
Number of Adoptions and Where Initiated:
Terminal-oriented Innovations

| | NUMBER OF ADOPTIONS | | | | | |
| | HIGH | | MEDIUM | | LOW | |
WHERE INITIATED	%	($\bar{x}$)	%	($\bar{x}$)	%	($\bar{x}$)
Teachers	55	(5.7)	77	(5.0)	84	(3.5)
Administrators	32	(3.3)	19	(1.3)	8	(0.3)
Collaborations	13	(1.3)	4	(0.3)	8	(0.3)
	100	(10.3)	100	(6.5)	100	(4.2)
Number of adoptions	$N = 31$		$N = 26$		$N = 25$	

special programs for slow or problem students, and professional teachers seemed to be more interested in what was new for collegebound students. Administrators sensed the needs for these special programs and were responsible for initiating many of them. Teachers were also important to the terminal-oriented innovation process. We don't mean to minimize their role. But it seems that innovation initiation by administrators made the difference between districts with a high number of adoptions and those with a low number of adoptions.

Other variables were also found to be important for the adoption of innovations for terminal students (chapter 4). Growth rate was important because it enabled the implementation of these new programs. The existence of nonteaching support staff was also important in proposal preparation and later implementation.

The most important finding in this chapter, however, is the role of administrators in educational innovation. Administrator initiative is not needed in districts with highly educated teachers and in districts considered innovative for collegebound students. Administrators only become involved when teachers are not active. However, administrators play a major role in districts considered innovative for terminal students. Administrators along with teachers seem to be sensing the needs of terminal students, and they propose innovations to satisfy these needs. These districts might be characterized as having had a top-down innovation process, a process with positive benefits for terminal students.

INFORMATION PROCESSING VERSUS PROBLEM SOLVING

During data collection we asked district superintendents where innovations were initiated in their school districts. At that time we didn't realize that different types of innovations tended to originate in different places within the school districts. We asked a single question pertaining to innovations in general. The superintendents estimated the percentage of innovations proposed by teachers, principals, superintendents, and others.

We combined the superintendent estimates of who proposed innovations into categories comparable to our other data (e.g., teachers who act as part-time department heads are combined into the teacher category; superintendents and principals are combined into the administrator category). Our interest is the teacher category. Teachers propose the largest proportion of innovations. Most remaining innovations are proposed by administrators.

Superintendents varied widely in their estimates of who initiated innovations. The estimates ranged from 5 percent to 90 percent proposed by teachers. Ten of the 13 superintendents estimated that 50 percent or more of innovations were proposed by the teachers in their districts. The average estimate by superintendents across districts was that 58 percent of innovations were proposed by teachers. The data in tables 5.1 and 5.2 indicate that teachers propose the large majority of educational innovations but only a minority of administrative innovations. When educational and administrative innovations are combined, approximately 58 percent are seen to be initiated by teachers. This is exactly the same as the 58 percent estimated by superintendents.

We went one step further and correlated each superintendent's estimate of innovation proposed by teachers with our actual figures for his district. The correlation coefficient for estimated with actual is .60 ($p = .014$). This correlation coefficient suggests to us that superintendents have some feeling for the innovation process that exists in their districts. If one superintendent had not erred very badly in his estimates, the correlation coefficient would have been even higher.

Our reason for comparing superintendent estimates with actual figures was to learn whether superintendents were accurate judges of the innovation process in their district. We were surprised they did so well. These districts are large; most have multiple schools. In addition, the superintendents' estimates were made in 1972, while our actual figures cover an eight-year span prior to 1972. But the proportion of innovations proposed by teachers did vary from district to district, and superintendents did seem to be tuned to the process in their district. We are justified in having confidence in their reports about innovation processes.

Our primary interest in asking these questions was to get some idea about the organizational motivation behind innovation adoption. We postulated incentives for innovation adoption in earlier chapters. The incentive to adopt an innovation is a function of the difference between aspiration and current performance. Incentives to innovate with the intent to improve performance can arise when great demands are placed on an organization or when new procedures are discovered that render current procedures obsolete.

We asked superintendents specifically about this aspect of the innovation process. Each superintendent estimated the proportion of innovations adopted in his district for each of two reasons: (1) as a result of searching for solutions to specific problems; and (2) as a result of organization members learning of innovations and then adopting them as a better way to do things. We wanted to obtain a sense of whether perceived problems provoke a search for new ideas, or whether ideas flow into the organization and seem good compared with current procedures. If ideas tend to come first, then continuous contact with the technological environment and a continuous influx of new ideas will be important and necessary for innovation. If problems come first, however, contact with the environment is still needed, but only inasmuch as it facilitates the search for problem solutions. Continuous innovation information-processing mechanisms may not be so important to innovation adoption.

Once again the superintendents varied considerably in their estimates of the problem-solving process in their districts. The estimates of innovations proposed as a solution to specific problems ranged from 10 percent to 100 percent of innovations adopted. The average estimate across districts was that 61 percent of innovations resulted from a search for solutions to specific problems. Approximately 39 percent resulted from having the idea before the problem. All but two superintendents estimated that 50 percent or more of innovations resulted from problems and search activities. These percentages suggest to us that both problem solving and information processing result in innovation but that problem-solving activities dominate.

How do differences in problem solving relate to other differences across school districts? We correlated the estimates of problem-solving frequency with teacher professionalism and with the number of innovations adopted for the 1968–72 period. We expected teacher professionalism to be positively related to innovation resulting from new ideas (information processing rather than problem solving). Professional teachers were expected to have greater exposure to the environment and to new ideas that would have made current procedures obsolete. Hence teacher professionalism should have been negatively related to the proportion of innovations resulting from problem-solving activities.

But the first correlation coefficient in table 5.12 shows quite the opposite ($r = .49$). The districts that innovate to solve problems tend to be the districts that have the highly educated teachers. After the fact, this finding makes sense. Part of the energy driving professionals to innovate are high standards of

TABLE 5.12
**Correlation of Problem-solving Innovation with
Teacher Professionalism and Adoption Frequency**

	PROBLEM-SOLVING ACTIVITY
Teacher professionalism	.49[a]
Number of adoptions	.43[b]

[a]Significant at .04 level
[b]Significant at .07 level

performance and high aspirations. High standards can lead to identification of areas where standards are not met and so problems are defined. Thus high goals and standards can be an incentive that provokes continuous search activity for new ideas to solve the identified problems.

The other correlation coefficient in table 5.12 reflects a positive relationship between problem solving and the number of innovations adopted ($r = .43$). This finding supports the same important role for problem-solving activity. School districts that innovate to solve problems with the intent of improving performance are the districts that adopt many innovations. The paradox is that those organizations energized to solve problems are the organizations most people would already rate as highly successful. Those organizations seemingly doing well also seem to be the ones that feel the urgency to improve their performance. This sense of urgency may come partly from high expectations in the community and partly from high professional standards within the organization.

We think this is further evidence in support of a rational model of innovation. Organizations innovate in an attempt to achieve goals, to meet requirements from the environment, or to improve upon past experience. High-performance organizations may actually feel the greatest incentive to innovate because their internal standards and performance expectations are highest. These findings tend to disconfirm the notion frequently expressed in the decision-making literature that organizations that are failing, or operating at a disadvantage, experience the greatest need to innovate and hence are the most innovative. It seems to be true that desire for improvement provides the impetus for innovation, but it is not just failing organizations that feel this incentive to innovate.

SUMMARY OF EMPIRICAL FINDINGS

In this chapter we have presented some data relevant to our speculations about innovation processes. The specific innovation process observed in a high school district is contingent to a large extent on innovation type and teacher professionalism. Educational innovations tend to percolate up from the bottom of the organization. Over 70 percent of the educational innovations originate with teachers. When average teacher professionalism is high, teachers propose over 90 percent of educational innovations; when teacher professionalism is low, the proportion initiated by teachers drops off significantly and administrators become more involved in the initiation of educational innovations. The percolate-up process for educational innovations and its relationship to teacher professionalism is true for innovations that benefit both collegebound and terminal students.

However, the relationship between who proposes educational innovations and the number of adoptions is not the same for innovations that benefit collegebound students and those that benefit terminal students. For college-oriented innovations a large number of adoptions are associated with teacher professionalism. Highly educated teachers seem to sense and to respond to the needs of collegebound students. This finding helps document and explain why teacher professionalism and decentralization are so important for college-oriented innovations in the regression analyses. Teachers do the work of introducing educational innovations for collegebound students. The administrators' role in these districts is to influence innovation by setting a climate conducive to innovation in the district, not by initiating innovations.

For terminal-oriented innovations the most innovative districts are characterized by administrator involvement in innovation initiation. Administrators apparently sense needs for innovation for terminal students and initiate innovations in response to those needs. Teachers also initiate terminal-oriented innovations, of course, but the activity of the administrators seems to make the difference between districts that adopt a large number of these innovations and those that adopt a small number.

Administrative innovations follow an entirely different process from educational innovations. Over 70 percent of the administrative innovations are initiated by administrators and are implemented downward. Teachers play a relatively minor role. Administrators tend to initiate more innovations in districts with

118

a low professional level, suggesting a top-down, centralized management process in those districts. The districts with a low professional level may require more administrative innovations because of fewer dollars, a less professional staff, and a more heterogeneous student population.

We also observed that a division of labor characterizes districts that adopt a large number of administrative innovations or innovations for collegebound students. The involvement of teachers in administrative innovations or administrators in college-oriented innovations is associated with fewer total adoptions of each innovation type. The adoption of a large number of innovations for terminal students, however, seems to result from the involvement of both teachers and administrators.

Finally, we observed that innovative districts innovate to solve perceived problems. Organizations that attempt to reach high standards of performance tend to adopt the most innovations. Innovations are also adopted in response to an awareness of new ideas.

Thus, the internal innovation process is a complex one. Different groups within the school organization tend to take the responsibility for initiating different kinds of innovations. The observed process of innovation depends upon innovation type, the professionalism of teachers, and the incentives impinging upon the organization.

NOTES

1. Christopher Argyris, *The Applicability of Organizational Sociology* (Cambridge, England: Cambridge University Press, 1972); and John Child, "Organizational Structure, Environment and Performance: The Role of Strategic Choice," *Sociology* 6: 1–22.
2. William M. Evan, "Organization Lag," *Human Organization* 25 (Spring 1966): 53.

6

Organizational
Innovation:
A Reexamination

Now that our data have been analyzed, we could proceed with a
restructuring of our theoretical model. Such a restructuring, however, would benefit from an examination of how these data relate to
findings and unresolved issues already in the literature on organizational innovation. In chapter 1 we discussed parts of the literature
relevant to our theoretical model, primarily other theoretical state-
ments but also some empirical work directly related either to our
theory or to our operationalization of that theory in the high school
district setting. It was not necessary to cover the larger body of
empirical work in order to derive our model, so that was ignored, as
were a number of issues we didn't think would be relevant.

In this chapter we shall explore how our findings and interpretations relate to other empirical research. We will give specific
attention to the issues of innovation type; organizational rationality;
professionalism; complexity; resistance to change; creativity; and
organizational structure. In the next chapter we will use these ideas
to restructure our theoretical model of organizational innovation.

THE IMPORTANCE OF INNOVATION TYPE

With hindsight, our most obvious finding, one that can potentially change future innovation research, is that innovation is
not a homogeneous category. All innovations share the char-

acteristic of newness, but beyond newness the array of innovations adopted by any organization may be a mixture of types
each having different attributes. Innovations may be adopted
to serve administrative purposes, to serve particular client
groups, or they may be adopted at the request of specialists
within the organization. Some types of innovation ideas percolate
up the organization, some are imposed from above, and other
types of ideas move in both directions. The consequence of this
heterogeneity is that the adoption of ideas from different innovation subcategories will be related to different organizational
and environmental factors and will follow different processes.
Studying one innovation category will produce markedly different
findings from the study of another category.

As we look at the innovation literature—even the most recent
literature—we observe only casual regard for the types of innovations studied. Researchers may strive to include all possible
innovations in the dependent variable, which might be called
the all-inclusive approach. We began this study the same way.
Another strategy is for researchers to ask an organizational informant to report on a few innovations adopted in the recent
past. The informant decides the number and type of innovations
to report, and the number of innovations reported constitutes
the dependent variable. These strategies seem simple enough
and may reveal something about the correlates of adoption. But
these strategies ignore the heterogeneous nature of innovations.
We expect that innovation types will be mixed together in an
unknown fashion. Consequently, the organizations will not be
compared on a common criterion of innovation, the findings will
obscure the correct correlates and underlying processes for each
type, and the complexity of the innovation phenomenon will be
understated.

It would not be fair to say that research that does not consider
innovation type is of no value. The innovation processes we
observed are rather robust, and if a certain type of innovation
dominates in a study of innovation, then the findings may be
representative for that type. But in order to unscramble the
underlying organizational processes associated with different
innovation types and to make increasingly finer discriminations

necessary for the advancement of the field, we feel it is essential in future research to consider the characteristics of the innovations being studied.

Obviously, a taxonomy of innovations would be useful. The basis for a typology appears to be emerging in the theoretical literature. Two notions are frequently mentioned—that of innovation type and that of innovation attribute. We have not found any definition distinguishing *type* from *attribute*, although Zaltman, Duncan, and Holbek provided a detailed discussion of types and attributes.[1] Figure 6.1 is the Zaltman, Duncan, and Holbek summary of innovation types, and figure 6.2 their summary of innovation attributes.

Types of innovations in terms of the state of the system

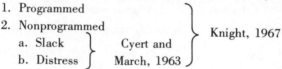

1. Programmed
2. Nonprogrammed
   a. Slack } Cyert and
   b. Distress } March, 1963 } Knight, 1967

Types of innovations in terms of their *initial focus*

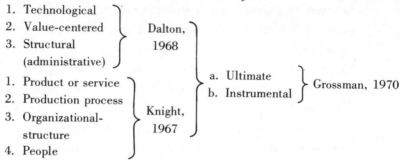

1. Technological
2. Value-centered } Dalton,
3. Structural } 1968
   (administrative)

1. Product or service
2. Production process
3. Organizational- } Knight,
   structure } 1967
4. People

a. Ultimate
b. Instrumental } Grossman, 1970

Types of innovations in terms of their *outcome or effect*

1. Performance radicalness } Knight,   i. Large scale } Harvey and
2. Structural radicalness } 1967   ii. Small scale } Mills, 1970
1. Variations (imply minor changes)
2. Reorientations (imply major changes)
   a. Systematic
   b. Idiosyncratic } Normann, 1971
   c. Marginal

FIGURE 6.1   Types of Innovations

SOURCE: Gerald Zaltman, Robert Duncan, and Jonny Holbek, *Innovations and Organizations* (New York: John Wiley & Sons, 1973), p. 31, with permission.

Financial cost	Perceived relative advantages	Publicness
Social cost	Demonstratability	Number of gatekeepers
Returns to investment	Terminality	Susceptibility to successions modification
Efficiency	Reversibility	
Risk and uncertainty	Divisibility	
Communicability	Degree of commitment	Gateway capacity
Clarity of results	Impact on interpersonal relationships	Pervasiveness
Compatibility		
Complexity		

FIGURE 6.2 Innovation Attributes

Source: Zaltman, Duncan, and Holbek, *Innovations and Organizations*, p. 47, with permission.

If we define *type* as members of a class and *attribute* as a characteristic of a member of a class, then we can reexamine the types and attributes in figures 6.1 and 6.2. It seems to us that types of innovations in terms of their *initial focus* (figure 6.1) are indeed types and all others in figure 6.1 can be considered as attributes of innovations or correlates of innovations (slack and distress innovations). Hence, innovation types would be: technical; organizational structure (administrative); and goal- (value-) centered innovations. Technical can be further subdivided into product and process, and people are subsumed under organizational structure.

Our research provides us with evidence of the usefulness of considering innovation type. Frequently, innovation adoption is postulated to be a function of the organic-mechanistic nature of the organization.[2] Organic organizations are characterized by member involvement in professional associations, decentralization and relative freedom at lower organizational levels, and a high degree of communication among organization members. Organic organizations are typically perceived to have characteristics that facilitate innovation. The decentralized districts with a high professional level in our sample are similar to the organic model. The organic organizations in our sample—those with a bottom-up innovation process—do tend to be the most innovative, *but only for educational innovations*. The organic-innovation relationship does not hold for other innovation types—especially administrative innovations—which follow a top-down process. An organic organizational climate may actually inhibit a top-down process and reduce the number of innovations normally adopted in this manner.

We can say that for our sample of organizations the distinctions between administrative and technical innovations, and between student groups served by technical innovations, were crucial in explaining innovation adoption. An investigator exploring the correlates and processes associated with one of these types will uncover a completely different innovation system than will another investigator exploring another type. Much additional research is needed to discover the full range of effects of the different types of innovations in different kinds of organizations.

The importance of the client group served to highlight an omission in the listing of types of innovations. In public service organizations the clients are "processed," and in some sense they also constitute the "product" of the organization. But just as product is distinguished from process in the manufacturing organization, client group served should be distinguished from process in the public service organization. Hence we feel technical innovations should be subdivided into product, process, and client served.

The various types of innovation can differ on any of the attributes listed in figures 6.1 and 6.2. The attributes we investigated seemed to be of little importance. We operationalized both cost and radicalness, and neither of these variables had any explanatory power for differences in adoption rates. Schools seemed to adopt innovations without regard to cost or change.

During the course of this study various discussants argued that radicalness is not a variable in educational organizations. They argued that really big innovations—the technological breakthroughs—don't seem to happen in education. Most educational innovations cluster at the low end of the radicalness continuum. In some respects this criticism is well founded. Most educational innovations were rated on the bottom half of the five-point Likert scale used to evaluate radicalness. But there were enough major educational changes taking place from 1958 to 1972 to provide considerable variance along the radicalness continuum. Open campus concepts, tracking systems, individualized instruction, the use of minicourses, pass-fail grading, modular scheduling concepts, and revised curricula, such as modern math and electives in English, were quite large changes. It seems, then, that innovations in education do vary according to the amount of change involved, but amount of change is not very important as an explanation for innovation adoption.

We suspect a connection may exist between innovation radicalness and the administrative-educational category in school organizations. Administrative innovations—PPBS (program, planning, and budgeting system), management by objectives (separate from PPBS), student involvement in administration, computerization, and community participation in school affairs—often require substantial changes in the administration of the school districts. On the average, administrative changes are somewhat more radical (involving a larger amount of change) than educational innovations.[3] Many administrative innovations are implemented throughout the organization. Perhaps radicalness becomes important when innovations are large enough to affect multiple departments in the organization. When several parts of the organization are involved, problems of agreement and coordination multiply dramatically. Administrators will have to be involved. Hence, many radical innovations, which affect all or most departments in the organization, are administrative in nature and initiated from the top, or at least have the involvement of top administrators. One reason we didn't find an important role for radicalness could have been that we only examined educational innovations in the correlation analysis.

Critics might argue that innovation cost, as well as radicalness, is small on the average in school organizations. This may be true, compared to manufacturing industries, but there were enough expensive innovations to give us considerable variance in cost. All courses that require special equipment—for example, film production, TV production, computer programming, driver's education, and power mechanics—were rated as expensive to adopt. So were teaching techniques that require special facilities—for example, language laboratories, dial-access retrieval systems (where students dial videotape lectures and teaching aids from study halls), separate classes for problem students, and resource centers. There are expensive as well as inexpensive innovations adopted across these districts. The absence of a correlation between cost and adoption in our school district sample cannot be explained by claiming lack of variance in dollar cost.

There are only two other empirical studies we know of that consider innovation attributes. Fliegal and Kivilan studied the adoption of 33 modern farming practices by 229 farmers in Pennsylvania.[4] They found that high cost did not act as a barrier to adoption. In fact, high cost was positively related to adoption. In addition, the slow rate of recovering costs did not decrease the rate of adoption. In either their study or ours innovation cost did not turn out to be an adoption barrier, as is usually presumed. Fliegal and Kivilan did find that divisibility for trial and potential for high return were positively associated with adoption. High eventual return was compatible with long-range profit goals for these farmers. Divisibility, which means the farmer could try the innovation in a stepwise fashion, reduced uncertainty and risk for the adopter.

Kaluzny, Veney, and Gentry evaluated the risk attributes in the adoption of new services in 23 health departments and 70 general hospitals.[5] They found that size was critical to the adoption of high-risk services in hospitals. Size served as a shield against possible failure, so large organizations could adopt risky innovations. They also found that cosmopolitan orientation and training of staff were positively correlated with the adoption of low-risk services in both health departments and hospitals.

Our conclusion for this section is that innovation attributes may affect innovation adoption to some extent. Obvious attributes, such as cost and change, do not receive empirical support as being important barriers to adoption. Attributes such as risk or profit potential, which relate to organizational goal achievement, do seem to have some effect on adoption. We feel that innovation types—administrative (organizational structure), technical (product, process, and client group served), and goal— are dramatically more important than innovation attributes. We suggest that it is no longer adequate for researchers to aggregate all kinds of innovations into a single dependent variable. It is much more meaningful to examine each innovation and to place it in a group of innovations according to some relevant typology. Much additional research is needed to sort out the various attributes and types and how they influence decisions to adopt innovations. A framework and the variables relevant to the process of adoption are shown in figure 6.3. Organizational environment and structure as well as the processes of innovation initiation and implementation should be exmained separately for each category of innovation type.

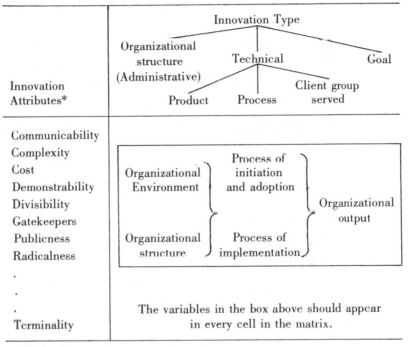

*Partial listing.

FIGURE 6.3 Organizational Variables and Innovation Types and Attributes

THE DRIVING FORCE OF RATIONALITY

Organizational rationality has been one of the most valuable explanatory concepts in the organization theory literature, though it has been little used to explain empirical innovation findings.

The concept of organizational rationality includes the supposition that organizations are goal-seeking mechanisms, so that organizational behavior is "rational" if goal achievement is enhanced. In any situation many behaviors may lead to goal achievement, and all such behaviors would be considered "rational," while those that result in a decrement in performance are not rational. Organizational innovation and rationality have infrequently been linked in the empirical studies of innovation because adoption of innovations is typically the dependent variable of interest and most often is not linked with degree of, or change in, goal achievement. This oversight may be due to choice or to circumstances, as in our case. We have no measure of how well schools prepare students to perform their life role. Indeed, we don't even have scores on a standardized achievement test to use as a proxy measure. None are available. Hence, strictly speaking, we have no basis for deciding whether any of the behaviors exhibited by the organizations in our sample are "rational" or not.

This definition of rationality leaves something to be desired. It implies that rationality can only be determined "after the fact." It implies that an observer could not judge which alternatives from a series of alternatives are rational and which are not until all have been tried and their effects on goal attainment noted. Such a definition is far too restrictive, since it says that a decision made under conditions of uncertainty will have been irrational if the desired outcome does not materialize. In other words, it would have been irrational to select the alternative with the highest expected value $[p(v)]$ if that value was subsequently not realized, if the $(1-p)$ event occurred.

We feel that organizational rationality should be defined as organization decision makers selecting alternatives that they perceive are related positively to goal attainment. Decision makers can make errors. Courses of action perceived to be beneficial can later turn out to have been detrimental, but when the decisions were made, they were rational. It is this latter interpretation of rationality we use in this study.

We have measures of elite goals for quality of education, we know how they related to community goals (education level), and we have measures of the frequency with which adopted innovations were perceived to relate to that goal structure. In other words, we feel we can say that in these districts adoption of innovations was *perceived* to be related positively to goal attainment, and so from our point of view innovation adoption in these organizations was rational behavior, it was a function of what the organization was trying to do. We feel this is a finding of some importance.

The finding is important not only in understanding adoption behavior, but it may also aid in understanding why innovations are not adopted, or not even considered for adoption. Considering our other major finding, that type of innovation is important, it may be that some types of innovations fit what the organization is trying to do, while other types do not. Failure to adopt may not be due to resistance to change, bureaucratic personalities, innovation cost, conflict over who benefits from the innovation, rules and regulations, lack of freedom and creativity for employees, the absence of new ideas, or structural barriers. The innovation may simply not be needed, so why adopt it?

Variables other than needs and incentives for innovations also play an important part in the explanation of innovation adoption. But since innovation is a heterogeneous category, and since different innovation categories serve different purposes within the organization, it makes eminent sense in future research to relate innovation functions to organizational goals and incentives. Then the variance unexplained by this fit can be related to other traditional variables believed to explain innovation.

One of the districts in our sample provides a striking example of how goals influence the number and kind of innovations adopted by an organization. This particular district was ranked as one of the most innovative in the 1959–64 period. In the 1968–72 period, however, this district ranked near the bottom in number of adoptions of educational innovations. The change in position was the greatest for any district in the sample. The district was fairly high on several of the important predictor variables in both periods, such as teacher professionalism, community education, and affluence (expenditures per pupil). The reason for the low number of educational innovations in the

1968–72 period was that a new superintendent had been hired in 1969 to install a program, planning, and budgeting system (PPBS) in the district. This signaled a change in organizational goals. The board wanted better control over expenditures, greater accountability, and greater value received for the dollars spent. To achieve this goal, they hired a superintendent experienced in program budgeting to install the program and reduce costs.

The result of the new budgeting system was an extreme efficiency orientation throughout the district and a very centralized decision-making process. All programs were to be costed and program success was to be measured and reported back to the superintendent. Nearly all decisions were made by the superintendent and/or the school board in order to ensure compliance with the new procedures. In addition a large share of the "nonessential" support staff were let go. These nonessential staff were curriculum coordinators, and it had been their job to play an integrative role across schools and across curriculum areas in the district.

Implementation of the new goals produced secondary changes in the organization that further inhibited educational innovation. There was a lack of freedom at the lower levels of the organization, there were no longer support staff to share ideas or help write innovation proposals, and there was strict accountability to the superintendent. These factors combined to practically close down the educational innovation process.

The changes that took place in the district also illustrate the rationality of innovation adoption. Educational innovations were adopted less frequently because the new goals and structure did not encourage educational innovation. Educational innovations no longer fitted what the organization was trying to do, which was to control costs. But the district was innovative in the area compatible with its goals. *This district was the first in our sample to implement PPBS, a very innovative act.* Clearly, compatibility between innovation and organizational goals can make adoption very easy; the lack of fit between innovation and organizational goals can serve as a huge barrier to adoption.

There is some other research evidence that innovation adoption is rational strategy to achieve goals. Myers and Marquis interviewed 'executives in 121 manufacturing firms about the important innovations adopted in recent years.[6] These interviews produced information on 567 product or process innovation adoptions. Seventy-five percent of the innovations were adopted in response to external market factors, such as anticipated demand or changes in demand, or in response to such production factors as high cost or changed processes. Two case studies of elementary schools reported that innovation resulted from environmental (client) pressure.[7] Gross, Giacquinta, and Bernstein observed that the attempted implementation of a major role change for elementary teachers in a primary school was the result of an influx of lower-class students into the school. The new role (innovation) was designed to cope with the new kind of student (change in goals). Bredo and Bredo reported a major school reorganization in response to student and parent expectations for greater school responsiveness.[7]

It seems fairly clear that rational processes are at work in organizations and that the perceived contribution to organizational goals—the need for innovation—is a major explanatory variable in innovation adoption. At this point we would like to probe the rational process in more detail. We want to consider (1) the sequence of events in the rational innovation process; and (2) which organizations experience the greatest need for innovation.

March and Simon made the original connection between innovation and the goal-seeking behavior of organizations.[8] They hypothesized that organization members make conscious decisions to obtain individual and organizational goals and that innovations are more likely to be adopted when existing procedures are deemed unsatisfactory for the achievement of goals. Dissatisfaction with existing procedures leads to search and problem-solving activity to find better alternatives.

Later theorists have elaborated on the March and Simon model. But the essential underlying innovation sequence is that members perceive a problem, and this perception leads to search activity, which results in a choice for or against innovation. Figure 6.4 shows an elaboration of the rational model taken from Zaltman, Duncan, and Holbek.

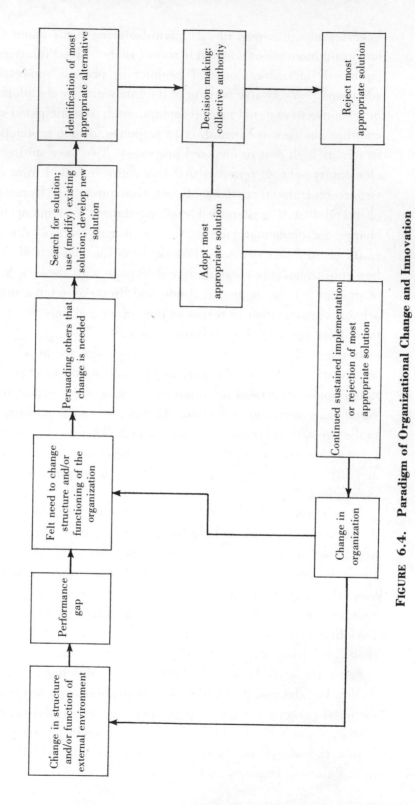

FIGURE 6.4. Paradigm of Organizational Change and Innovation

Source: Zaltman, Duncan, and Holbek. *Innovations and Organizations*, p. 5, with permission.

We wonder whether figure 6.4 presents a complete picture of the rational innovation process. Certainly for many innovations it is right, but the superintendents in our sample reported that 39 percent of the innovations were not the result of searching for a solution to a problem. The problem–search–innovation sequence doesn't account for those innovations. Meyers and Marquis reported that in 25 percent of innovation adoptions information inputs, rather than search, evoked the idea.[9] A similar finding was reported by Utterback for 32 innovations in the musical instrument industry.[10] For about 25 percent of innovation adoptions Utterback reported an awareness of a technical advantage that stimulated adoption.

What seems to be happening is that for some significant portion of innovation adoptions the idea arrives first. A problem isn't recognized prior to that time, and search activity does not explain awareness. This sequence of events does not run counter to norms of rationality. The need for the innovation still influences the decision to adopt. The presence of new ideas seems to stimulate the recognition that goal attainment is lower than it might be. This additional sequence is shown in figure 6.5 and could be combined with the figure 6.4 model quite nicely.

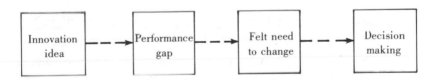

FIGURE 6.5. Alternative Innovation Sequence

It makes little difference if the idea enters the organization first and "creates" the problem or whether the problem arises and stimulates search for new ideas; adoption of innovation is seen as a rational process. There is, however, disagreement on the organizational conditions under which rational behavior leads to innovation adoption.

March and Simon hypothesized that innovations are most likely to be adopted when existing procedures are perceived as unsatisfactory. As does most everyone, we agree with this proposition. What we disagree with is when innovation solutions will be adopted in response to the perceived unsatisfactory procedures. Cyert and March predicted that unsuccessful firms will actually be more innovative than successful firms because failure induces search, which ordinarily results in solution.[11] Knight adopted a similar perspective and predicted that distress will lead to the adoption of certain kinds of innovations.[12] Harvey and Mills proposed that organizations operate under different conditions of threat.[13] Organizations operating under high threat will often be faced with novel problems and hence will adopt novel (innovative) solutions. Variables that represent high threat to an organization are small size relative to competitors, high degree of competition in the market situation, young age relative to competitors, and rapid technological change. Thus an organization characterized as small, young, and operating in a competitive market in an uncertain technological environment is expected to be very innovative because of high threat conditions.

The prediction derived from the rational problem-solving model that innovation is a function of distress and threat does not receive support in the empirical literature. In the school districts in our sample the adoption of innovations for collegebound students most often occurred in those districts with highly educated teachers, more dollars, and highly educated communities. The schools adopting educational innovations would normally be rated as high-quality, successful school districts, not those that experience distress or failure. There is a great deal of similar evidence in the literature. Large organizations, for example, tend to be more innovative than small organizations.[14] Good financial health has been found associated with innovative adoption in hospitals and welfare agencies (but unrelated in another study of hospitals and a study of manufacturing firms).[15] At least six studies of high schools have linked adoption of innovations to greater availability of resources.[16] Several studies have also reported a positive relationship between innovation adoption and the professionalism and cosmopolitan orientation of employees.[17]

Why doesn't distress or failure lead to innovation, and why do apparently successful organizations innovate? The answer is that successful as well as distressed organizations feel dissatisfaction with existing procedures. In times of distress dissatisfaction with procedures is obvious, and search is frequently quick and designed to yield immediate relief. Such search activity usually develops only one or two alternatives.[18] Furthermore, short-term search activity is not very effective in developing the best alternatives available in the technological environment.[19] The search procedure is likely to lead decision makers to try something that is in their immediate repertoire, a noninnovative solution.

Successful organizations have experienced high levels of performance and presumably have high aspirations for future performance. (We don't know which came first, success or high aspirations.) In our sample the apparently successful organizations also had a relatively larger group of highly professional employees. Highly professional employees tend to have higher standards of performance than do less professional employees. However these high standards evolve, successful organizations apparently feel the greater need to improve upon existing procedures. The felt need to improve procedures is probably not a temporary phenomenon. Organizations with high aspirations probably experience continuous dissatisfaction with current performance. Such dissatisfaction implies that organization members will be on the lookout for better procedures. Highly professional employees will know where to look for superior alternatives, and they will better be able to recognize and identify superior alternatives. If the decision makers perceive more efficient goal attainment as a result of the proposed alternative, adoption will follow.

Our perception of rational innovative behavior, then, takes on a somewhat different perspective from past theorizing. Rational innovation behavior is not a simple reaction to problems with search and decisions for change. Rational behavior means structuring the organization and channeling organizational energy toward the importation and proposal of ideas on a continuous

basis, *if* the organization maintains high standards of performance and dissatisfaction with current procedures. Rational innovation behavior for organizations with lower aspirations and
fewer dissatisfactions is less search for ideas and less frequent
adoption of innovations.

PROFESSIONALISM, ORGANIZATIONAL COMPLEXITY, AND RESISTANCE TO CHANGE

Employee professionalism, organizational complexity, and resistance to change are variables frequently used to explain
adoption or nonadoption of innovations. Hage and Aiken have
contributed much to our understanding of organizational innovation with their empirical research and theoretical framework.[20]
They have devoted considerable attention to the concepts of
professionalism and complexity, but their conclusions differ
somewhat from ours. By exploring these differences we hope
to increase our understanding of how these variables affect the
innovation process. One cautionary note: In this dicussion we
will oversimplify the richness of the Hage and Aiken arguments
and the evolution of their ideas. We can't avoid it. We don't
feel we do their ideas any gross injustice, but we do select only
limited portions of their work to contrast with our own ideas.
Specifically, we are going to compare our findings about how
professionalism and complexity influence the adoption of high
school innovations with their findings about new program
changes.

We will then turn to the notion of resistance to change and
give special attention to the theoretical argument concerning
complexity proposed by Zaltman, Duncan, and Holbek.[21] They
elaborated the Hage and Aiken complexity argument and relate
complexity specifically to facilitation and resistance to innovation.

Professionalism and Complexity

The first problem is a definitional one. In his axiomatic theory
of organizations Hage has described organizational complexity
as follows:

The *complexity*, or specialization, in an organization is measured by the number of occupational specialties included and the length of training required by each. The greater the number of occupations and the longer the period of training required, the more complex the organization.[22]

We find a similar definition in Hage and Aiken's book on organizational change:

The complexity of an organization refers to the level of knowledge and expertise in an organization. There are two complementary aspects of complexity: the number of occupational specialties in an organization and the degree of professionalism in each.[23]

In these definitions the two distinct concepts—length of professional training and the number of occupational specialties in the organization—are combined. Why not leave these two variables separate? Why not conceptualize two separate variables both of which independently might affect innovation—organizational complexity and employee professionalism? The common thread holding these concepts together seems to be the notion of knowledge. Specialization of work and length of training are assumed to be positively related to each other, and each variable captures something of the notion of the complexity of knowledge within the organization.

This particular thread is a weak one, however. There is no reason to believe that occupational diversity and length of training are positively related or are measures of a common construct. In many organizations the specialization of labor into different tasks leads to routine work that requires little training. In our school district sample the relationship between number of specialties and degree of professionalism is not statistically significant. We suspect the same was true in the welfare agencies studied by Hage and Aiken because the number of occupational specialties was positively related to program change ($r = .48$), while professional training was not ($r = .14$).[24] They experienced a similar finding in their follow-up study of these organizations. The number of occupational specialties was strongly related to program change ($r = .59$), while professional training was not ($r = .19$).[25]

One reason for treating length of training and occupational diversity as separate concepts is that they result from different organizational processes. For the most part, complexity is a function of organizational size and environmental heterogeneity. Large organizations and organizations in heterogeneous environments usually require a wide range of specialties and services. Professionalism, however, frequently results from other factors: from having a sophisticated or difficult-to-operate core technology or from having sufficient resources to afford highly trained personnel. If complexity and professionalism are indeed functions of different organizational processes, isn't it reasonable to determine if they differentially affect other organizational variables, such as adoption of innovation?

Interestingly enough, Hage and Aiken's operationalization of their variable, complexity, utilized a measure of the number of jobs and a separate measure of the number of years of education. Their operationalization has closer correspondence to our definition of complexity and professionalism than to their own. If their operationalization is like ours, why bother comparing the studies? The comparison is necessary because they found complexity to be considerably more important than length of professional training. In our study professionalism was found to be very important, while organizational complexity was not.

The different findings probably stem from differences in the way the dependent variables were treated. Hage and Aiken combined all new programs that met their criterion for newness into the dependent variable. They did not separate innovations by type, and some of what they classed as innovations we would have categorized as organizational change. Hage and Aiken simply incorporated programs that had been adopted in the five years prior to their survey.

Categorizing organizational change as innovation is probably less important than failing to account for types of innovations. It could be argued that an organization with 15 different functions is likely to adopt more changes than an organization engaged in only 5 separate functions. Diversity within the organization increases the possible number of changes that could be applicable to the organization. Organizational size is probably also a factor because complex organizations tend to be the largest organizations. If changes are made within departments, there is more opportunity to observe change (on a simple probabilistic basis) in large, complex organizations, everything else being equal. We don't want to stand or fall on that argument, however, for it can easily be argued that most changes cross departmental lines and are therefore less likely to occur in large organizations. No, for us the major argument is that type of innovation was not accounted for.

In our analysis we divided the total innovation package into innovation groups that served different functions within the organization and served different client groups. By analyzing only educational innovations, for instance, and innovations that benefit collegebound students in particular, the educational level (professionalism) of teachers became important. Teachers, especially highly educated teachers, initiated innovations for collegebound students. Professionalism had little to do with the number of administrative innovations or with the number of innovations that benefited terminal students. Had we aggregated all kinds of innovations into a single innovation index, professionalism would have shown only a weak relationship to innovation, if it had shown any relationship at all, but size and complexity would have explained variance in adoption of innovations. However, it would have been inaccurate to impute a causal role to size and complexity, especially for those innovations that benefited collegebound students.

The contradictory findings between our study and that of Hage and Aiken illustrate how a good typology of innovations can enhance our understanding of the processes underlying innovation. In future research if innovations are subdivided according to the functions they serve in the organization, we feel that professionalism within that particular function will be important to innovation adoption. Further, we suggest that a causal connection between organizational complexity and innovation adoption is spurious.

We don't expect easily to win converts to a downgrading of the role of organizational complexity. Much has been written about the importance of conflict, diversity, and cross-fertilization as important antecedents to innovation. Heterogeneity of ideas is presumed to bring more alternatives to bear in decision situations. This is an attractive scenario but one whose veracity we doubt.

First, we expect the exchange of ideas between occupational specialties to decrease as the differentiation between specialties increases. Cross-fertilization is most likely to occur when occupational groups are similar because they can understand and communicate with one another. It is similarity that facilitates exchange. Lawrence and Lorsch provided evidence that occupational differences are associated with problems of communication, understanding, and empathy.[26] Rather than a facilitating factor, they found differentiation to be a barrier that had to be overcome in the goal attainment process. Second, many innovations pertain to a specific occupational area, and the innovations applicable to each area enter the organization via members of that specialty. Thus, the important exposure and exchange relationships for occupational specialties are with the external environment—with outside professionals in the same specialty. More ideas will enter the specialty from outside the organization than from other occupational groups in the same organization. Third, as employee professionalism increases, employees are more resistant to influence from outside their specialty. As expertise increases, employees become more autonomous and less susceptible to external influence. They decide among themselves what will be adopted or not, and they feel they are the people best qualified to make that decision. Finally, complexity inhibits the adoption of innovations that affect multiple specialties. Wilson; and Zaltman, Duncan, and Holbek pointed out that problems of cooperation and implementation increase as occupational diversity increases.[27] For these reasons we believe that complexity adds little to the causal process of adoption.

We don't wish to argue that *all* differentiation inhibits innovation. We do want to argue that professionalism and complexity are separate concepts and that the professional level of employees within occupational specialties is important to innovation. It is the specialization and expertise within functions that is important, not the diversity among functions.

Using the notion of specialization, it is possible to explain contradictory findings in the professionalism literature. Several studies have attributed successful innovation to the professionalism of organization members.[28] The studies in which positive associations between professionalism and innovation were reported dealt primarily with new programs and other technical innovations that were more likely to be pushed for adoption by professional employees. Zald and Denton, in a study of the YMCA, however, and Corwin in a study of the Teacher Corps did not find positive relationships between professionalism and innovation.[29] These inconsistent findings can be explained by the types of innovations studied and the relative autonomy of employee groups.

Zald and Denton were studying the introduction of new organizational goals into the YMCA, which is an organizational change and is outside the expertise of professionals in the technical core. In fact, Zald and Denton reported that an absence of professionalism among lower members facilitated the goal change process. In Corwin's study innovations were introduced by Teacher Corps interns who were assigned to schools to act as catalysts to influence teachers to adopt innovations. This kind of influence is not particularly effective with highly professional teachers, who are responsible for their own initiatives and who are familiar with their tasks.

As a final illustration concerning the influences of professionalism and complexity on innovation, we will reanalyze a case example used by Hage and Aiken.

Case of a College. During the middle of the nineteenth century, American colleges faced a continual decline in enrollment. At the same time the proportion of the population attending college was increasing. More and more Americans were going to Europe to study. A large number of these were attending the new German universities, such as the University of Berlin, in which it was possible to study any one of a number of new sciences. In other words, American colleges were not competing effectively. The demand for their services was declining. This had not gone unnoticed, having been mentioned in a speech by the president of Brown as early as the 1850s. But the resistance was so great to the new sciences among the existing faculties of American colleges that it was difficult to introduce these new occupational specialties to American universities.

Shortly after the end of the Civil War in the United States, Harvard needed a new president. At this time Harvard had not suffered as much as the other New England colleges; its enrollments were keeping pace with the growth in population. The selection of Charles Eliot, the first president who was not a clergyman, represented a sharp break with the past. He had studied science and, at the time of his selection, was teaching chemistry at a newly founded college, Massachusetts Institute of Technology. Eliot was young, only thirty-five at the time. Whether these were factors important for Eliot's selection by the Harvard board is hard to say. But the fact that Eliot had an entirely different career sequence meant that he came to Harvard with a different perspective from many of his new colleagues.

Within the first few years Eliot introduced a series of changes. The most important, from our perspective, were those that resulted in radical changes in organizational complexity. He doubled the size of the faculty, hiring mostly young men trained in new academic disciplines. Instead of relying on the existing faculty to make recommendations, Eliot went out of his way to secure men with different intellectual perspectives. He introduced not only men of the new sciences but also men in the new social sciences such as economics.

The power structure of Harvard was altered in several ways by Eliot. He created the new position of dean and delegated considerable authority to him. Eliot attended faculty meetings and increased the number of these meetings, with many complaints being registered by the old faculty. If Eliot met resistance to a particular idea, he would let the matter rest and bring it up again at a later date. In these meetings, the majority vote counted. Thus there was decentralization of decision making.

A number of student regulations were eliminated: the rules manual was reduced from forty pages to five; compulsory chapel was eliminated; perhaps the most dramatic change was the abolishing of the fixed curriculum instruction. Gradually the concept of electives was introduced into American education.[30]

Hage and Aiken provided the following analysis:

It would be easy to see these changes as a consequence of Eliot's leadership, and this certainly was an important factor in bringing about the radical alteration in the social structure of Harvard. But it is important to recognize that what Eliot did was to increase the complexity of the organization and to decentralize its structure. Once new occupational specialties were brought in, new ideas were generated by the men in these specialties. Gradually research laboratories were introduced. The new dean of the law school and his faculty introduced the famous case method, which later became the method for most law schools in the United States. And finally the medical school curriculum was revised. Once Eliot had increased the complexity of the college, the development of new programs continued of its own accord. These new programs gradually led to the development of a graduate school in 1890. And thus Harvard became Harvard University.

There was an important environmental factor that facilitated the introduction of new programs: the competition between universities for good men. During the period of Eliot's forty years as president of Harvard, two new universities—Johns Hopkins and the University of Chicago—were created. These new universities attempted to hire leading faculty members away from Harvard. When men received offers from other schools, they used this as a bargaining device to support the implementation of their new ideas. A Harvard man, after receiving an offer from Johns Hopkins, obtained research support that later led to his winning a Nobel Prize. Thus the competition between organizations helps maintain a high rate of program change in a complex organization.[31]

It seems apparent from the Harvard case that pressure from the external environment—the felt need to meet the European competition—provided the impetus for the innovation sequence. This is congruent with our theory that incentives, or needs, are present and important for explaining innovation. Another incentive facing the Harvard Administration was the desire to keep the high-quality faculty.

What innovations are involved in this case? The innovations seem to fall into two categories—the initial administrative changes and the later educational changes. The initial changes include: (1) selection of a new president who was young and not a clergyman, a major change that decreased the traditional religious influence of college education; (2) the introduction of new academic departments (increased complexity); (3) the creation of new administrative positions; and (4) the decentralization of decision making to the faculty (this apparently took place after the major administrative changes were in place). Later educational innovations included: (1) the introduction of electives; (2) the case method in the law school; (3) a new medical curriculum; (4) research laboratories; and (5) a graduate school.

Harvard certainly adopted a significant number of innovations during this period and would have been classified as an innovative college. However, are Hage and Aiken justified in imputing major causal influence to organizational complexity? Can occupational diversity combined with employee professionalism account for this innovation activity?

The initial series of innovations, which included the decision to add new academic departments (increased occupational diversity), are all top-down innovations. This is similar to our findings in high schools. Changes in the organization itself tend to originate with administrators. Organizational complexity is a consequence, not a cause, of these changes. The *absence* of occupational diversity and a highly professional faculty probably made implementation of these initial changes easier.

Some of the later educational changes pertained to specific departments within the university, for example, the law school case method and the new medical curriculum. These changes apparently originated within the respective departments, were bottom-up, and were probably due in large part to the professional level of faculty members in those departments. Exchange among departments such as law and medicine probably had little influence on these innovations. To us, professionalism rather than organizational complexity seems to be a relatively more important explanatory variable in this case, and we think this will typically be observed when innovations affecting the technical core are involved.

We've devoted considerable attention to the professionalism–complexity issue because if the Hage and Aiken view is correct, then the process fostering innovation adoption is one of diversity, conflict, and cross-fertilization within the organization. If our view is correct, then the process involves specialization, expertise, and years of training. In the literature one can find innovation "explained" by a number of other variables and processes, but we feel these effects are spurious on a causal level and are observed only because the effects of professionalism, rationality, and type of innovation have not been properly accounted for.

Resistance to Change

The notion of resistance to change has been discussed extensively by Zaltman, Duncan, and Holbek and by Wilson.[32] Zaltman, Duncan, and Holbek define organizational complexity as Hage and Aiken did (job diversity *and* employee professionalism). They argued that high complexity, low formalization, and decentralization have a positive influence on the number of ideas initiated in the organization. These same characteristics, however, have a negative influence on the actual adoption and implementation of innovation. This is similar to Wilson's argument that the process that facilitates ideas in the organization may also inhibit later adoption. Many ideas will be proposed but never adopted because of conflict and disagreement among organization members and because centralized authority and formalized procedures are not sufficient to ensure implementation.[33]

They believed the organization's dilemma is to maintain an influx of new ideas and simultaneously to secure adoption of these ideas. To do that they might conclude that an organization may have to change structures continually in order to accommodate both aspects of innovation, or that organizations may have to maintain separate groups charged with each role in the innovation process.

Much has been written about resistance to change in organizations and the various ways to overcome these problems. Most of the ideas originate in the literature on individual behavior and change. People are presumed to prefer the familiar and to resist new behavior. Change in the organization is thus a very sticky process. Intervention may be required; an outside change agent can help overcome organizational inertia. People go along with changes only when they participate and when the change has some benefit for them.

We did not specifically study the process of resistance in our school district sample. Our attention was drawn to the notion of resistance by the noticeable lack of resistance that we observed. The highly innovative districts seemed to adopt innovations quickly and easily. And the less innovative districts did not seem to experience resistance either. Innovations just didn't seem to be proposed as often, and innovation wasn't as important to these districts.

We also have some harder evidence on this matter. In chapter 2 we reported that virtually all innovation proposals were adopted in these school districts. It was not possible to use separate measures of innovation proposals and innovation adoption because they were the same. This finding is inconsistent with the hypothesis that organizations must be organized one way to encourage proposals and another way to achieve adoption and implementation. This finding leads us to suggest that organizing to facilitate innovation proposals is the best technique for increasing organizational innovation.

The hypothesis that different circumstances would encourage proposals and adoptions seems reasonable enough, but there appear to be two flaws in this argument. One flaw is the failure to consider innovation type and organizational location. The reason the Zaltman et al. argument is not supported by our data becomes clear when technical innovations are distinguished from administrative innovations. Low formalization, decentralization, and high complexity (professionalism) are suited to both initiation *and* adoption of innovations within the technical core. The opposite structural conditions facilitate innovation in the administrative domain. High formalization, centralization, and low complexity (professionalism) fit the initiation and adoption of innovations which pertain to the organization itself. These innovations often are pushed onto the technical core. For both types of innovations, proposals tend to be approved and implemented because the people who are involved with the innovations, the local experts, are within the respective domains and have a hand in initiating the changes.

The other flaw in this argument seems to be the assumption that proposals and adoptions are independent, which they are not. Proposals are necessary antecedents to adoptions, and adoption decisions reinforce innovation proposals. Organization participants will not continue proposing technical innovations under circumstances of low formalization, high complexity, and decentralization if the proposals are never adopted. And high formalization, low complexity, and centralization have little to offer the innovation process if there are no proposals to be implemented. Proposals and adoptions are interdependent, and a learning process takes place. Organization participants learn whether innovations are important to the organization. They also learn which types of proposals are acceptable. At this point in our thinking we feel the important task for the innovative organization is to ensure an adequate supply of innovation proposals of the type compatible with organizational goals.

It could be that the interdependence between proposals and adoptions is greatest for certain organizational types. In school organizations such as we studied, objective cost-benefit information is minimal. It is difficult to tell whether innovations actually improve the education of students, so the risk of failure is low. In organizations where innovations are risky, expensive, and where the contribution of the innovation can be measured, differing organizational circumstances may be important for the proposal and adoption stages. This would tend to be the case for technical innovations in for-profit organizations. However, even in those circumstances adoptions and proposals will not be completely independent. Proposals will influence adoptions and vice versa, so that some equilibrium point will be reached in terms of the number of innovations initiated and adopted in the organization.

Our data are compatible with the economic model of organizational change rather than with the behavioral model of change. The economic view of organizational change suggests that organizations are quite flexible and can incorporate whatever behavior alternatives help achieve organizational goals. Organizations welcome new techniques if the new techniques really add something to performance. Some organizations actually seem to reach out for new techniques just because they are new. Resistance to change is not a big problem. The major barriers to innovation are lack of information on new techniques and lack of fit between new techniques and organizational goals.

A noticeable absence of resistance to change has been reported in other studies. Gross, Giacquinta, and Bernstein observed that teachers did not resist the implementation of a new teaching role in a primary school.[34] There were structural barriers to implementation, but resistance on the part of organization employees was not a problem. The teachers welcomed the new technique, which could help them deal more effectively with students. Mintzberg studied five top managers.[35] He reported that the managers kept an average of 50 improvement projects moving along. These managers were continuously involved in finding new and better techniques for use in their organizations. MacDonald, McLeod, and Nininger worked with managers in five municipalities.[36] They found that managers welcomed and enjoyed change when they had the necessary information and assistance and when changes were supported by higher managers in the organization.

Earlier in this chapter we suggested that there is a major barrier to change in organizations when innovations do not fit the goals of the organization. Consequently the innovation is of little value to the organization. Innovations may not be resisted because of foot dragging and natural resistance to change on the part of organization participants. Much of the organizational resistance-to-change literature assumes that organizations should be adopting new techniques. But only a small subset of available new ideas may fit organizational needs. If investigators are studying innovations or changes that are not in line with organizational goals, we can imagine a great deal of intervention is needed to implement the changes. The intervention will have to overcome the fact that organization members don't want or need the innovation. This is resistance to be sure, but not resistance to change. This is resistance to those things that don't contribute to organizational performance.

Our conclusion is that organizations do not need separate structural configurations for the initiation and implementation stages of innovation. The initiation of appropriate ideas is critical to innovation. In our sample few ideas that were initiated and pushed for adoption, and that were potentially useful for the organization, were rejected. We do not suggest that innovations are adopted effortlessly. But resistance to change is not the major innovation barrier some people believe it to be, and it is probably not an appropriate strategy to structure organizations in a rigid manner in anticipation of overcoming resistance. If innovation is important to an organization, it is more effective to structure the organization to continually learn about new ideas that can be proposed for adoption.

CREATIVITY

One source of organizational innovation is the creative potential of organization members. It is often argued that organizations should be designed to encourage individual creativity. In this way the full abilities of organization members will be harnessed, which in turn will lead to greater organizational responsiveness and effectiveness. Those concerned with the creativitiy of organization members emphasize free, open, psychologically supportive organizational circumstances to enable creativity and self-actualization to flourish.[37] Other variables that are expected to facilitate this process include mutual trust and a lack of control, decentralization, and free resources to devote to problem solving.[38]

For the average organization employee a relaxed, supportive climate; good interpersonal relations; no pressure; and lack of control may simply mean the freedom to avoid the hard work, the routine, the parts that aren't fun—all to the detriment of the organization. In most organizations, given norms of rationality, the requirements for predictability and certainty will conflict with widespread freedom for organization members. In most cases organizations will be successful if routinization takes precedence over exhilarating personal experiences of organization members. Successful organizations utilize their memberships to do the vast amounts of necessary routine work rather than to produce great insights.

The importance of predictability and routine, despite the value placed upon individual creativity in our culture, was expressed by Maslow.

Sometimes creativeness can be a horrible nuisance. It can be a troublesome, dangerous, messy thing, as I learned once from a "creative" research assistant who gummed up research that had been underway for over a year. She got "creative" and changed the whole thing in the middle without even telling me about it. She so gummed up all the data that a year's work was lost completely. On the whole, we want the trains to run on time and, generally, we want dentists not to be creative. A friend of mine had an operation a couple of years ago, and he still remembers feeling uneasy and afraid until he met his surgeon. Fortunately, he turned out to be a nice obsessional type of man, very precise, perfectly neat with a little hair-line moustache, every hair in place, a perfectly straight, controlled and sober man. My friend then heaved a sigh of relief—this was not a "creative" man. Here was a man who would do a normal, routine, pedestrian operation, not play any tricks or try any novelties or experiments or do any new sewing techniques or anything like that. This is important, I think, in our society where, with our division of labor, we ought to be able to take orders and to carry through a program and be predictable. It is also important for each of us, not only in our capacity as creative workers, but also as students of creativeness with a tendency to deify the one side of the creative process—the enthusiastic, the great insight, the illumination, the good idea, the moment in the middle of the night when you get the great inspiration—and of underplaying the two years of hard sweaty labor that then is necessary to make anything useful out of the bright idea.

In simple terms of time, bright ideas really take a small proportion of our time. Most time is spent on hard work. My impression is that our students don't know this. It may be that these dead cats have been brought to my door more because my students so frequently identify with me, because I have written about peak experiences and inspirations and so on, that they feel that this is the only way to live. Life without daily or hourly peak experiences, that's no life, so they think they can't do work that is boring.

Some student tells me, "No I don't want to do that because I don't enjoy it," and then I get purple in the face and fly up in a rage—"Damn it, you do it, or I'll fire you"—and he feels I am betraying my own principles. In making a more measured and balanced picture of creativeness, we workers with creativity have to be responsible for the impressions we make upon other people. Apparently one impression that we are making on them is that creativeness consists of lightning striking you on the head in one great glorious moment. The fact that the people who create are good workers tends to be lost.[39]

If successful organizations are not organized to foster creativity, how then do we observe innovative organizations? In our sample of school districts most innovations adopted were created outside the organization. A diffusion process seemed to describe how most ideas entered these school districts. The names of many innovations indicate where creation took place. Harvard Project Physics, the Carnegie Philosophy Program, and the University of Illinois Committee on Secondary Mathematics (modern math) are three examples.

There is other evidence that most ideas are borrowed by innovative organizations. Miller surveyed the use of 49 innovations by 16 low-carbon steel companies.[40] He reported a correlation coefficient of .98 between frequency of total innovation adoption and frequency of borrowed innovation. He concluded that there is great dependence between organizations and their technological environments. Miller also examined 468 patents that were applicable to low-carbon steel producers. He found that 80 percent of those patents originated outside the low-carbon steel industry. There is even significant technological interdependence across industries.

Studies of other technological advances reveal a similar interdependence between organization and environment. DuPont might be regarded as one of the most creative of organizations. Mueller reported that of 25 major product innovations brought out by DuPont during the period 1920–50 only 10 originated within the firm.[41] The ideas for the other 15 innovations originated outside but were further developed by DuPont. Hamberg studied the creation of 13 major innovations in the American steel industry between 1940 and 1955.[42] Seven of these innovations originated within the steel industry. Peck reported a similar finding in the aluminum industry where only one of seven major innovations actually originated there.[43]

What seems to be going on is something like this: The common technological environment cuts across industry lines. For example, the technological environment of the high school district is continuously infused with ideas from all other high schools, colleges and universities, federal government agencies, independent not-for-profit agencies like Rand Corporation, and for-profit learning and testing agencies. No single high school district, regardless of its creativity, could match this idea output. The district, to be innovative and rational, should set up some process to monitor the environment and to evaluate the various ideas in relation to its own goals.

In our sample of organizations the highly professional teacher performed that function for educational innovations. Administrators performed that function for administrative innovations. We found that decentralization and professionalism were related to educational innovation, while teacher free time was not. (Creativity is supposedly greatest when organization members have time for creative thinking.) This implies that professional teachers were not given more free time but were given greater latitude in determining how their work was to be done, so that knowledge of ideas created elsewhere could be translated into new ways of performing the work.

For us, the dilemma over how to organize to foster efficiency and simultaneously foster creativity is not difficult to resolve. One organizes for efficiency and includes professionals familiar with the core technology so that technical changes and innovations can and will be evaluated and introduced for their ability to contribute to efficiency. In those cases where originality is essential to organizational survival, such as introducing new products in a rapidly changing marketplace, specialized groups can be charged with the creative function. But even in these organizations exposure to ideas created elsewhere is necessary because creativity is not a very reliable source of innovation. Mansfield's study of research and development laboratories indicated that only a modest proportion of the new projects undertaken ever met with success. Only one project in eight was ultimately successful in the marketplace.[44]

ORGANIZATIONAL STRUCTURE

Decentralization

Decentralization has a very strong relationship to the adoption of innovations for collegebound students. We believe the effect of decentralization is to increase the bottom-up flow of innovations through the organization. Decentralization is most important for innovations for collegebound students because these innovations are proposed by teachers. The decentralization finding is basically a replication of other research on organizational innovation.

However, we must add that decentralization is not related to other types of innovation—notably innovation that administrators tend to initiate. In chapter 4 decentralization was not related to innovation for terminal students, and in chapter 5 most administrative innovations were proposed in school districts with a low level of teacher professionalism. Hence decentralization is important for innovations that typically originate at lower levels of the organization. For innovations that are typically implemented from the top down, decentralization offers no advantage, and may act as a barrier to adoption.

Slack Resources

Our earlier conjecture about stocking the organization with professionals in order to innovate seems quite defensible when we look at role played (and not played) by slack resources in our organizations. Contrary to theory, slack resources (operationalized as increases in expenditures per pupil over time period studied) are unrelated to innovation, and elites' perception of slack resources is negatively related to innovation. Extra dollars in the system are not used to purchase innovations, and the perception of extra dollars is not associated with more frequent innovation approval. We did find, however, that school district affluence—the total dollars spent per pupil—makes a substantial difference to educational innovations for collegebound students, which was the major innovation category and the category most often initiated by teachers. The association of organizational affluence and innovation has previously been noted in other studies. [45]

Why are free resources, perceived free resources, and innovation cost (chapter 2) either unrelated or negatively related to college-oriented innovation, while total expenditures are positively related? The reason is that the causal linkage goes from dollars to people, who in turn cause innovation to occur. District wealth is important because of the people it allows the district to obtain—highly educated teachers and a separate support staff. The superintendent and school board feel overextended by the large salary expenditures, but the effect on educational innovation is very positive. Highly educated teachers want to innovate, and the presence of a support staff group facilitates the innovation process. These participants provide innovation energy. They get the innovation process going. Innovation does not require free resources so much as it requires people to push innovation. Top administrators tend to approve what the professional teachers want, and they manage to work the innovation into the system somehow. In effect, innovation requires some financial investment, not in plant and equipment, but in salaries for support staff and professional teachers. Innovation adoption is a function of the people in the district rather than the presence of available dollars for equipment purchases.

If our interpretation of these findings is correct, then government policies that earmark dollars for innovation hardware in the hope of stimulating innovation in public organizations will miss the mark. The dollar cost of innovation is seldom a barrier to adoption. Organization members must want to innovate. To stimulate innovation, dollars should be provided to increase the professional level of employees, or to hire special coordinators (facilitators) charged with generating innovation activity in the organization. Then ideas can be initiated to fit the goals of the organization. The appropriate people will provide a greater stimulus to innovation than will the presence of free dollars in the system.

Support Staff

A variable about which there has been conjecture but little hard evidence is the presence of a special support group, or consulting group, in the school district. Our findings for this group were extremely positive for the adoption of educational innovations. The presence of a special group playing a coordinating role in the high school districts seems to make a real and positive difference to the number of innovations adopted.

The support staff are typically part of the district superintendent's staff. They report directly to the superintendent and are not under the influence of principals in the individual high schools. Sometimes an assistant superintendent for education is hired to supervise this consulting group. The relationship of the group to the rest of the organization is shown in figure 6.6.

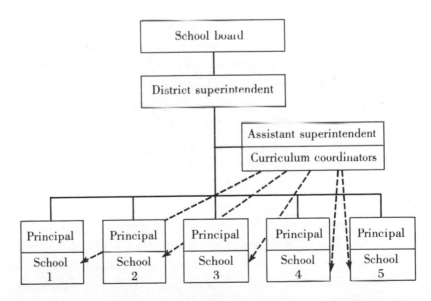

FIGURE 6.6 Relationship of Support Staff to the High Schools in the District

In the typical support group each member is responsible for a specific curriculum area. One individual might be in charge of math, for example, and another in charge of physical education. These individuals are certified teachers but are free of all teaching responsibilities. Their full-time job is to act as coordinators and consultants in their particular curriculum area. They also help coordinate across curriculum areas when the need arises. These people are usually called, appropriately, curriculum coordinators or curriculum supervisors.

When we were in the school districts tracing down innovations, the support staff frequently became a topic of conversation. The coordinators were close to the teachers in their respective curriculum areas and were the people to whom we were referred for information about specific innovation adoptions. The coordinators were also perceived to be expensive by top administrators. They required from 5 to 15 full-time salaries, plus an assistant superintendent for supervision, plus clerical support and office facilities. Superintendents wondered aloud whether gains from such a group were worth the costs. Support staff members were usually selected from among senior teachers and consequently drew high salaries, and they taught no classes at all.

We do not have a cost-benefit analysis to determine whether the benefits of a support group outweighed the cost. But we can restate that the relative size of the support group was substantially associated with the adoption of innovations for both collegebound and terminal students throughout these districts. This effect was in addition to the other factors found to be important to the adoption of these kinds of innovations.

The coordinators arranged frequent meetings with small groups of teachers and department heads to exchange ideas and information. The coordinators also did the research work and proposal preparation for ideas the teachers wanted approved by the district superintendent and school board. Coordinators seldom proposed their own ideas for adoption. Coordinators also did extensive research work and proposal preparation for top administrators, thereby facilitating the trickle-down of administrative changes as well.

The effectiveness of staff support groups, we believe, was in large part due to their role as facilitators and integrators. In the role of facilitators staff members encouraged the communication process that led to idea generation and proposal preparation. This ensured a large supply of innovation ideas to apply to perceived problems and to increase the effectiveness and quality of education in the district. In the role of integrators staff members helped provide a connection between administrative goals for education and the types of innovation proposals introduced into the system by teachers. The support group encouraged the innovation process by representing administrative interests to teachers and teacher interests to administration. In this way the support group kept innovations and goals aligned and ensured a high percentage of innovation approvals.

We suspect that the presence of specialized groups can have an equally positive effect on innovation in other types of organizations. Specialists could be hired to coordinate, advise, and assist specific technological areas in many kinds of public organizations. The presence of such a group adds energy to the initial innovation steps of conception and proposal. Establishing a staff support group is one way to design the organization so that ideas are continuously interjected into the decision process. The group also keeps ideas aligned with the goals of the organization. Consequently the frequency of innovation adoption can be substantially increased.

Differentiation and Integration

The fact that the support staff is necessary to innovation is interesting and, again, seems to provide evidence favorable to our interpretation of how complexity relates to innovation.

Conflict and disagreement presumably arise from the varying orientations developed by people in different departments and jobs and because coordination among these departmental or job units is poor. Lorsch and Lawrence described these conditions as problems of differentiation and integration.[46] Differentiation refers to the differences in cognitive orientation and formal structures among organizational departments and is normally considered a barrier to interdepartmental communication and cooperation. Integration refers to the quality of collaboration that exists among departments. Lorsch and Lawrence concluded that highly innovative organizations have higher levels of both differentiation and integration than less innovative organizations. Lorsch and Lawrence were studying new product innovation that was created within the organization and that required collaboration by the research and development, manufacturing, and marketing departments. The new product innovations were considered quite radical because implementation required cooperation and change by each major department in the organization.

One cannot conclude that because differentiation is greatest in innovative organizations that complexity causes innovation. Each of the major departments studied by Lorsch and Lawrence—research and development, manufacturing, marketing—were highly specialized and expert in doing their respective jobs. This specialization and expertise is what produced the innovation, which is similar to what we found for innovative teachers in high schools. Differentiation led to problems of collaboration in the Lorsch and Lawrence study, however, because of the type of innovation involved. Successful innovators had to have mechanisms for integrating the differences. The innovative organizations were able to achieve collaboration among departments in order to bring about innovation.

We were studying a different kind of organization and a different kind of innovation than were Lorsch and Lawrence, yet the notion of differentiation and integration seems to explain some of the innovation activity in these high schools. We saw that teachers proposed the greatest number of innovations for collegebound students when educational innovations were the exclusive domain of teachers. Highly educated teachers were differentiated from administrators, and this differentiation was associated with greater numbers of innovations. Administrators became involved in innovation for collegebound students in some school districts, and the result was fewer adoptions. Administrator involvement did not result in as many innovations as when a greater division of innovation labor between teachers and administrators was observed.

Integration, however, was also present in the districts with highly professional teachers. Innovations for collegebound students were compatible with community and administrative expectations. The innovations that were proposed were integrated within the goals of the high school district. This integration was in large part due to the activity of staff support groups, which acted as a buffer between administrative goals and the types of innovation proposals introduced by teachers.

It seems that teacher professionalism is a key aspect of differentiation in school organizations. Professional teachers have more influence over educational changes and initiate a larger proportion of educational innovations. In less professional districts administrators initiate more innovations. The kinds of innovation initiated by administrators tend to reflect the goals of the administrators and the domain of administrators. Where administrators are active, the technical innovations proposed tend to serve administrative needs or a minority group (terminal students) not well served by the teachers.

Another finding is that differentiation tends to be *vertical* in school districts. In our organizations differentiation was between teacher and administration; in Lorsch and Lawrence's manufacturing firms differentiation was horizontal between the respective technical groups. The organization design to achieve integration will depend on the direction of differentiation. In manufacturing firms integrative personnel located between technical groups is an effective device. In school districts integrative personnel working from the superintendent's office can achieve necessary coordination of technical people with administration. Vertical differentiation may represent the major requirement for integration in many small and medium-sized public organizations because administration and the technical core represent the major organizational functions. Horizontal differentiation will dominate in large for-profit organizations that contain three or more major technical functions.

NOTES

1. Gerald Zaltman, Robert Duncan and Jonny Holbek, *Innovations and Organizations* (New York: John Wiley & Sons, 1973), chap. 1.
2. Michael Aiken and Jerald Hage, "The Organic Organization and Innovation," *Sociology* 5 (January 1971):63–82.
3. Richard L. Daft, "The Process of Organizational Innovation: An Empirical Study of 13 High School Districts" (Ph.D. diss., University of Chicago, 1974).
4. Frederick C. Fliegel and Joseph E. Kivilan, "Attributes of Innovation as Factors in Diffusion," *American Journal of Sociology* 72 (November 1966):235–48.
5. Arnold D. Kaluzny, James . Veney, and John T. Gentry, "Innovation of Health Services: A Comparative Study of Hospitals and Health Departments" (Paper presented at the University of North Carolina Health Services Research Center Symposium on Innovation in Health Care Organizations, Chapel Hill, N.C., 18–19 May 1972).
6. Sumner Myers and Donald G. Marquis, *Successful Industrial Innovations* (Washington, D.C.: National Science Foundation, NSF 69–17, 1969).
7. Neal Gross, Joseph B. Giacquinta, and Marilyn Bernstein, *Implementing Organizational Innovations: A Sociological Analysis of Planned Educational Change* (New York: Basic Books, 1971); Anneke Bredo and Eric Bredo, "Effects of Environment and Structure on the Process of Innovation," in *Managing Change in Educational Organizations*, eds. J. V. Baldridge and T. E. Deal (Berkely, Calif.: McCutchan, 1975).
8. James March and Herbert Simon, *Organizations* (New York: John Wiley & Sons, 1958), chap. 7.
9. Myers and Marquis, *Successful Industrial Innovations*.
10. James M. Utterback, "The Process of Technological Innovation within the Firm," *Academy of Management Journal* 14 (March 1971):75–88.
11. R. M. Cyert and James March, *A Behavioral Theory of the Firm* (Englewood Cliffs, N.J.: Prentice-Hall, 1963).
12. Kenneth Knight, "A Descriptive Model of the Intra-Firm Innovation Process," *Journal of Business* (October 1967):479–96.
13. Edward Harvey and Russell Mills, "Patterns of Organizational Adaptation: A Political Perspective," in *Power in Organizations*, ed. Mayer N. Zald (Nashville, Tenn.: Vanderbilt University Press, 1970).
14. Selwyn W. Becker and Frank Stafford, "Some Determinants of Organizational Success," *Journal of Business* 40 (October 1967):511–18; Jerald Hage and Michael Aiken, "Program Change and Organizational Properties," *American Journal of Sociology* 72 (March 1967):503–19; Kaluzny, Veney, and Gentry, "Innovations of Health Services"; Lawrence B. Mohr, "Determinants of Innovation in Organizations," *American Political Science Review* 63 (March 1969):11–126; Edwin Mansfield, "Size of Firm, Market Structure, and Innovation," *Journal of Political Economy* 61 (December 1963): 556–76; Robert A. Peterson, William Rudeluis, and Glenn L. Wood, "The Spread of Marketing Innovations in a Service Industry," *Journal of Business* 45 (October 1972):485–96; J. Victor Baldridge and Robert A. Burnham, "Organizational Innovation: Individual, Organizational and Environmental Impacts," *Administrative Science*

Quarterly 20 (June 1975):165–76; and Ronald G. Corwin, "Innovation in Organizations: The Case of Schools," *Sociology of Education* 48 (Winter 1975):1–37.

15. Martin M. Rosner, "Administrative Controls and Innovation," *Behavioral Science* 12 (January 1968):36–43; Aiken and Hage, "The Organic Organization and Innovation"; Mohr, "Determinants of Innovation in Organizations"; Kaluzny et al., "Innovation of Health Services"; and Edwin Mansfield, "Technical Change and the Rate of Innovation," *Econometrics* 29 (October 1961):741–66.

16. Samuel F. Christie and Jay D. Scribner, "A Social System Analysis of Innovation in 16 School Districts" (Paper presented at the annual meeting of the American Educational Research Association, Los Angeles, Calif., February 1959); Larry W. Hughes, "A Study of Administrative Arrangements in Different Types of School Districts" (Columbus, Ohio; Ohio State University Microfilms, 1965); James C. Laflant, "School District Innovativeness and Expectations for the School Board Role" (Paper presented at the American Educational Research Association, New York, N.Y., 16 February 1967); Homer M. Johnson and R. Lavern Marcum, "Organizational Climate and the Adoption of Educational Innovations" (Paper presented at the American Educational Research Association, Los Angeles, Calif., 5–8 February 1969); P. R. Mort and Francis G. Cornell, *American Schools in Transition* (New York: Bureau of Publications, Teachers College, Columbia University 1941); and Paul P. Preising. "The Relationship of Staff Tenure and Administrative Succession to Structural Innovation" (Paper presented at the American Educational Research Association, Los Angeles, Calif., 5–8 February 1969).

17. William Evan and Guy Black, "Innovation in Business Organizations: Some Factors Associated with Success or Failure of Staff Proposals," *Journal of Business* 40 (October 1967):519–30; Hage and Aiken, "Program Change and Organizational Properties"; Harvey M. Sapolsky, "Organizational Structure and Innovation," *Journal of Business* 41 (October 1967):497–510; Kaluzny, Veney, and Gentry, "Innovation of Health Services"; Robert E. Mytinger, *Innovation in Local Health Services* (Washington, D.C.: Government Printing Office, Public Health Service Publication 1664-2, 1968).

18. Cyert and March, *Behavioral Theory of the Firm*.

19. R. M. Cyert, W. R. Dill, and J. C. March, "The Role of Expectations in Business Decision Making," *Administrative Science Quarterly* 3 (December 1958):307–40; and Harvey and Mills, "Patterns of Organizational Adaptation."

20. Hage and Aiken, "Program Change and Organizational Properties"; Jerald Hage and Michael Aiken, *Social Change in Complex Organizations* (New York: Random House, 1970); Aiken and Hage, "The Organic Organization and Innovation"; and Jerald Hage and Robert Dewar, "Elite Values versus Organizational Structure in Predicting Innovation," *Administrative Science Quarterly* 18 (September 1973): 279–90.

21. Zaltman, Duncan, and Holbek, *Innovations and Organizations*.

22. Jerald Hage, "An Axiomatic Theory of Organizations," *Administrative Science Quarterly* 10 (December 1965):294.

23. Hage and Aiken, *Social Change in Complex Organizations*, pp. 32–33.

24. Hage and Aiken, "Program Change and Organizational Properties."

25. Aiken and Hage, "The Organic Organization and Innovation," p. 70.

26. Paul Lawrence and Jay W. Lorsch, *Organization and Environment* (Homewood, Ill.: Richard D. Irwin, 1969).

27. James Q. Wilson, "Innovation in Organizations: Notes toward a Theory," in *Approaches to Organizational Design*, ed. James D. Thompson (Pittsburgh:

University of Pittsburgh Press, 1966); and Zaltman, Duncan, and Holbek, *Innovations and Organizations*, chap. 3.

28. Evan and Black, "Innovation in Business Organizations"; Hage and Aiken, "Program Change and Organizational Properties"; Kaluzny, Veney, and Gentry, "Innovation in Health Services"; and Mytinger, *Innovation in Local Health Services*.

29. Mayer N. Zald and Patricia Denton, "From Evangelism to General Service; The Transformation of the YMCA." *Administrative Science Quarterly* 7 (September 1963):214–34; and Ronald G. Corwin, "Strategies for Organizational Innovation; An Empirical Comparison." *American Sociological Review* 37 (August 1972):441–54.

30. Hage and Aiken, *Social Change in Complex Organizations*, pp. 82–84.

31. Ibid., pp. 84–85.

32. A nice review of the resistance-to-change literature can be found in Zaltman, Duncan, and Holbek, *Innovations and Organizations*, pp. 85–102.

33. Zaltman, Duncan, and Holbek, *Innovations and Organizations*; and Wilson, "Innovation in Organizations."

34. Gross et al., *Implementing Organizational Innovations*.

35. Henry Mintzberg, *The Nature of Managerial Work* (New York: Harper & Row, 1973).

36. V. N. MacDonald, G. McLeod, and J. R. Nininger, "Organizational Change in Municipal Government" (Manuscript in progress, Queen's University, Kingston, Ont. Canada).

37. Christopher Argyris, *Organization and Innovation* (Homewood, Ill.: Richard D. Irwin, 1965); Herbert A. Shepard, "Innovation-Resisting and Innovation-Producing Organizations," *Journal of Business* 40 (October 1967):470–77.

38. Harold Guetzkow, "The Creative Person in Organizations," in *The Creative Organization*, ed. Gary A. Steiner (Chicago: University of Chicago Press, 1965); and Victor Thompson, "Bureaucracy and Innovation," *Administrative Science Quarterly* 10 (June 1965):1–20.

39. A. H. Maslow, "A Holistic Approach to Creativity," in *Climate for Creativity*, ed. Calvin Taylor (New York: Pergamon Press, 1972), p. 293.

40. Roger Miller, *Innovation, Organization and Environment* (Sherbrooke, P.Q., Canada: Institut de Recherche et de Perfectionnement en Administration, Université de Sherbrooke, 1971).

41. W. F. Mueller, "The Origins of the Basic Inventions Underlying DuPont's Major Product and Process Innovations, 1920–1950," in *The Rate and Direction of the Inventive Activity: Economic and Social Factors*, ed. R. Nelson (Princeton, N.J.: Princeton University Press, 1962).

42. D. Hamberg, "Invention in the Industrial Research Laboratory," *Journal of Political Economy* 71 (April 1963):95–115.

43. M. Peck, "Inventions in the Post-war American Aluminum Industry," in *Rate and Direction of Inventive Activity*.

44. Edwin Mansfield et al., *Research and Innovation in the Modern Corporation* (New York: W. W. Norton, 1971), p. 57.

45. Rosner, "Administrative Controls and Innovation"; Mohr, "Determinants of Innovation in Organizations"; Christie and Scribner, "A Social System Analysis of Innovation in 16 School Districts"; Hughes. "A Study of Administrative Arrangements in Different Types of School Districts"; Laflant, "School District Innovativeness"; Johnson and Marcum, "Organizational Climate"; Mort and Cornell, *American Schools in Transition*; and Preising, "Relationship of Staff Tenure and Administrative Succession to Structural Innovation."

46. Jay W. Lorsch and Paul R. Lawrence, "Organizing for Product Innovation," in *Organizational Structure and Design*, ed. Gene W. Dalton, Paul R. Lawrence, and Jay W. Lorsch (Homewood, Ill.: Richard D. Irwin, 1970).

7

Revising the Theory: Garbage Cans, Idea Champions, and Innovations

In chapters 3, 4, and 5 we explored our data as carefully as we could in an attempt to gain an understanding about the environmental and organizational factors that influence innovation. We also attempted to gain insight into the internal organizational processes associated with the proposal and adoption of innovations. Our attempts at understanding began with our theoretical model, in which the important environmental and organizational variables were identified. This model was like a road map, telling us where to look and what to measure. We found there was merit in our general proposition that innovation is a function of incentives to innovate, the number of innovation alternatives in the decision process, and organizational enabler variables; although incentives and innovation alternatives seem to be more potent explanatory concepts than enabler variables for the school district sample.

In other words, our road map was pretty good. But like many maps of uncharted territory, much subtlety and complexity was omitted. One assumption implicit in our model was that if the incentives and enablers existed, then the organization's actors would respond in more or less similar and predictable fashion. We thought naïvely, that with appropriate incentives and enablers, across a variety of organizational settings, and for any and all innovations, the same kinds of people would do the proposing and the same kinds of others the adopting. Neat, simple, precise, and predictable—but wrong.

We did not foresee the disorganized nature of the innovation processes that occur in an organization, or even that there are processes. Innovation action takes place in different areas within the organization. Different types of innovations follow different routes to adoption. Organizational and environmental variables may predict one type of innovation but not another. The innovation processes seem to be rational for the organization in the sense that they yield innovations in line with organizational goals, but these processes are not rational in the classical sense of a felt problem followed by search and then the careful consideration of several alternatives.

A revised theory of organizational innovation is needed. The revision, first, must be consistent with our empirical findings and, second, explain why innovation choices are consistent with organizational goals when innovation adoption is a pluralistic and somewhat disorganized activity. Third, it must detail how organizational and environmental factors influence the behavior of organization participants to produce or not to produce innovation adoption.

In reviewing our findings, we are struck by the compatibility between them and two depictions of organizational processes: Cohen, March, and Olsen's garbage can model of organizational decision making, and Weick's view of educational organizations as loosely coupled systems.[1] A loosely coupled system is one in which the subparts are relatively independent, so that actions taken in one subpart have little effect, or are relatively slow to effect, another subpart. Weick noted that the idea of loose coupling is evoked by such terms (among others) as *decentralization, delegation* and *planned unresponsiveness*. He deduced that loosely coupled systems preserve independent sensing elements, know their environments better and hence respond quickly, although this could lead to making many faddish responses; that they may be good for localized adaptation but as a result lose the benefits of standardization; that they can retain more novel solutions, but their diffusion through the organization might be difficult.

Weick's depiction evokes many rich images, but it is not yet well enough elaborated to escape the "either this or that" nature of the propositions. Organization conditions were described and organization behavior predicted to be either one set of events or another, or both. The richness in description was achieved at the cost of precision in prediction. The garbage can model is applied to organizations whose subparts appear to function as organized anarchies, obviously loosely coupled systems. The garbage can model is less rich than Weick's description, but because sharper predictions can be drawn from it, we will lay greater emphasis on that model. Our data, however, are quite compatible with both models.

THE GARBAGE CAN MODEL

The garbage can model was devised to explain decision behavior in organized anarchies, organizations characterized by problematic preferences, unclear technology, and fluid participation. Organized anarchies experience uncertainty about specific organizational goals and about how to achieve organizational goals. Alternatives may be inconsistent and ill defined. Consequently, decision makers do not necessarily take action on the basis of preferences. They may discover what they prefer by taking action and learning what works. Unclear technology leads to considerable trial-and-error behavior as a device for finding preferences. Organized anarchies are also characterized by fluid participation. Organization members come and go, and with them travel perceptions, ideas, problems, and experience. For participants within the system there are diverse demands upon their energy, so that participation in specific problems is also fluid. Under these conditions, "one can view a choice opportunity as a garbage can into which various kinds of problems and solutions are dumped."[2]

Cohen, March, and Olsen applied the garbage can model to university organizations. High school organizations probably do not display the characteristics of organized anarchies to the extent universities do. But goals in high school education are by no means precise, nor is the technology used to achieve educational goals. And fluid participation does occur, especially in rapidly growing school districts. No organization fits the organized anarchy model completely. But Cohen, March, and Olsen maintained that these organizational traits do characterize many organizations part of the time and that the organized anarchy model is particularly conspicuous in public and educational organizations.

The important theoretical breakthrough of the garbage can model is that it disconnects problems, solutions, and decision makers from each other, unlike traditional decision theory. Specific decisions do not follow an orderly process from problem to solution but are outcomes of several relatively independent streams of events within the organization. Cohen, March, and Olsen described four of these streams.

1. *Problems*. Problems are the concern of people inside and outside the organization. They arise over issues of lifestyle; family; frustrations of work; careers; group relations within the organization; distribution of status, jobs, and money; ideology; or current crises of mankind as interpreted by the mass media or the next door neighbor. All require attention. Problems are, however, distinct from choices; and they may not be resolved when choices are made.

2. *Solutions*. A solution is somebody's product. A computer is not just a solution to a problem in payroll management, discovered when needed. It is an answer actively looking for a question. The creation of need is not a curiosity of the market in consumer products; it is a general phenomenon of processes of choice. Despite the dictum that you cannot find the answer until you have formulated the question well, you often do not know what the question is in organizational problem-solving until you know the answer.

3. *Participants*. Participants come and go. Since every entrance is an exit somewhere else, the distribution of entrances depends on the attributes of the choice being left as much as it does on the attributes of the new choice. Substantial variation in participation stems from other demands on the participants' time (rather than from features of the decision under study).

4. *Choice Opportunities*. These are occasions when an organization is expected to produce behavior that can be called a decision. Opportunities arise regularly, and any organization has ways of declaring an occasion for choice. Contracts must be signed; people

hired, promoted, or fired; money spent; and responsibilities allocated.[3]

Our concern is not with all choices influenced by these streams but only the subset of decisions that pertain to innovation adoptions. Problems are traditionally believed to ignite the innovation sequence. Some urgent problems that hit the organized anarchy undoubtedly lead to search behavior. The problem thereby connects with potential solutions, and an innovation decision is made.

But that process may explain only a portion of innovation adoptions. A solution may not solve the problem when cause-effect relationships are uncertain. The decision to adopt is then only a temporary garbage can in which to dispose of that problem. Further, many problems hang around organized anarchies and do not stimulate search at all. There may be more problems than can be processed at any one time. Some problems will not receive attention because other pressing problems push ahead in the queue. Other problems are dormant in the organization. Organization members get accustomed to them and no longer think of them as requiring search and solution. On the other hand, organization participants may occasionally preoccupy themselves with specific problems that they believe are critically important, and consequently they maintain continuous search behavior and attach solution after solution to the problem in an attempt to resolve it.

Solutions are innovation ideas. The stream of innovation ideas into and through the organization exists independent of problems. Ideas may be brought into the organization by new personnel, or they may be discovered by existing personnel. Innovation solutions may occasionally be invented within the organization. Organization members may be attracted to certain ideas and push these ideas for adoption. Attraction to an idea may cause the member to look for a problem to which the innovation can be attached as a solution, or the participant may present the idea as an opportunity for improved organizational performance. Under conditions of uncertainty ideas can be tried in order to learn whether they are preferable to existing procedures.

The entire innovation process hinges upon organization participants. Participants have to make the connection between ideas, problems, and innovation choices. Ideas have to be proposed, attached to problems, and choices made. Participants in the organization have to make the right connections in order for innovation to proceed.

Choice opportunities require formal decisions about innovation. Choice opportunities require that the decision system respond to a decision expectation. Choice opportunities can be precipitated by the proposal of an idea for adoption by an employee, an equipment manufacturer who wants an answer on the purchase of new equipment, or university faculty members who want an answer on whether to proceed with the creation of a new academic department. The formalized innovation decision situation requires the presence of an idea—a decision alternative—and an expectation for a decision, but the decision situation does not necessarily require the presence of an urgent problem.

We believe there are two identifiable decision stages in which employees participate. The formal choice opportunity is actually the second stage in the decision process. This is the decision where a choice is made among several alternatives and is the decision most often studied and reported upon in the organization theory literature.

The first stage is the decision by a participant to propose an idea, or to connect an idea to a problem, and ask for approval. Out in the organization, away from traditional power centers and formal decision makers, an organization participant decides to act. This initial decision creates an expectation that the formal decision system will make a choice for or against innovation. Both the initial decision to create a choice opportunity and the later formal choice have to be made in order for innovation to proceed. At this point in our thinking, we suspect that the initial decision, made without fanfare in the hinterland of the organization, is the more important decision for explaining innovation. Yet we know virtually nothing about the decision to propose an innovation, perhaps because the following, formal decision is easier to observe, quantify, and evaluate. We hope to see future studies of the decision that precipitates the innovation sequence.

To these ideas we would like to add the notion of territory. The event streams that influence innovation are not monolithic. Organizations divide tasks into territories or domains. Each territory has goals, tasks, ideas, problems, and participants separate from other territories. Territories may be established to deal with specific environmental sectors or to deal with specialized organizational tasks. These differences in tasks, goals, etc., differentiate territories from one another.

Territory is important in explaining how organization participants and decision makers allocate their attention to problems, ideas, and decisions. Participants can disregard events not pertinent to their domain. They can refer some problems, ideas, and requests to other territories in the organization, or they can ignore them altogether. Administrators can limit their attention to the domain of coordination and control and to the external events relevant to the administrative function. Teachers involved with the instruction of collegebound students will attend to ideas and problems pertinent to this task. They will connect ideas to problems and request decisions pertaining to innovations for collegebound students. They will tend to ignore other types of ideas and problems. This is not a phenomenon limited to educational organizations. Departments of marketing, purchasing, and research and development in all types of organizations attend to certain problem and idea streams and ignore others.

However, organizational territories are by no means completely independent. The attachment of ideas to problems in one territory can also generate a decision opportunity elsewhere. Lower-level departments may have to obtain approval from higher-level administrators before adopting an innovation. The desire to try the innovation creates a decision opportunity for top administrators. And large innovations may involve implementation throughout several territories. Proposal of these innovations will generate a ripple of decision expectations throughout the organization. In figure 7.1 we represent the differentiation of an organization into territories and the streams of problems, innovation ideas, and decision expectations that flow into each.

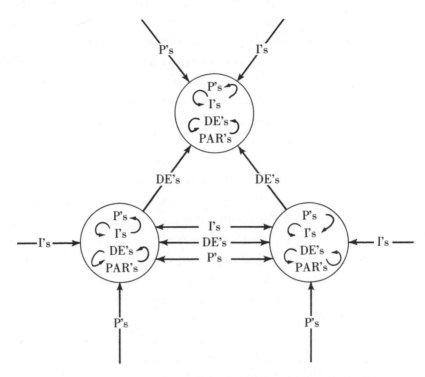

FIGURE 7.1 Sketch of Territories and Major Innovation Streams
I = ideas; P = problems; DE = Decision expectations; and PAR = participants.
→ indicates influence; ◠ indicates turbulence.

Territorial rights and boundaries will affect the streams of ideas, problems, and decision expectations. Exclusive territorial rights and sharp boundaries will be associated with increased differentiation between organizational groups, and with greater demarcation between idea and problem streams into each territory. We assume that territorial rights and boundaries will partially be a function of the participants' expertise in their respective area, and participants' power and influence relative to other territories. As expertise and influence increase, exclusive rights to the decision activity within the territory will be established. As expertise and influence diminish, differentiation of the group decreases and there will be less specialized innovation activity within the territory; more ideas, problems, and decisions will tend to be pushed upon the group from other areas.

In our high school sample there seemed to be two major functional territories—administrative and teaching. The relative influence of each group on innovation adoption was not equal across districts. Teachers had almost exclusive rights to the educational domain in districts where teachers were highly educated (mostly master's degree holders). Well over 90 percent of educational innovations were initiated by teachers in these districts. As average teacher education dropped, administrators were more likely to be involved with innovations in the educational domain. A similar situation existed for administrative innovations. When the teachers had lower average education, administrators had exclusive rights over the administrative innovations. But as average teacher education increased, the relative influence of administrators over their own domain decreased, and teachers became involved to some extent in the initiation of administrative innovations.

The balance of innovation influence, and the exclusiveness of each organizational territory, seem to be a function of employee professionalism. The professional level in a territory relative to other organizational territories alters the pattern of innovation initiation and decision expectations in the organization. Professionalism also determines the penetrability of the territory. We expect this pattern of innovation influence to generalize to other types of organizations. For example, if a manufacturing organization has a specialized manufacturing engineering department populated with highly educated and expert engineers, we would expect most innovation ideas for manufacturing to be initiated from within this engineering group. These ideas would then translate into decision expectations for the manufacturing department. There would be few ideas pushed in the opposite direction—from manufacturing onto the specialized engineers.

Much can be understood about the innovation process in an organization simply by knowing the expertise level in the various functional areas. Innovation type is also terribly important because innovations have to fit the function of the territory. Innovation choice opportunities can only serve as garbage cans

if the innovations are of the right type. Organization members can dump problems into them when the problem fits the garbage can and when the member can bring both garbage can and problem together.

Influences other than professionalism, such as environmental variables and organizational structure, are also important to the explanation of innovation in the garbage can framework, because these variables influence the flow of the problem, idea, and decision expectation streams. Certain organizational structure variables also affect the linkages among these streams within territories and the degree of coordination across organizational territories.

Environmental variables probably have the most direct effect on the idea and problem streams. Rapid change in the client sector, for example, will translate into frequent problems for the organization and will provide incentives to try new ideas. Rapid change in the technological sector will provide a swift flow of ideas in the idea stream. More ideas will be available to improve performance, and of course, if competitors are implementing these innovations, there will be additional incentives to adopt them. Increasing either problems or ideas will lead to increased innovation choice opportunities.

Because of environmental differences and the resulting influence on the flow of ideas and problems into the organization, organizations in one industry will certainly adopt innovations at a different rate from organizations in another industry. There is nothing new in this observation, but it does indicate that investigators must use great care when interpreting the number of innovation adoptions among different types of organizations. An investigator might find that the number of innovations is correlated with low formalization among a diverse sample of organizations, for example, but there is no justification for imputing a causal role to formalization. Low formalization and frequent innovations may both result from rapid environmental changes. It seems legitimate to impute causality only to organizational structure variables, such as formalization, when the environment—hence the frequency of problems and ideas—is similar for all organizations in the sample.

We also expect the environment to have a differential effect on individual territories within the same organization. Organizational departments that deal with rapidly changing environmental sectors will in all likelihood tend to adopt more innovations than other organizational units. In our high school sample, educational innovations appeared at a much greater rate than administrative innovations. And within the educational function more innovations tended to benefit collegebound clients than the terminal clients. Again, these kinds of differences mean that investigators must use caution when interpreting innovation findings. If innovations adopted by different organizational territories are combined in a single innovation index, there is the possibility of making spurious inferences.

Assuming that environmental variables and innovation type can be controlled for, then several organizational variables might be expected to influence the adoption of innovations. We have already discussed professionalism and how it influences innovation patterns and relative power among organizational territories. But professionalism is also important to the number of problems perceived to need solutions and to the number of ideas generated as solutions to the perceived problems. The data in chapter 5 indicate that professionals seem to have high standards of performance and, hence, see problems and shortcomings where others do not. Consequently, they are willing to try innovations as solutions or improvements. They also seem to have a bigger repertoire of innovation ideas, presumably because of their expertise and increased exposure to professional ideas, and so generate larger numbers of ideas for trial. Combined with these traits is the the professionals' greater independence and initiative. They not only see problems and are aware of solutions, but they connect the problem to the innovation and push for the change. Thus the presence of professionals in an organizational unit increases the frequency of formal innovation choice opportunities.

Other organizational structure variables also influence the innovativeness of the organization by influencing the flow of problems, ideas, or decision expectations. In our high school sample curriculum coordinators performed an integrative function and thereby increased the number of ideas and the number of choice opportunities in the organization. Coordinators brought teachers together to share ideas; they occasionally suggested ideas to teachers and helped both teachers and administrators prepare proposals for desired changes. This facilitation of the idea- and proposal-generating steps in the innovation process increases the number of innovation decision expectations in the system and thereby adds to the number of innovations adopted.

Slack resources are another example. The presence of slack, or so-called free, resources in the system has no discernable impact on innovation because dollars do not directly generate ideas or problems. But the sheer amount of resources in the organization—the affluence—does affect innovation because revenues influence the type of people recruited and the resulting organizational structure. Professional employees and coordinating groups cost money. Affluent districts have these and other people and consequently enjoy the benefits of greater energy devoted to innovation ideas and choice opportunities.

In high schools the critical innovation activities are those that lead to a choice opportunity. Most proposed innovations are adopted. The final choice is nearly always made in favor of adoption. In other types of organizations other variables, such as free resources, may be relatively more important. It may not be enough simply to initiate a proposal when such things as expensive new equipment or a risky new product are involved. The formal choice could go against the proposal if sufficient slack is not available. We expect that initiating a choice opportunity is an important explanation for innovation in most organizations, but initiation may not be the single most important step for all types of innovations and organizations.

ORGANIZATIONAL GOALS

The second issue that must be addressed by the theory of innovation is how innovations congruent with organizational goals are adopted. In a simple bureaucratic model innovation decisions are processed through a central decision authority, and departmental goals supposedly add up to overall organizational goals. But the process we observed in high schools, which probably characterizes many types of organizations, is not so simple. Innovation ideas enter the organization in different functional areas. Each functional area concerns itself with problems relevant to itself without clear connection to other areas. Decisions at the top of the hierarchy frequently reflect whatever the lower-level experts want to do. There is little conscious effort to coordinate one group with another. Few specific innovation requests are turned down. The entire innovation process seemed to be pluralistic, and at least parts of it are decentralized to various functional areas. There seems to be no single person or mechanism that orchestrates the innovation process in order to ensure congruence with organizational goals.

One explanation for congruence may be that innovations partially determine organizational goals. Influential groups in the organization initiate innovations, and influential groups thereby indicate their preferences for the direction the organization should take. In the organized anarchy described by Cohen, March, and Olsen action dictates preferences rather than vice versa. This seems to be at least partially confirmed by our high school sample. The highly educated teachers initiate educational innovations. These teachers are interested in college preparation. Consequently these teachers provide a push toward college preparation, which is reflected in the innovations that are proposed and adopted. The innovation behavior of the influential groups within the organization thereby shape to some extent the goals of the organization.

Of course, organizational goals are not determined solely from within the organization. A second explanation for congruence between innovation adoption and organizational goals lies in the structure of the organization and its hiring practices, which reflect past administrative efforts to serve organization clients. In our high school sample the acquisition of highly educated teachers in the first place partly reflected the goal of serving high socio-economic status communities and collegebound students. Goals of cost cutting, efficiency, and value received would be reflected in hiring practices that acquired teachers with lower education and lower salaries.

Finally, underlying both directions of influence between organizational goals and innovation—innovations shape goals, and goals shape innovations—is the learning process. Innovations can be tried by teachers and, if adopted, the teachers learn to innovate in that direction. Teachers will also learn to avoid areas of innovation rejection. Likewise, acceptance of innovative programs by the clients of the organization and success in improving levels of organizational performance will reinforce innovation efforts.

Thus, our impression is that innovations are indeed congruent with organizational goals, but the explanation for this congruence is complex. Congruence is not the result of tight control by one person or control mechanism within the organization. Innovation is a rather diffuse, pluralistic process that reflects larger organizational relationships. The dominance of organizational groups, the needs of clients, the educational level of employees, and the administrative goals influence one another. Hence, innovation activity and organizational goals are compatible, and identification of one should enable the researcher to predict quite successfully the other.

INDIVIDUAL BEHAVIOR AND INNOVATION

George Homans argued that if our macro-social-science theories are to really explain social phenomena, then at some point these theories have to incorporate individual behavior.[4] A complete economic theory of demand, for example, would not simply relate the price of a good to the demand for the good but must explain how the price impinges upon individuals, how individuals decide and behave in response to the price, and how the accumulation of individual behaviors produce a demand at the aggregate level. Incorporating the individual in macrotheories is not simply psychological reductionism, which most sociologists loathe. Homans was saying that good theory, complete theory, uses individual behavior to fill in the intervening links between the observable macrovariables. Filling in the intervening links is the only way to "explain" the observed social system phenomena.

The implication of this argument for organizational innovation is that relating organizational structure and environment to innovation adoption does not constitute an explanation for innovation. Nor is it adequate to relate the flow of ideas or problems to the number of innovations adopted. The relationship between structure and innovation or between the number of ideas and innovation do not just happen. Individual actors are making decisions and behaving in a way that enables us to observe the relationships at the macrolevel. Somehow we have to include individual actors in our explanation of organizational innovation.

We cannot offer a complete theory that includes all possible intervening links between environmental variables, organizational structure variables, and innovation. Nor do we have data on individual behavior other than where innovations are initiated. But we do have one idea that seems compatible with our data and which brings individuals into the explanation of organizational innovations.

The thrust of our theory thus far in this chapter is quite simple: Environmental and organizational variables influence the frequency of innovation adoption by influencing the frequency of ideas, problems, and decision expectations within the organization. The individual within the organization has to be involved because someone must perceive the idea or the problem and translate it into a proposal that requires a decision about adoption. Thus, the role of the individual organization participant is critical. In addition to sensing the idea or the need for the innovation, someone must gain the support of relevant organization members. Some individual has to want the innovation badly enough to do the groundwork necessary to carry the innovation forward to adoption. We are going to call the individual who connects the idea to the problem and who carries the idea forward to approval the *idea champion*.

We received our first real insight into this role after our high school data were collected and analyzed. One of our students,

Patricia Bradshaw, studied the process whereby new departments were created in university organizations.[5] She identified 30 new departments in five universities and traced the history of these departments to their inceptions. Ten departments were administrative and 20 were academic. Bradshaw gathered information from informants who had participated in the creation of the departments. When she followed the thread of historical development to where the ideas originated in the university, she found that it was invariably tied to someone who badly wanted the new department to be established. In 28 of the 30 departments she was able to identify clearly some individual who championed the innovation and without whom the new department would never have been established. This individual was credited with doing the necessary legwork, with persuading reluctant colleagues, and with giving the idea the necessary impetus to reach approval and implementation.

At this point we do not know very much about idea champions, such as their motives, their styles, and in general, how they differ from their organizational colleagues who prefer to stand pat. But we are struck by the importance of these people to innovation. It seems obvious that somebody has to take the idea and push it through to adoption. In the university study Bradshaw concluded that the possibility of the organization implementing a new department depended upon whether a champion picked up the idea. This seemed to be more important to eventual adoption than other traditional variables, such as the size of the organization or finances.

The notion of some individual who champions an idea is not new. This type of individual has been associated with successful creation of new products in research and development organizations.[6] Yet, this notion is nowhere to be seen in the organizational innovation literature. The idea champion fits our theory perfectly because it brings the individual into the picture. This explains how the right connections take place and how innovation is made to happen. The idea and the problem connect in the head of the idea champion. It is the champion who then provides the energy to generate a proposal and places a requirement on the formal organizational system for a decision to innovate. It is also the idea champion who makes the necessary contacts with affected organization members.

We find this an attractive notion because it helps us explain the empirical findings in our earlier chapters. Decentralization, for example, was related to the adoption of educational innovation because there was more freedom for teachers to champion their ideas. The presence of highly educated teachers in the school districts very likely influenced innovation because the highly educated teachers tended to be expert and autonomous, and more likely to champion their ideas. Most organizational circumstances can be related, at least partly, to the adoption of innovation by how they influence the ability or frequency of idea champions.

Another attractive aspect of the idea champion is that it does not require creative organization participants in order for the organization to be innovative. There is much literature on the need for creativity in organizations. Yet creativity does not seem to us a very useful concept for explaining organizational innovation. The role of champion has little to do with creativity. Bradshaw found that the idea champion borrows the idea for a new department elsewhere. The idea champion is not necessarily even an opinion leader. His or her distinguishing characteristic is to connect the idea to a perceived need and then to manage the idea to the point of its gaining acceptance. The champion has to be persistent, persuasive, and willing to push on others to accept the innovation.

Thus, an organizational climate and structure that provides freedom and participation at the lower organizational levels very likely leads to increased innovation because this type of organization fosters the championship of ideas, not because this type of organization increases the amount of creativity or the number of inventions within the organization. This seems to us an important departure from other explanations of innovation. We find the same organizational variables, such as professionalism and decentralization, to be important for an entirely different reason. An organizational context that leads to greater numbers of innovations will tend to be one that rewards idea champions for proposed innovations. Thus the organization need not be structured to support the rather difficult process of creativity; it can simply be structured to provide incentives for the proposal of new ideas to solve problems. And, innovation activity can be reduced in an organization, or in a given department, by designing the structure to discourage and inhibit the idea champions.

The idea champion is not unlike the "change agent" concept that is found in the organizational development literature. The change agent is typically an outsider and a specialist in organizational development. By coming into the organization and gaining support of members, and by pushing and persuading and working within the organization, the change agent brings about change. When this role is taken over by individuals within the organization, then the type of technical and administrative innovations described in our study will tend to be observed. To make an organization continually innovative will require organizational circumstances that support internal idea champions. We doubt that continual innovation can be sustained by outside agents. We hope that future researchers undertake to explore the characteristics of idea champions, their strategies, and the organizational circumstances that encourage or inhibit this type of activity.

NOTES

1. Michael D. Cohen, James G. March, and Johan P. Olsen, "A Garbage Can Model of Organizational Choice," *Administrative Science Quarterly* 17 (March 1972):1–25; Michael D. Cohen and James G. March, *Leadership and Ambiguity: The American College President* (New York: McGraw-Hill, 1974); and Karl E. Weick, "Educational Organizations as Loosely Coupled Systems," *Administrative Science Quarterly* 21 (March 1976):1–19.
2. Cohen, March, and Olsen, "Garbage Can Model of Organizational Choice," p. 2.
3. Ibid., p. 3.
4. George C. Homans, *The Nature of Social Sciene* (New York: Harcourt, Brace & World, 1967).
5. Patricia J. Bradshaw, "The Process of Organizational Differentiation: A Study of New Departments in Ontario Universities" (Bachelor of Commerce thesis, Queen's University, Kingston, Ont., Canada, 1976). Some of her data are also

reported in Richard L. Daft and Patricia J. Bradshaw, "University Innovation: The Institutionalization of New Departments," working paper, Queen's University.

6. Science Policy Research Unit, University of Sussex, *Success and Failure in Industrial Innovation*, Report on Project SAPPHO (London: Center for the Study of Industrial Innovation, 1972); Staff of *Innovation* magazine, *Managing Advancing Technology*, (New York: American Management Association, 1972), vol. 1, *Strategies and Tactics of Product Innovation*, and Richard L. Daft, *Research and Development in the Transportation Industry: A Case Study of Canadian National* (Kingston, Ont., Canada: Canadian Institute of Guided Ground Transport, Report No. 75-17, 1975).

8

The Innovative
Organization:
How to Do It

In the early chapters of this book we posited a process of how
and why organizations innovate, and we examined some data
to see if our posited process was a good description of reality.
We found that it was reasonably good, but not all the pieces
of the puzzle fitted together as neatly as we would have liked.
To that end we presented a revised process of how and why
organizations innovate, one that we think is a better description
of reality. But all our positing has been on the theoretical level.
What of the real world? How do you actually go about building
an innovative organization? Surely our theories and our data
should enable us to answer the question, What do we do next
if we want to build an innovative organization? Although our
theorizing is quite general, and relevant to all organizations, our
data are specific to one type of organization, the high school
district. The high school district as an organization is idiosyncratic enough so that inferences drawn from data about them
might not be descriptive of all organizations. To reduce possibly
erroneous inferences and generalizations, we shall describe at
some length how to develop an innovative high school district.
We shall do so by relying on our data, on our intuitions and
theories, and where useful, on existing literature about innovative school districts. The major part of our discussion will
pertain to educational (technical) innovations because this is
the dominant form of innovation in high schools. We will consider

administrative innovations separately. Then, hopefully without introducing too much error, we will generalize to other types of organizations. We will close the chapter by shifting our attention to strategies individual organization participants can use to achieve adoption of their ideas.

EDUCATIONAL INNOVATIONS

The first question to be answered is Where does one start? What part of the system does one first examine to see if its condition is appropriate to innovation? One obvious first place to look is where system goals are determined. According to the model of organizational functioning presented by Becker and Neuhauser, the owners of the organization determine its goals.[1] In this case the owners are the people residing in the district and, through them, the school board. According to this model if the people and their school board desire high-quality education, and if they feel that innovation is one way to achieve it, then they, functioning both as owners and as the environment with which the school organization must interact, provide the necessary incentive to innovate. This view—that a stimulus from outside the organization is the necessary beginning of the innovation process—is the one with which we began this study, and it is compatible with the views of others who write about the general process of innovation in organizations. Terreberry, for instance, argued that organizational change is largely externally induced, since in order to survive, organizations must adapt to increasingly turbulent environments.[2] Zaltman, Duncan, and Holbek, as another example, also concluded that interaction between the organization and its environment is crucial to the innovation process.[3]

The position that the environment determines innovativeness is not entirely consistent with the extensive literature dealing specifically with innovation in educational organizations, nor is it completely consistent with our garbage can model of innovation, in which organizational innovation may occur without the presence of outside stimuli. In the education literature the

184

district superintendent is relatively more important in the adoption of innovations than is the school board or the citizenry. Pincus's view of the public school provides us with clues as to why this might be the case. He said that (for the most part) public schools are a de facto local monopoly; the aims of schooling are unclear (no consensus about priorities); the technology of schooling is unclear; and finally, because the effects of influences like heredity and other environmental learning experiences and opportunities are not held constant, it is difficult to measure the effects of schooling on people's lives and learning. Pincus also said that "like other self-perpetuating bureaucracies, . . . the schools are a labor-intensive craft industry whose managers often present to the outside world the impression that their craft is highly specialized, that its functions cannot be carried out by replacements whether in the form of uncertified labor or machines."[4]

If this is an accurate view of public school systems, we can come to two conclusions:

1. Following the logic of the entrepreneurial theory, under conditions where procedures to obtain the organization's goal are difficult to specify, it is logical to delegate authority to specify procedures to an expert (professional).[5]
2. The uncertainties in goal priorities and technology are the precise conditions that make operative the garbage can model of organizational decision making.

There is evidence that authority to operate the school system is substantially delegated to the superintendent. First, in many studies the superintendent is found to be of prime importance, and second, school boards are not found important. In fact, in one study of 48 communities where adoptions had occurred in the systems the typical participation of school boards was followership, and the next most frequent position that of ignorance. Leadership appeared in only 8 out of 183 cases, active support in 23. Another study of 249 potential adoptions also led to the conclusion that the typical position of school boards was ignorance. Leadership appeared in only 2 instances.[6] Comparing administrator, teacher, citizen, and school board importance in the adoption of 64 innovations, Laflant found school boards least important and administrators most important.[7]

The importance of the superintendent is found at both theoretical and empirical levels. Griffiths has stressed the top–down nature of change in school systems, while Carlson saw the necessity for top administrators to be change agents if change is to occur. Both Carlson and Griffiths found the change agent role more frequently played by superintendents recently arrived from outside the system.[8]

However, there is little agreement on how the change agent's role is played. A. D. Little Inc., from interviews with teachers and principals in eight school districts, concluded that the superintendent can be a barrier but not an idea champion, that superintendent support is necessary but not sufficient for innovation.[9] Gross, Giacquinda, and Bernstein, after studying a major innovation in a laboratory school, concluded that the administrator role is particularly important in establishing conditions conducive to innovation and in rewarding innovative efforts.[10]

In short, there seems more consensus that the superintendent is important, but there is less agreement on what he has to do to be important in the innovation process. Two somewhat different roles seem to be played by the administrator in the innovation process. One role is that of organizational leader who establishes innovation goals and gives credibility and support to innovation activity by other people in the organization. Administrators thereby influence innovation without actually introducing innovation. We might call this the indirect innovation role of administrators. The other role is that of innovator. Administrators make their organization innovative by initiating innovations for adoption. Top administrators' exposure, status, and rank place them in a position to introduce change. They are exposed to new ideas, and their ideas count. We can call the administrators' actual initiation of innovations their direct innovation role.

Our findings indicate that the top administrator role in organizational innovation is quite complex and is a function of much more than education, or whether the administrator has been hired from within or without. The ideal innovation role to be played by administrators depends heavily upon specific organizational circumstances. In some cases administrators might do best by actively initiating innovations; in other cases administrators would do well to stay out of the way of lower organization members.

Using our data and the garbage can model, we shall detail what it is superintendents are supposed to do in order to build innovative districts. But let us answer the first question, Where does one start if one wants to develop an innovative school district? Seemingly, the first thing to do is either to have or to get a superintendent who wants his district to be an innovative one.

Based only upon our data, that is, the positive relationship between elite attitudes toward innovation and adoption of educational innovations, having a positive attitude toward innovation would seem to be a sufficient criterion (all other things being equal) for the superintendent. But not according to the garbage can model. That model also demands that the superintendent perceive the goals of a high school district as relatively uncertain, difficult to ascertain, or with changing priorities, and also that the path leading to attainment of these goals be relatively unclear.

We can illustrate the importance of the second set of criteria with a hypothetical example. It's quite easy to imagine a high school superintendent who, when asked if he wants an innovative district, responds with a resounding yes. This same person could also be quite certain about his district's goals and how to achieve them. He knows what ought to be taught, and he knows precisely how it ought to be taught. Using only our data about attitudes, we would predict that this superintendent would have an innovative district; but if we extrapolate from the garbage can model, we would make the opposite prediction. The certainty with which the superintendent approaches the task of education will restrict proposals and innovation choice opportunities. Our hypothetical example is not so hypothetical in a slightly different setting.

Street, Vinter, and Perrow described the markedly different climates that existed in two organizations with identical inputs—delinquent boys.[11] In the first institution boys were handled with rigid regulation and discipline. The boys were constantly watched, marched about, and taught to say "yes sir" and "no sir," and they were frequently counted and inspected. The boys had to ask permission for small routine requests, such as going to the bathroom. There were strict rules for all behavior. The boys were not allowed to talk during meals. Punishments for rule infractions were frequently physical, such as a paddling in front of the other boys. Runaways had their heads shaved in addition to paddling, and they were sentenced to a diet of bread and water and were put in isolation.

This style for handling delinquent boys was perfectly compatible with the organization's goals and with members' perceptions and beliefs about their task. The goals were to maintain order and to teach the delinquent respect. Members believed boys were delinquent because they lacked respect and obedience. They also believed that respect and obedience could be taught through rigid regulation and discipline. Innovation in this setting would have to be in line with these beliefs and goals. But there is little need for innovation. The administrators and other organization members perceived that they knew exactly how to straighten the boys out. They were not uncertain about their task, nor were they striving to improve individual performance or to increase organizational effectiveness. Innovations had little room for adoption in this organizational climate.

The other institution, however, approached the task quite differently. The delinquents were free to talk at mealtime, and they frequently griped about the food. The boys were permitted to horse around at bedtime, and they were allowed to resolve many of their own problems with the other boys, so that quarrels would occasionally erupt. Rules and regulations were minimized. Supervision was also minimal. The boys had room to move around in psychologically. This institution also used specialists in psychology and social work. There were few sanctions for misbehavior. Treats might be withdrawn, but some infractions were not punished at all.

Once again the style for handling delinquent boys was compatible with the goals and beliefs of organization members. Members believed that the delinquent's problems were psychological. Obedience and respect for authority had little to do with these problems. Staff members saw each delinquent as unique. They had to learn about each boy, to delve deeply into his past and personality. Staff members believed the necessary changes could be brought about in the boy's personality through understanding, empathy, and a permissive environment. There was a great deal of uncertainty regarding the personality change process. The task was complex, yet the aspirations of staff members were high. Innovation in this environment would be welcomed. Members didn't already have the answers. Innovations could help members to achieve their goals and do their job well.

Thus the two institutions, which from the outside appear to be doing virtually the same task, actually have very different goals, beliefs, and climates. This illustration points out that it is not just innovation goals per se that lead to innovation by organization members. The perception of the task, the uncertainty about the process, and the aspirations of organization members all combine to create a climate that can favor or inhibit innovation. This climate cannot easily be manipulated, but organization administrators, who have more power than other organization members and who can influence structure and hiring, can do much to bring about an innovation climate if it is desired.

These perceptions about goals and technology interact with attitudes toward innovation. To a large extent administrators have to sense environmental needs and translate these needs into internal goals. The school board, superintendent, and principals are buffers between school and community and learn from community members the kinds of services desired. Administrators and board members receive complaints and generally have direct interaction with the community. The particular goals determined by administrators are then communicated to lower organization members. If administrators were no more than conduits, the goals within the organization would be a perfect reflection of the needs and desires of the larger community. But our data suggest that administrator attributes have an independent effect on innovation adoption. Elite attitudes and personal goals can influence perception of what the community wishes and how these perceptions are translated into organizational goals.

It is possible to oversimplify the role in innovation and the influence of practicing administrators. We have discussed evidence that communities and boards delegate, almost abdicate, to the superintendent, who consequently has freedom to maneuver. This freedom, however, is far from absolute; the community context places constraints on his actions. When community residents (owners) absolutely do not support educational innovation, either attitudinally or financially, or when residents insist upon educational goals antithetical to educational innovation—cost cutting, rigid curriculum, traditional teaching methods—administrators won't achieve a high level of innovation. We believe our recommendations for superintendent behavior will increase innovation in most districts, but as a practical matter, superintendents cannot achieve the same level of innovation in every community setting.

We can conclude that step one in building an innovative high school district is to get (or have) a superintendent who has positive attitudes toward educational innovations, who has high aspirations for educational quality, and who perceives that there is a great deal of uncertainty associated with the goals of the district and, further, that the technology associated with attaining those goals also has many uncertainties.

Now that we have identified the kind of superintendent we want in order to build an innovative school district, what is the next step? The next step, or series of steps, is up to the superintendent. The superintendent knows how uncertain is the technology of transmitting knowledge and of getting young people ready to cope with adult realities. He need not deliberately set out to be innovative or to have an innovative district. He wants to transmit knowledge effectively and to augment the socialization process of high schoolers effectively. Recognizing the difficulties, the superintendent rationally decides that the best way to do so is to hire the most competent people he can find.

If he can find and hire the people best versed in the "state of the art," then his best course of action is to hire them and then let *them* determine how to transmit knowledge and how to ready high schoolers for college, jobs, or whatever else life has to offer.

These two almost simultaneous decisions to hire professionals and to let them run the technical core will have important consequences for the high school organization. If they are implemented, it will mean, first, that the organization will have a higher than average proportion of "professionals," teachers with education beyond the four undergraduate college years. Many of them will have master's degrees and some perhaps even Ph.D.'s. Second, these professionals will have authority and responsibility for running the technology of the organization, for transforming ninth graders into alumni able to cope with the demands of the next stages of their lives. In other words, the organization will be relatively decentralized. Decentralization goes hand in hand with employee professionalism. Teachers will only be loosely coupled to administrators. The freedom to influence curriculum and teaching techniques will enable teachers to champion ideas that will become innovation choice opportunities for the district.

The decision to increase the professional level of teachers requires a long-term commitment. Changing the composition of the teaching component may take several years unless the district is growing rapidly. But the decision, which will mean hiring new teachers and upgrading present teachers, will ultimately have substantial impact on district performance. Not only innovation but the quality of education appears to be positively related to teacher education.[12]

Having made this decision, the superintendent realizes that implementation requires resources. The constraints of the external environment may be felt at this point. If the superintendent finds himself in an affluent district with many slack resources, his task is relatively easy. But even in affluent districts unused resources are difficult to find. School boards and members of the community don't provide school districts with more resources than are necessary to implement ongoing or planned programs, no matter how rich they are. So the superintendent has to lobby for his programs. He has to aid in the actual acquisition of resources.

The superintendent, or members of his administrative staff, could apply for special state or federal funding. They could prepare position papers detailing needs in the community that require new courses or personnel. These papers would be used to convince the board that more resources are necessary. The school board then might vote to increase property taxes in the community. Administrators could prepare arguments for why a bond issue is necessary and then spend time speaking before groups of citizens in an effort to attract votes for the issue. In other words, the high school administration could attempt to influence the external environment in order to increase the flow of revenues into the organization.

There is some empirical evidence that this is a correct supposition, both in schools and other organizations. Mintzberg observed the behavior of five top managers. He found that one third to one half of top manager contacts were with groups or individuals outside the organization.[13] The administrators apparently served as a direct buffer with certain elements in the external environment. Two of the administrators studied by Mintzberg were heads of not-for-profit organizations—a hospital and a school district. In these two organizations he observed even greater interaction outside the organization, and a greater proportion of this interaction was with boards of directors and community recipients of the organization's services. Our visits to some of the 13 districts in our sample provided additional evidence for the revenue-producing orientation of top administrators. One superintendent reported that his assistants had successfully influenced legislation at the state capitol to increase support for summer school programs. This particular district made extensive use of summer school. Another superintendent and his principals were nearly impossible to see. They were working almost full time in the community to win voter acceptance of a bond issue. They were speaking to any group that would listen to their appeal.

It is almost impossible to attract more revenues single-handedly. If the administrative staff devotes full time to "administering the system" when the new superintendent first joins the organization, then the time and effort to develop position papers, grant proposals, etc., will require additional administrative help. So we have a paradox. One side effect of the decision to recruit a highly professional staff is the need first to expand the administrative component of the organization to attract the revenues necessary to implement the decision. When revenues are scarce, it is often necessary to invest in administrators, not teachers. There is some evidence that this strategy works. In a longitudinal study of school districts, those with the largest administrative components realized the largest increases in future revenues.[14]

Let us presume that the newly acquired administrators in our hypothetical district are successful in increasing revenues for the school district. Let us further presume that the increased funds are used to recruit teachers with master's degrees. The M.A.-degreed teachers are recruited both to replace non-M.A.-degreed teachers who leave the district due to natural attrition, and to fill the additional needs of the district due to (assumed) population growth. We can also expect, in line with the superintendent's views about the uncertainty of the technology of schooling, that the teachers are given authority and responsibility (within system limits) over classroom decisions. How do these events fit the garbage can model of innovation?

The garbage can model requires four things: (1) the organization recognize the existence of problems; (2) solutions must be proposed (which may or may not solve problems); (3) members participate fluidly in multiple proposals of solutions and naming of problems; and (4) choice opportunities arise—the organization can make a decision.

Now let us show how the superintendent's initial decisions affect these factors. First, he increases the proportion of "professionals" in the organization and, second, he gives them increased authority and responsibility over the organization's technology.

The M.A. degree can be taken as a proxy for many things. But we need merely assume, first, that the M.A. degree represents greater commitment to the field and hence greater continuing self-education through the reading of journals and attendance at meetings and, second, that it represents greater knowledge of problems associated with high school education and greater knowledge of potential solutions, partial solutions, and even perhaps already discarded solutions that may fit a not yet identified problem.

Havelock stated that knowledge input to the organization can be facilitated by increasing professionalism. It will also increase striving to "keep up" with what outside colleagues are doing.[15] Professionalism is not only associated with bringing ideas into the organization, but it is also associated with adopting and using them. Corwin, in a regression analysis of innovation adoption in 131 schools, found that teacher characteristics (including number of teachers with M.A.'s) independently explained 12 percent of the variance in innovation.[16]

If these assumptions are correct, then the newly acquired teachers will quickly identify problems, problems the organization didn't even know it had until these teachers were recruited. Further, they will be acquainted with many solutions, some of which may fit the newly identified problems, some of which may fit older, well-identified but unsolved problems, and some of which may not fit any problems. Many solutions will be proposed, which will provide opportunities for the district to make innovation choices.

Given that they have some autonomy over the technology, they may implement minor solutions immediately, but to the extent the problems or solutions involve two or more participants or cross departmental lines, some coordination, cooperation, and accommodation will be necessary. Further, if the solution requires expenditure of resources (human or monetary), approval must be sought. Almost all educational changes fall into the latter category. These effects, identifying problems and solutions, stem from each professional's greater individual knowledge.

There are also effects from the individual professionals' commitment to the field (interacting with their greater knowledge). In addition to their continuing self-education, they will have greater motivation to discuss among themselves the problems and solutions. They will frequently "talk shop," on both an informal and a formal basis. As a result, there will be a pooling of solutions and problems, and perhaps new connections will be made. Idea champions will develop the beginning agreements for the necessary accommodations if the solution is to be adopted. They will develop the necessary support for and consensus about the various solutions. And finally, when solutions are desired by the group and requests are made of the superintendent, they will discover a high rate of program approval.

We were fortunate to observe in our sample a school district that displayed several of the characteristics just described. Over 75 percent of the teaching staff had M.A.'s. The top administrators made it known that they expected their district to become one of the best school districts in North America. The administrators utilized the ideas and energy of the entire teaching staff by having a two- to three-month series of meetings each year. The meetings started out as small groups at the bottom levels of the district. Everyone participated in the discussions at some point. Students were also encouraged to participate (but their participation was not significant). The purpose of the meetings was to air new ideas, make proposals, and to raise problems that needed solutions. Subsequent meetings were held by middle- and higher-level personnel in the district. Through these meetings problems and solutions were passed up the hierarchy for decisions. The series of meetings, beginning at the bottom of the organization and working up to the top, acted as a huge garbage can into which all possible problems and proposals were dumped. This procedure was very effective for generating bottom-up innovations. The district was one of the most innovative in our sample for college-oriented innovations.

This particular district had several important characteristics. The superintendent and principals had goals of innovation adoption. They had high aspirations for district quality. They were uncertain about the education process and provided mechanisms to change it. They already had highly educated teachers. The series of meetings constituted enforced decentralization of the responsibility for problem and solution identification to teachers. The meetings provided opportunity for solutions and problems to be aired and connected to one another. The meetings also acquainted teachers with others' ideas, and they engendered acceptance of them. The result was what aspiring innovative districts should seek: an ample supply of choice opportunities. Approval and implementation were typically a foregone conclusion.

Not all districts run so smoothly, of course. Professional teachers can be hired, and they can learn that in order to present the superintendent with an innovation proposal, a great deal of paperwork is necessary—outlining the proposal, the probable benefits, the costs, and how personnel will be coordinated both within and between departments. Thus, they may find in many cases that they cannot both teach and develop full-fledged proposals for change without additional support.

Here, again, elite attitudes toward innovation play a critical role. The teachers may propose change, and the administrators may say they'd be glad to consider it *if* they get 20 copies of the proposal, which should contain complete plans and justifications necessary to satisfy the board, community members, and all interested state or federal agencies. At this point the teachers should change their request. Instead of the educational innovation they were proposing, they should now request additional support staff: support staff in the form of clerical help and office facilities, and more importantly in the form of nonteaching certified teachers whose role would be to coordinate curriculum areas and to aid in the development of proposals. The superintendent's attitude toward innovation will determine whether he will expend the effort necessary to attract the additional resources to acquire the support staff. In our sample the innovative districts paid full-time salaries for 5 to 15 certified nonteaching staff.

An effective group of certified support staff can make a substantial difference to district innovativeness. One district in our sample heavily depended upon support staff to facilitate innovation. Each support staff member was in charge of a subject matter area but did not have formal authority over teachers. Support staff met frequently with groups of teachers and department heads. These meetings would bring together personnel from different school buildings to exchange ideas and information. Support staff stayed abreast of developments, both nationally and in Cook County, in their respective curriculum areas. They also did detailed research work for ideas that teachers wanted adopted. This research work along with proposal preparation made it easy for teachers to make serious proposals for change. Staff members also did detailed research and preparation for ideas that administrators wanted to implement. The net effect of these activities was very positive. Across the full range of innovations—college oriented, terminal oriented, administrative—this district was the most innovative in our sample.

This district also had several other factors favorable to innovation. The administrators were uncertain about the best way to educate students, and they decentralized authority to teachers. Administrators also had high aspirations for district quality. Approximately 61 percent of the teachers had master's degrees, which was not as high a percentage as some districts. But certified support staff served to draw out ideas and problems from teachers and translate ideas into proposals. Support staff typically did not propose their own ideas for adoption. They worked through the teachers for educational innovations; teachers decided what was to be proposed. This strategy tended to assure acceptance of the innovation by other teachers.

In many respects there is less uncertainty associated with acquiring the proper resources, both money and people, than with putting them together so that they are innovative. Part of the strategy lies in keeping the organization relatively decentralized, in giving relatively greater authority and responsibility to the teachers than usually might be the case. Decentralization accomplishes at least three things: First, because teachers have responsibility for the technology, they must think about problems, possible problems, solutions, and possible solutions that are presented to them. They can't simply report the problem, file it, and forget it. Second, if their solutions are successful, it will make their work easier (more pleasant, more effective, more satisfying, etc.) so they have an incentive to continue proposing solutions. Third, because decentralized organizations cannot be coordinated by memos and directives from above, the

teachers have to talk to one another in order to coordinate

ordinary curriculum and other matters. This facilitates the discussion of problems and solutions and the development of consensus within the teacher group.

To summarize briefly, the strategies described thus far concern the administrators' indirect role in innovation. Educational innovation is a consequence of several activities within the school organization—high aspirations, uncertainty about the education process, innovation goals, professional teachers, certified support staff, and decentralization. Additional administrator activities are more directly related to innovation initiation and adoption.

After recruiting professionals and providing them with support staff it is crucial that they do not receive too many negative reinforcements in response to their proposals for change. The choice opportunities presented to the organization should result in a relatively high proportion of positive reinforcements. This is necessary if the teachers are to feel that they function in a climate conducive to innovation because even decentralized professionals will stop making proposals if none or nearly none of the proposals is accepted. Hence, initially, it is necessary for the new superintendent to be aware of emerging proposals and to encourage completion of those proposals that he can endorse and that he feels the board (or whoever else might have veto power) also can endorse. Creating this climate conducive to innovation is the difficult part for the superintendent. Depending on how large the system is, he must do it personally or else make certain that he has selected assistants and principals who can do it for him.

Once the system has gotten over the initial hurdles—increasing revenues, increasing the proportion of professional staff and support staff, encouraging proposals, and finally, adopting and implementing a reasonable number of early proposals—maintaining an innovative system seems to be relatively simple. The professional teaching staff will continue to generate garbage cans, that is, choice opportunities, into which problems can be stowed. And the superintendent needn't fear running out of problems, for the professional staff will continue to find new ones or rediscover old, unsolved or inadequately solved problems to make necessary the almost continuous review of new solutions and the creation of new garbage cans into which the problems can be stowed.

As we have seen from our data, the cost and change associated with educational innovations are not barriers to adoption, so encouraging continued innovation in the system is mostly a matter of participants wanting to innovate and of their having a willingness to expend the energy necessary to make the change. Getting a system to the point where it is an innovative one is the difficult and expensive part. It is expensive to hire administrative support, a larger professional staff, and a certified nonteaching support staff; and it is difficult, initially, to encourage and create the atmosphere conducive to generating choice opportunities for the organization. Again, once choice opportunities are presented to the organization and several of them realized, their continued generation rests upon the willingness of the elites to administer change continuously.

Administration of change often requires mediation between conflicting views, or at least differing priorities, within the staff and administration, between administration and board or community, etc. These differing interests or priorities stem from the one variable in the garbage can model of innovation so far ignored in this chapter, that of territoriality.

In chapter 7 we discussed how the idea of domains or territories affects innovation in an organization; how sharp territorial boundaries and expert personnel restrict entry into the territory of ideas or influence from outside the territory. In our sample of school districts we found that the teachers' territory seemed confined primarily to educational innovations. Further, the innovations (and presumably the teachers) were oriented toward students planning to enter college. Administrative innovations and innovations to benefit terminal students seemed to be outside the teachers' territory, and if they occurred, they frequently originated with administrators.

Hence, to maintain a "balanced" innovative school district, the superintendent must pay attention to the territories abandoned by the highly professional teachers. The superintendent must be aware of the number and proportion of students whose formal education probably will terminate with high school. He must assess the community's attitude toward these students and their education, and he must inform himself about developments in the environment relevant to this territory. When the absolute number of such students justifies the expenditures necessary to build a good program for their education, the superintendent himself may have to introduce innovations in the system.

These innovations are typically costlier than other educational innovations (presumably because they require greater investments in equipment or transportation), so the superintendent's problem won't be resistance to the change per se but resistance to the change if it is perceived to be deterimental to changes dear to the professionals' territory. But this is the same task the superintendent has been performing all along the way, mediating between conflicting interests and priorities within his faculty and between faculty and administration.

There is one additional situation where superintendents and other administrators will have to take a direct role in educational innovation. In many districts the problem of scarce resources is serious. Even with substantial effort administrators may have a difficult time increasing revenues sufficiently to change the composition of teachers toward greater professionalism. Stable or shrinking enrollments add to this problem. When the teachers are relatively low on professionalism, and when they are not actively initiating innovations, then a different set of strategies will apply.

Administrators will have to supply the initiative for the adoption of mainstream educational innovations. One technique is to collaborate with teachers. The administrator acts as a sponsor of the idea and obtains teacher cooperation during the proposal and implementation of the idea. The teachers become partners in the innovation process. Collaboration requires that the administrator initiate the idea and involve teachers in the innovation activity. Administrators can also sponsor idea champions within the teacher ranks. The administrator might plant the idea with teachers and provide incentives for completion. The superintendents we talked with in our school district sample indicated that they found collaboration an effective device when teachers did not initiate ideas of their own. Collaboration is best suited to initiating innovations that affect people in another territory, such as administrators initiating innovations that affect teachers.

As a last resort, the most direct method for achieving adoption of educational innovations is for administrators simply to impose them upon the teachers. Teachers would not be involved in the process at all. We saw in chapter 5 that this strategy will not make a school district innovative compared with districts where teachers are active innovation initiators. But this strategy will ensure the adoption of a selected subset of innovations that administrators wish to see adopted in their district.

A summary of strategies both direct and indirect that school administrators can follow to encourage adoption of educational innovations is in table 8.1 (see page 202).

ADMINISTRATIVE INNOVATIONS

We begin this section with the understanding that not very much is known about the initiation, adoption, and implementation of administrative innovations. Administrative innovations have not been studied often, so there is not a concrete body of literature to turn to for guidance. Most of our recommendations will be based upon the analysis in chapter 5, where we examined the origin of innovation proposals. We will also make recommendations based upon inferences from the garbage can organizational process.

What seems clear is that administrators have to take the initiative for the adoption of administrative innovations. Administration is their turf, and if anyone is to initiate change, it usually will be administrators. In our high school sample administrators were involved in over 80 percent of the administrative proposals. Administrators are the local experts with regard to problems and solutions in the administrative territory. In order for the district to be forward and progressive in the

TABLE 8.1

Summary of Administrator Strategies for Educational Innovation

When teacher professionalism (education) is high

Indirect innovation activities include:
  decentralization and freedom for teachers (loose coupling)
  uncertainty about "correct" education process
  high aspirations for educational performance
  positive attitude and expressed goal of innovation
  employment of a certified support staff (curriculum coordinators)
  recognition and reward for innovators (idea champions)

Direct innovation activities include:
  approval of teacher proposals
  initiation of innovations for client groups not served by teachers (e.g., terminal students)

When teacher professionalism is low

Indirect activities should also include:
  exploitation of additional revenues to increase educational level of teachers and to obtain support staff (the initial investment may have to be in additional administrators)

Direct activities should also include:
  scanning of the environment for new ideas
  collaboration with teachers on innovation proposals
  initiation of educational innovations for major client groups

---

administrative domain, the administrator role has to be a direct one, scanning the external environment for new developments and introducing those developments that are promising.

There is some other evidence that administrative innovations have to be introduced by administrators, not by others in the organization, such as technical personnel or board members. Bradshaw found that nine of ten new administrative departments in five universities were initiated and championed by top administrators.[17] Clark observed that the successful implementation of new organizational structural designs was associated with administrative sponsors who had a cosmopolitan orientation and a good knowledge of organization science.[18] These findings support our interpretation that innovation is a function of task specialization and expertise. Innovations are introduced by organization members involved in a particular function, and innovation frequency increases as expertise and professionalism within the function increases. Hence it is up to administrators to be aware of ideas and problems and to generate choice opportunities for administrative changes in the school district.

One of the structural barriers to innovation is the time required to prepare the proposal and gain its acceptance. In school organizations there are two additional strategies that administrators can use to facilitate the innovation process. First, utilize support staff to do the proposal preparation and detail work. These people can be curriculum coordinators or middle-level administrators. The important thing is that top administrators sponsor and push administrative innovations. They should not avoid innovation activity because of the detail work involved. The use of support staff can greatly ease this process. In our school district sample the districts with large support staff groups reported that these groups worked on administrative proposals as well as educational proposals for board approval.

Second, collaboration with teachers may smooth implementation of administrative changes that affect teachers. Many administrative changes, of course, will only affect the administrative processes and administrators themselves. Teachers need not be involved in these innovations. But when teachers are directly influenced, such as in changes in merit pay, facilities, or scheduling, teacher involvement will tend to increase teacher understanding and acceptance of innovation.

There is one other finding concerning administrative innovation that may be relevant to the administrator strategy. More administrative innovations were adopted in our sample when teacher professionalism was relatively low. What this probably means is that administrators have relatively more influence and greater centralization in districts with few professional teachers. The teaching component will tend to be tightly coupled to the administrative component. Hence, top-down changes may be easier to install under circumstances of low teacher professionalism.

Table 8.2 contains a summary of administrator strategies for administrative innovation.

TABLE 8.2
Summary of Administrator Strategies for Administrative Innovation

Direct innovation activities include:

  scanning of environment for new ideas

  initiation of administrative innovations

  collaboration with teachers when innovation affects them

  recognition and reward for innovation by other administrators

Indirect innovation activities include:

  obtaining and utilizing certified support staff

  centralization of authority and tight coupling (this may reduce educational
    innovation, however)

NONSCHOOL ORGANIZATIONS

Other types of organizations can become innovative by following the suggestions in tables 8.1 and 8.2 if their goal structures and technologies are similar to school districts. This will typically be the case in public and not-for-profit organizations where college-trained individuals populate the core technology and provide specialized services to the public. It can be argued that school organizations are somewhat unique because both goals and technology are uncertain.[19] Other not-for-profit organizations, such as hospitals trying to provide high quality medical care, may have unclear technologies also, but the goal structure is better understood and perhaps more measurable. Other organizations, such as for-profit manufacturing organizations, tend to have relatively clear goals and well-understood technology.[20]

Unique as high schools are, we feel three of our findings can be generalized to apply to most organizations. First, managers should take advantage of specialization and expertise in order to generate innovation choice opportunities. Simply put, this means they should hire groups of professionals to work in those areas where innovation is of primary importance. A group of manufacturing engineers may be charged with innovation in the manufacturing process, and personnel specialists for innovations in human resource management. Specialists are aware of new developments, and they perceive problems; hence, most innovations will enter the organization through them. Clark has suggested that this same strategy applies to organizational innovations.[21] He suggested that a separate organizational design group, working within the management function, be established and charged with the continuous evaluation and modification of organizational structure. In this way the organization can become self-designing and does not have to rely on external consultants. Whatever the area of expertise, specialists must be given freedom (loose coupling) to observe problems, discover solutions, and propose innovation alternatives.

The second suggestion is for managers to impose a sense of uncertainty on the organizational system combined with high standards of performance and a positive value for innovation. Uncertainty about the best way to do things and acknowledgment that better techniques may be available free the system to search and experiment. High performance standards create a performance gap, a need for innovation, even if things seem to be working pretty well. Aspirations for even better performance will stimulate search and problem awareness. Search and problem awareness eventually lead to innovation choice opportunities.

Managers must remember that leadership is social influence, that they have a continuing impact upon the organizational culture whether they realize it or not. On the basis of cues emitted in meetings, letters, decisions, speeches, memos, announcements, and telephone conversations, leaders convey a set of values, meanings, and interpretations to organization participants. Leadership in many respects is truly a language game.[22] The organizational direction and organizational values conveyed by leaders can have substantial impact on the perception of problems, the willingness to consider solutions, and the availability of innovation choice opportunities.

Third, the use of specialists and the implementation of appropriate innovation value structures may not plug every important innovation gap. Change in some areas may not be progressing satisfactorily. In this case administrators can act themselves either by initiating solutions or by sponsoring someone else. Mintzberg, for example, reported that top managers typically were involved in 50 improvement projects.[23] For most of these projects someone other than the top manager was supported and encouraged by the top manager to carry the project forward. As the projects were completed and implemented, new projects were undertaken. The point is that managers usually will have to be directly involved in innovation to some extent.

What about innovation in specific nonschool settings? Because the situation with clear goals and unclear technology is similar to the school district one, we will consider it first. As we have already stated, it is necessary that the ruling elites have a positive attitude toward innovation; otherwise managerial effort may be directed toward cost saving rather than toward testing and accepting innovative proposals. Where technology is uncertain, it is a good managerial strategy to hire a professional staff and to delegate responsibility for the technology to them. This certainly is the case in an organization like a hospital, where the goal, quality of care, is relatively certain but the technology is uncertain—it has been said that only 20 percent of medical interventions have highly predictable outcomes.

In the hospital organization the board and the administration hire professional staff—M.D.'s—and delegate to them responsibility for patient care. By and large these professionals are dedicated to their profession and will continue programs of self-education. They will be aware of new developments in the field, especially if the administrator and chief of staff provide financial support and plans for exposure through continuing education programs.

We saw in school organizations that the dominant innovation issue is how to generate new solutions and innovation choice opportunities. Once the choice opportunities are generated, almost any of them can be adopted because of the ambiguity in the system. It is likely that some acceptable goal or some acceptable outcome can be ascribed to the innovation to justify its adoption so long as the professional group supports its adoption. But where goals are clear, and outcomes relatively measurable, proposed solutions must be relevant to the goal in order to justify adoption. When the technology is uncertain, the connection to goals may be difficult. Hence the concomitant issue is not to generate choice opportunities willy-nilly, but to establish mechanisms that will enable tests of the solution, so that the connection to organizational goals can be established. To this end the top administrators will encourage both formal and informal communication. The primary goals and direction of the organization must be clear to organization participants who will be proposing innovations. Perhaps committees for the review of proposals can be established. These committees will evaluate proposals, propose tests for alternatives, and evaluate the outcome of the tests. Their major function will be evaluative, that is, they will evaluate a proposal's contribution to the organizational goal. Even if the outcome of the evaluation is relatively subjective, the evaluation must be attempted and a concensus obtained; otherwise factionalism will develop over the adoption of presumably inferior alternatives to the detriment of the organization. A management by objectives process whereby the objectives and the proposed contributions of the innovation are evaluated before adoption is another alternative.

The necessity for rigorous evaluation of proposals will reduce innovation frequency. This is an unfortunate aspect of certainty. Goal certainty reduces the options available for innovation and requires a more rigorous criterion for adoption. Typically, organizations with certain goals might be expected to adopt fewer innovations than those with uncertain goals.

In organizations having both clear goals and well-understood technologies there will be two dominant issues. First, there will necessarily be a lower rate of innovation than in organizations experiencing ambiguity in goals and process. The problem, then, is to generate solutions where there apparently are no problems, and to do so may mean to attempt to reduce uncertainty in the technology. Clearly, it is necessary to have chief operating executives or managers who perceive that the technology is not as certain as it appears, that it is almost always possible to find better ways of getting something done. This attitude must become general throughout the organization. One formal way to get this attitude transmitted to the lower levels of the organization, and hence to draw upon their potential solutions, is the Scanlon plan.[24] Essentially, this plan encourages suggestions for better ways to do the work and then, following a prearranged formula, distributes a portion of the benefits derived from the suggestion to nearly all personnel in the organization. Whatever method chosen by the manager, the idea must be communicated that technologies can be improved and that proposing changes in the technology can lead to rewards. (The professionals in our school districts had incentives as a function of their commitment to their fields and disciplines, as well as pay and promotion opportunities.)

Most innovations originating with the lowest-level production workers will be related to production problems rather than to organizationwide or environmentally connected problems. Many desired innovations, however, may pertain to several groups within the organization in for-profit manufacturing firms. When technologies are well understood, there will be clear interdependencies among work units. Production cannot innovate separately from marketing in the same way high school teachers could propose innovations in school organizations. The teaching function was often a loosely coupled, autonomous territory.

Organizationwide problems should be addressed by people higher up in the organizations or by participants from several groups. One of the executive's problems is to increase fluidity of participation across rigid territorial or departmental boundaries. The executive could assemble teams focused on particular problems or particular solutions. When the manager is the head of such a team, he is responsible for the proposed solution. He could also rate each team member for search and innovativeness. As innovations are implemented, problem teams can be dissolved. New teams and new team leaders can be assembled as new problems or major new proposed solutions arise.

The reason for the team approach, we repeat, is that many innovations cut across department lines. We do not believe that a team approach is the most important element in creating innovations. We have already discussed how expertise and specialization are responsible for the awareness of solutions and the perceptions of problems. Mixing managers from various departments together is a strategy of collaboration and implementation, similar to what we saw happen with superintendents and teachers when the innovation affected both areas. In a manufacturing organization a team could be made up of a lawyer, a controller, a sales manager, and an engineer—all working on a marketing problem, or a capital budgeting problem, which will eventually affect their areas. Presumably their participation will increase integration and smooth implementation.

The strategy of organizing around innovations or problems with interdepartmental teams will increase communication and cooperation within the organization. Interorganizational communication is also vital. To infuse new ideas into the organization from outside, the organization could establish an exchange program with other organizations in similar activities as well as with those in very different ones. Many excellent ideas originate outside the technology of the organization that eventually adopts it. A manager could get leave to work in one of the cooperating organizations, which would send someone to replace him. Each unit would get the benefit of the visitor's experience, and when the original member returned, he would bring fresh ideas from his contacts in the other organization. Problems of secrecy could inhibit the process, but exchanges would be concerned with solving new problems and learning about new solutions rather than giving secrets.

These various strategies are all designed to present the executive or his immediate subordinates with a large number of innovation choice opportunities. Should they make choices in favor of innovation and reward those who present the organization with the opportunities, they will establish a climate conducive to continued innovation. The long-range task will be similar to the school superintendent's; to approve proposals and to mediate conflicting interests and priorities.

THE IDEA CHAMPION

Throughout this book we have been concerned with the top manager perspective, that is, how leaders can behave and design their organization to increase innovation. Now we turn to the individual organization participant who is aware of a problem or is aware of an innovation that he or she would like to see adopted. This person could be a middle manager, a teacher, a foreman, an engineer, or a salesman—anyone associated with the organization who wants to see a change occur. The person who actually brings about the change is referred to as an idea champion. The following are some tentative ideas that seem to be associated with successful championship.

First, the implementation of innovations requires an investment of effort. Cohen and March described the organizational anarchy as energy poor.[25] Insufficient energy to do all desired tasks is probably true to some extent for most organizations. The successful idea champion will work hard on his or her innovations over an extended period of time. We assume organization members are not naturally resistant to change. We assume most organization members are interested in the success of their department and their organization. But even without deep-seated resistance to change, the innovations will be implemented gradually. People take time to get used to a new idea and to change their behavior from the old to the new. To be successful, idea champions have to spend effort to see the idea through and to bring about necessary role changes.

Cohen and March argued that energy will pay off in other ways as well. By investing energy the idea champion builds up a claim—an equity, so to speak—in the outcome. For organization decision makers to refuse to approve the innovation will be inconsistent with the effort devoted to bringing the change about. Moreover, the champion becomes the local expert on the innovation. He knows about the innovation and has the information relevant to it. As people hear about the idea, they will come to the idea champion for information and advice rather than spending their own energy evaluating the idea. The superior information and the past effort expended by the idea champion can have a significant positive influence on the eventual acceptance of the innovation.

Second, the idea champion must be persistent. The successful idea champion should take the long view and should not be deterred by initial defeats. Bradshaw found that adopting and making functional a small administrative department in a university could easily take a year. Implementating new academic departments could take several years.[26] Implementating operations research and industrial engineering innovations in a major transportation organization typically took over a year as well.[27] Expectations for overnight victory will lead to disillusionment. Most innovations in most organizations take time. Most innovations in most organizations will probably not be welcomed with open arms in the initial stages. Persistence will be required to bring about the required change.

Persistence is also important because organizations change over time. Participants come and go. Initial failures can be turned into victories when reluctant organization participants leave. Organizational problems and opportunities also change, which enables later adoption.

Third, the idea champion should believe in the innovation. This characteristic was observable in the idea champions in universities and in a transportation organization.[28] The commitment to and belief in the value of the innovation appeared to be genuine. The champion seldom displayed any uncertainty about the appropriateness or the benefits from adoption. Idea champions are not necessarily objective in their evaluation of the idea. The successful champion will be convinced of the rightness and legitimacy of his or her approach, and this may be sustained on the basis of faith rather than logic. Belief is a valuable asset, considering the time and the effort required to implement major organizational changes.

Fourth, sponsorship. The successful idea champion will expend his or her energy enlisting the support of influential individuals. Organization members in positions of responsibility and power (either hierarchical or social) can give momentum to innovations by providing support to the idea champion's activity. Appropriate sponsorship will bring about the desired acquiescence of reluctant organization members.

Sponsorship can lead to successful innovation from both sides. Idea champions can seek high-level and influential sponsors for their ideas, and influential managers can bring about change by actively sponsoring projects for lower-level personnel.

Fifth, collaborations may be necessary when the innovation impinges upon individuals in another territory. A university professor who wants to bring about an administrative change will be well advised to collaborate with an administrator in the affected department. Likewise, operations research specialists who want to implement changes in the manufacturing process would be well advised to collaborate with someone in the production department. Involvement of individuals from the affected territory increases understanding and acceptance and smooths the implementation process.

Finally, there will be rewards for success. There is the personal gratification associated with involvement in organizational change and improved performance. In addition, tangible rewards frequently follow. In the case of university departments, the idea champion frequently became the head of the new department.[29] The advancement in careers for idea champions has also been observed in the American military.[30] Rewards might also include the esteem and recognition associated with the new technology. Individuals associated with the successful innovation are able to present themselves as the "hidden hand" behind the innovation.[31] The time and effort devoted to innovation will typically be rewarded if the idea is seen through to successful implementation.

EPILOGUE

We began this book with a brief discussion and three questions about bureaucracy: Are there conditions under which a bureaucracy innovates? Must a bureaucratic mechanism undergo change before innovations can be adopted? If so, how does one change a bureaucracy? Now we would like to close this book with three tentative answers.

The answer to the first question we believe to be yes. And this answer is a long way from where we began this study. At that time we would have agreed with most organization theorists that bureaucracy stifles innovation and change. Now we think innovation adoption is contingent upon the type of innovation and the location of adoption.

Conditions of bureaucracy, which typically include centralization of authority with upper-level administrators, formalized rules and procedures, little participation, and routine technical work, are suited to innovation in the administrative domain. We suspect that bureaucracies can adapt more quickly than non-bureaucracies to changes in goals, policies, structure, control systems, and personnel because top administrators are the internal experts in these matters, and they have the authority to proceed. The bureaucratic form of organization may be ideal for organizations that must be poised to implement administrative rather than technical changes to survive.

Bureaucracy does not appear to induce change within the technical core, however. Technical innovation adoptions appear to correspond to a traditional model of innovation, which emphasizes decentralization of authority (loose coupling), low formalization, and nonroutine work. Hence we do not expect bureaucracies to compare favorably with nonbureaucracies in the adoption of innovations in the technical domain.

The answers to the second and third questions involve contingencies also. Bureaucratic mechanisms need not undergo change so long as a top-down innovation process is required. Most administrative innovations and a few technical innovations can be adopted this way. But nonbureaucratic forms appear to be appropriate for the continuous upward proposal of innovations from within the technical core.

How does one change a bureaucracy to encourage this upward movement of ideas? We don't have the final answer. This chapter has been devoted to suggestions that should help—hiring professional employees, hiring support staff, stressing high aspirations, stressing technological uncertainty, stressing a positive value for innovation, decentralizing, and rewarding idea champions. But bureaucracies exist for a reason, and one should not expect wholesale innovations within them even if strategies to increase innovation are adopted. Perhaps the best that can be hoped for is that bureaucracies can be made to innovate administratively, thus reducing and making more efficient the bureaucratic mechanism. Then perhaps the point will be reached when the bureaucratic mechanism is so reduced that technical innovation becomes feasible.

NOTES

1. Selwyn W. Becker and Duncan Neuhauser, *The Efficient Organization* (New York: Elsevier, 1975).
2. Shirley Terreberry, "The Evolution of Organizational Environments," *Administrative Science Quarterly* 12 (March 1968).
3. Gerald Zaltman, Robert Duncan, and Jonny Holbek, *Innovations and Organizations* (New York: John Wiley & Sons, 1973).
4. John Pincus, "Incentives for Innovation in Public Schools," *Review of Educational Research* 44 (Winter 1974):115.
5. Becker and Neuhauser, *The Efficient Organization*.
6. P. R. Mort and F. G. Cornell, *American Schools in Transition* (New York: Bureau of Publications, Teachers College, Columbia University, 1941).
7. James C. Laflant, "School District Innovativeness and Expectations for the School Board Role" (Paper presented at the American Educational Research Association, New York, N.Y., 16 February 1967).
8. Daniel Griffiths, "Administrative Theory and Change in Organizations," in *Innovation in Education*, ed. Matthew Miles (New York: Bureau of Publications, Teachers College, Columbia University, 1964); and Richard O. Carlson, "Barriers to Change in Public Schools," in *Change Process in Public Schools* (Eugene, Oreg.: University of Oregon Center for Advanced Study of Educational Administration, 1965).
9. Arthur D. Little Inc., *A Model for Innovation Adoption in Public School Districts* (Boston: Arthur D. Little, 1968).
10. Neal Gross, Joseph D. Giacquinda, and Marilyn Bernstein, "Complex Organizations: The Implementation of Major Organizational Innovations" (Paper presented at the American Sociological Association, Boston, August 1968.
11. David Street, Robert Vinter, and Charles Perrow, *Organization for Treatment* (New York: Free Press, 1966).
12. C. E. Bidwell and J. D. Kasarda, "School District Organization and Student Achievement," *American Sociological Review* 40 (February 1975):55–70; S. M. Goodwin, *The Assessment of School Quality* (Albany: New York State Education Department, 1959); and Richard L. Daft and Selwyn W. Becker, "High School District Characteristics and Perceived District Quality," Working paper, University of Chicago, 1976.
13. Henry Mintzberg, *The Nature of Managerial Work* (New York: Harper & Row, 1973).
14. Richard L. Daft and Selwyn W. Becker, "Organization Structure and Environment: A Theory and Longitudinal Test" (Paper presented at the Academy of Management, Kissimee, Fla., 14–17 August 1977).
15. Ronald G. Havelock. *Planning for Innovation* (Ann Arbor, Mich.: University of Michigan Institute for Social Research, 1971), pp. 6–15.
16. Ronald G. Corwin, "Innovation in Organizations: The Case of Schools." *Sociology of Education* 48 (1975):1–37.
17. Patricia J. Bradshaw, "The Process of Organizational Differentiation: A Study of New Departments in Ontario Universities" (Bachelor of Commerce thesis, Queen's University, Kingston, Ont., Canada, 1976).

18. Peter Clark, "Organizational Design: A Review of Key Problems," *Administration and Society* 7 (August 1975):213–56.
19. Pincus, "Incentives for Innovation," p. 115.
20. It is difficult to find an organization that has a clear technology and unclear goals.
21. Peter A. Clark, *Organizational Design: Theory and Practice* (London: Tavistock, 1972).
22. Louis R. Pondy, "Leadership Is a Language Game," in *Leadership: Where Else Can We Go?*, ed. M. McCalland and M. Lombardo (Greensboro, N.C.: Center for Creative Leadership, 1976).
23. Mintzberg, *The Nature of Managerial Work*, p. 159.
24. George Strauss and Leonard R. Sayles, *Personnel: The Human Problems of Management* (Englewood Cliffs, N.J.: Prentice Hall, 1960), pp. 670–74.
25. Michael D. Cohen and James G. March, *Leadership and Ambiguity: The American College President* (New York: McGraw-Hill, 1974).
26. Bradshaw, "The Process of Organizational Differentiation."
27. Richard L. Daft, *Research and Development in Transportation Industry: A Case Study of Canadian National* (Kingston, Ont., Canada: Canadian Institute of Guided Ground Transport, Report No. 75-17, 1975).
28. Bradshaw, "The Process of Organizational Differentiation"; and Daft, *Research and Development in the Transportation Industry*.
29. Bradshaw, "The Process of Organizational Differentiation."
30. M. Janowitz, *The Professional Soldier: A Social and Political Portrait* (New York: Free Press, 1960).
31. Peter Clark, "Organizational Design."

APPENDIX A

SUPERINTENDENT AND SCHOOL BOARD QUESTIONNAIRES

HIGH SCHOOL INNOVATION STUDY
Superintendent Questionnaire

Name _____ School District _____

1. Do you think your school district is more or less innovative than other local high
   school districts? (circle one)

                            More...1
                            Less...2
                            About the same...............................3

   Considering your answer, is that good or bad? (circle one)

                            Good...6
                            Bad..7

   Why? Code for question 1: 0 = prefers less innovation than at present
   _____ 1 = present innovation rate okay
   _____ 2 = prefers more innovation than at present

2. In general, how would you characterize the contribution of <u>educational innovations</u>
   (new courses, teaching methods, programs) to the education of high school students
   in your district? (circle one)

   Innovations nearly always improve the quality of education...................5
   Innovations improve the quality of education most of the time................4
   Innovations quite often improve the quality of education.....................3
   Innovations occasionally improve the quality of education....................2
   Very seldom if ever do innovations actually improve the quality of education.1

3. If there were no financial or organizational obstacles to the adoption of innovations in your high school district, what would be your personal preference for the
   adoption of <u>recently developed</u> innovations? (circle one)

   Probably not adopt any innovations until they are proven elsewhere...........1
   Occasionally adopt first, but usually wait until proven elsewhere............2
   Frequently be one of the first schools to adopt:............................3
   Nearly always be one of the first schools to adopt recent innovations.......4

4. Do you think your school district spends more or less money educating each student
   than other suburban Cook County high school districts? (circle one)

                            More...1
                            Less...2
                            About the same...............................3

   Considering your answer, is that good or bad? (circle one)

                            Good...6
                            Bad..7

   Why? _____
   _____
   _____

5. In terms of educational quality, which of the following best describes your aspirations for your high school district? (circle one)

    Be one of the best schools in the country....................................4
    Be above average in quality...3
    Average quality is sufficient...2
    Somewhat below average would be okay..1

6. Some people consider the amount of money spent per pupil in a school district a good indicator of the quality of education provided to students. How important would you rate the role of money in providing a good education to students? (circle one)

                        Very important..............................1
                        Fairly important............................2
                        Not too important...........................3
                        Not important at all........................4

7. Could a school principal in this district normally make the following changes in his school without approval from the superintendent's office or school board? (put a check mark in the appropriate blank)

	Yes	No
Add a two course sequence in a new foreign language (if teacher available)	6*	___
Make a major curriculum change (e.g., APEX in English or PSSC in physics)	___	___
Let teachers team up in a course to take advantage of each other's expertise	___	___
Utilize volunteer experts as speakers	3	___
	1	___
Change from part-time department heads to full-time division heads or vice versa	___	___
Replace regular classwork for 3 days with mini courses	___	___
Add a new math course (if teacher available)	___	___
Require written course objectives from teachers	2	___
Permit two teachers from different areas to offer an interdisciplinary course	___	___
Adopt an open campus (students come and go as they wish)	4	___
Permit teachers to develop individualized instruction with the use of contracts	___	___
Hire a teacher at mid-year to teach a new course	7	___
Adopt a social science course wherein students work part-time in community social agencies	___	___
Have an open lunch period	5	___
Assign a designated smoking area for students	8	___
Make an agreement with a contractor for students to build a house and sell it	___	___

8. How would you rate the financial well-being of your district over the last 4 years? (circle one)

    We have been severely short of money...1
    We have needed some additional income to meet our needs......................2
    Income has been just adequate..3
    Income has been fully adequate to meet our needs.............................4
    We have had more than enough money coming in.................................5

* Numbers identify items in Guttman scale for decentralization. A yes response to larger numbered items means greater decentralization.

9. Of the innovations that are adopted anywhere in this high school district, where do the proposals originate? Please give your best estimate of the percentage of proposals that originated with each of the following groups (i.e., 10%, 45%, etc.)

_____ % teachers

_____ % superintendent

_____ % principals

_____ % department heads

_____ % other administrative staff

_____ % parents

_____ % consultants

_____ % other

10. Considering innovation proposals over the last 3-4 years, which of the following would you say has the most influence on the final decision of whether to adopt? (circle one)

```
Principals...................................1
Teachers....................................2
Superintendent..............................3
School Board................................4
Department heads............................5
Other administrative staff.................6
```

11. Which has the second most influence on whether to adopt? (circle one)

```
Principals...................................1
Teachers....................................2
Superintendent..............................3
School Board................................4
Department heads............................5
Other administrative staff.................6
```

12. Which has the third most influence on whether to adopt? (circle one)

```
Principals...................................1
Teachers....................................2
Superintendent..............................3
School Board................................4
Department heads............................5
Other administrative staff.................6
```

13. How often are new programs evaluated? (circle one)

```
Nearly all new programs are evaluated........................................1
Most new programs are evaluated..............................................2
About half the new programs are evaluated....................................3
Fewer than half are evaluated................................................4
Only a few if any programs evaluated.........................................5
```

14. When evaluations of new programs are made, how often are the results provided to you? (circle one)

Nearly always...............................1
Most of the time............................2
About half the time.........................3
Less than half the time.....................4
Seldom if ever..............................5

15. Finally, we would like to know something about why innovations get adopted. Sometimes innovations get adopted as a solution to a specific problem, other times it seems that innovations are adopted because people learn of them and they seem to be a good idea. What proportion of the innovations adopted in this district would you say fall into each category?

_____ % innovations result from searching for a solution to a problem

_____ % learned of innovation from other sources and adopted as a better way to do things

16. Your education (circle one):

Bachelor's Degree--B.A., B.S., B.E., etc..1
Master's Degree--M.A., M.S., M.B.A., etc..2
Professional Degree--LL.B., J.D., etc...3
Doctorate--Ph.D., Ed.D., M.D., J.S.D., D.B.A., etc..............................4

17. How many professional educational association meetings do you attend in a year?

_____

HIGH SCHOOL INNOVATION STUDY

School Board Questionnaire

Name _____ School District _____

1. Do you think your school district is more or less innovative than other local high school districts? (circle one)

                    More...1
                    Less...2
                    About the same...............................3

Considering your answer, is that good or bad? (circle one)

                    Good...6
                    Bad..7

Why? ___ Code for question 1: 0 = prefers less innovation than at present ___
_____ 1 = present innovation rate okay _____
_____ 2 = prefers more innovation than at present _____

2. In general, how would you characterize the contribution of <u>educational innovations</u> (new courses, teaching methods, programs) to the education of high school students in your district? (circle one)

      Innovations nearly always improve the quality of education...................5
      Innovations improve the quality of education most of the time................4
      Innovations quite often improve the quality of education.....................3
      Innovations occasionally improve the quality of education....................2
      Very seldom if ever do innovations actually improve the quality of education.1

3. If there were no financial or organizational obstacles to the adoption of innovations in your high school district, what would be your personal preference for the adoption of <u>recently developed</u> innovations? (circle one)

      Probably not adopt any innovations until they are proven elsewhere...........1
      Occasionally adopt first, but usually wait until proven elsewhere............2
      Frequently be one of the first schools to adopt.............................3
      Nearly always be one of the first schools to adopt recent innovations........4

4. Do you think your school district spends more or less money educating each student than other suburban Cook County high school districts? (circle one)

                    More...1
                    Less...2
                    About the same...............................3

Considering your answer, is that good or bad? (circle one)

                    Good...6
                    Bad..7

Why? _____
_____
_____

5. In terms of educational quality, which of the following best describes your aspirations for your high school district? (circle one)

> Be one of the best schools in the country.........................4
> Be above average in quality.......................................3
> Average quality is sufficient.....................................2
> Somewhat below average would be okay..............................1

6. Some people consider the amount of money spent per pupil in a school district a good indicator of the quality of education provided to students. How important would you rate the role of money in providing a good education to students? (circle one)

> Very important........................1
> Fairly important......................2
> Not too important.....................3
> Not important at all..................4

7. How would you rate the financial well-being of your district over the last 4 years? (circle one)

> We have been severely short of money..............................1
> We have needed some additional income to meet our needs...........2
> Income has been just adequate.....................................3
> Income has been fully adequate to meet our needs..................4
> We have had more than enough money coming in......................5

8. Which of the following best describes your educational attainment? (circle one)

> High school...1
> Attended college for one year or more but didn't graduate.........2
> Bachelor's Degree--B.A., B.S., B.E., B.Phar., etc.................3
> Master's Degree--M.A., M.S., M.B.A., etc..........................4
> Professional Degree--LL.B., J.D., etc.............................5
> Doctorate--Ph.D., Ed.D., M.D., J.S.D., D.B.A., etc................6

9. What kind of work do you do (e.g., college teacher, wheat farmer, clothing buyer for department store). If housewife please give husband's occupation. _____

_____

_____

_____

10. Which of the following best describes your employer? (circle any that apply)

> I am self-employed, or in business owned by my family.............a
> Private company with 100 or more employees........................b
> Private company with fewer than 100 employees.....................c
> Professional partnership..d
> Research organization or institute................................e
> College or University or Junior College...........................f

cont'd on next page

```
Elementary or Secondary School or School System.............................g
Hospital or Clinic...........................................................h
Church, Welfare, or other non-profit organization............................i
Federal Government (U.S.)....................................................j
State or Local Government....................................................k
Other (specify) _____ l
```

11. How many professional educational association meetings (e.g., IASB meetings) do you attend in a year? _____

APPENDIX B

MASTER INNOVATION CHECKLISTS

THE UNIVERSITY OF CHICAGO

DATE

To   High School Districts   DEPARTMENT

FROM Richard Daft   DEPARTMENT The Graduate School of Business

IN RE: Study of High School Innovation

Attached is a master list of new courses and programs reported to me by the schools in the study. To complete the study we need the information contained in the five columns to the right of the innovation list.

Column 1: If a listed innovation has been seriously considered for adoption anywhere in your district, please indicate as nearly as possible the calendar year it was first considered in this column. We need to know if and when the innovation was considered even if it was never adopted.

Column 2: For those innovations that have been adopted anywhere in your district, please write the year of adoption here.

Column 3: If the innovation was adopted and then dropped, indicated the year dropped in this column.

Columns 4 & 5: Who brought the idea into the school district and who approved its adoption should go in these columns. Ascertaining who originated the idea in the school will probably be difficult for some innovations, so when you don't know the originator, leave column 4 blank. You may use the following codes for columns 4 & 5:

        T = teaching staff (teachers, aids, parttime dept. heads)
        P = principal or his non-teaching staff
        S = superintendent or his assistants and staff
       ST = students
        B = school board
        C = consultants or other outsiders
        O = other

Innovations Checklist

(** New in 1968-72 period)

	year first considered-if ever-even if never adopted	year, if adopted	year, if dropped	w/whom originated	who approved
Curriculum	1	2	3	4	5
Mathematics:					
Computer programming					
**Transformational geometry					
Slide rule					
Advanced seminar (topic reflects student interest)					
Science:					
**Harvard project physics					
Zoology					
VD education					
Geology					
Genetics					
Horticulture					
**Physics sequence for non-college bound					
Chemistry sequence for non-college bound					
**Oceanography					
**Environment					
**Organic chemistry					
**Microbiology					
After-school projects					
Physics & chemistry					
**Science by topic					
Science seminar (topic reflects student interest)					
English; Speech:					
**APEX or modification (wide variety of short courses replace traditional required English courses)					
**Black literature					
Great books					
Film study					
Mass media					
Broadcasting					
Mime					
Advanced reading skills					
Capsule English (overview of English for top college-bound seniors)					
Social Studies:					
**Social Science practicum (students work in social agencies w/o pay)					
Black studies program (integrate black contributions into regular courses)					
**Philosophy program (Carnegie)					
Introduction to teaching					
**Black history					
Mexican-American history					
Political science					
**International relations					
Law					
Economics					
Anthropology					
Urban studies					
**Community affairs					
Social science seminar (topic reflects student interest)					

Innovations Checklist

(** New in 1968-72 period)

	year first considered-if ever-even if never adopted 1	year, if adopted 2	year, if dropped 3	w/whom originated 4	who approved 5

Curriculum

Music; Art; Theatre:
- Theatre workshop
- Jazz bands
- **Use photography in design
- Contemporary materials in sculpture
- Art history
- Advanced photography
- Media (sculpture, ceramics, painting)
- **Black drama
- Music literature
- Music drama workshops
- Vocal techniques
- Contemporary music

Business; Industrial Arts; Home Economics; P.E.:
- **Elective courses in Phys. Ed.
- Marketing
- Retailing
- Work experience
- Welding
- Power mechanics
- **Power mechanics for girls
- **Build house & sell it
- Printing
- **Turf management
- Practical architecture (survey setting, design home, help build it)
- **Cosmotology
- Family foods
- Experimental foods
- Personal & social development
- Clothing
- Clothing for teens
- **Home economics seminars
- Child care
- Home economics for boys (co-ed or bachelor living)

Interdisciplinary:
- History-literature
- Humanities program
- Psychology & children's literature

Teaching Methods

Individualized instruction:
- student can contract for a course
  - --to be taken in addition to regular load
  - --to break a course conflict
  - --to take a course not normally offered

Regular offerings on individualized basis in following subjects (continuous progress performance-based curriculum):
- Reading
- English
- Foreign language

Innovations Checklist

(**New in 1968-72 period)

Teaching Methods

	year first considered-if ever-even if never adopted	year, if adopted	year, if dropped	w/whom originated	who approved
	1	2	3	4	5

Teaching Methods

    Mathematics

    Science

    Social studies

    Vocational

    Music

    Other _____

High school students tutor elementary students

Top high school students give tutorial assistance to slower high school students

Use teaching (instructional) assistants

Laboratory approach (games, calculators, etc.) in math at lower levels

** Utilize computer in math

Cooperative (team) teaching for expertise:

    English

    Foreign languages

    Mathematics

    Science

    Social studies

    Vocational

    Music--art

    Other _____

** Mini or short courses

** Suspend classes for 2-3 days & replace w/diverse mini courses

For disadvantaged or problem students:

    Cooperative work agreement (to get students interested)

    Program to identify potential failures among the incoming freshman & give special attention

    Special instruction for students w/poor basic skills

    **Separate facilities for pregnant girls

    **Separate facilities for problem students

    Program for expelled students (correspondence, etc.)

    Afternoon or evening classes for problem students

    **Group meetings/counseling of parents of problem students

    Teacher training in behavior modification

Student Resources

Community resource program (utilize community facilities in education for students)

Resource centers:

    Reading/communication

    English

    Foreign languages

    Mathematics

Innovations Checklist

Student Resources

	year first considered-if ever-even if never adopted	year, if adopted	year, if dropped	w/whom originated	who approved
	1	2	3	4	5

Science

Social studies

Music--art

Other _____

Students may audit courses

Non-credit courses

** Volunteer talent pool (utilize volunteer experts to speak, tutor, assist in schools)

Paid speakers in subject matter areas

** Dial access retreival system

Cooperative teacher education program (w/teacher training institutions--in-service & college credit for staff, and participate in student-teacher training)

Driver education simulators

Off-road driving range

Mobile trailers for drivers ed. simulators

Fulltime psychologist
        speech therapist
        social worker
        college consultant
        vocational consultant
        reading specialist
        learning disabilities teacher

Extend school year:
  ** Tuition free summer school
     High school credit courses at night
     Late afternoon & night courses available to day students

School nursery for study of pre-school children

Staff utilization (teachers paid to assist students with non-credit projects on evenings & weekends)

Paid teacher summer workshops for curriculum improvement

Other Educational

Open campus concepts:
  ** Open lunch
  ** Unassigned time within school
  ** Students may enter or leave campus as they wish

**Pass/fail option

**Senior option program (in lieu of 4th major seniors may do part-time work, independent study, community service, or study in another institution)

Credit for foreign students in native language (they go to advanced course)

Innovations Checklist

(**New in 1968-72 period)

	year first considered-if ever-even if never adopted 1	year, if adopted 2	year, if dropped 3	w/whom originated 4	who approved 5

Other Educational

Basic education for adults (residents can take whatever courses they want or need)

Students may test out of courses

Early graduation program

Manpower development training program for community residents

Program to humanize education (in-service training, rap sessions, emphasis on black-white relations & other interpersonal issues)

Program to personalize education (emphasis on positive teacher-pupil relationships)

Organizational

Management by objectives:
    for administrators
    for teachers

Staggered salary review

Management reorganization

Full-time division heads

K-12 curriculum coordinator

Program budgeting (PPBS)

Flexible or variable scheduling

Block scheduling

Modular scheduling

** Self-scheduling (student selects section & time)

** Designated student smoking area

Professional for union negotiations

Computer system of parent notification of absences

Program of total racial integration

Student & parent involvement:
    ** Students appointed to sit at school board meetings
    Students advise on curriculum proposals
    Students on disciplinary appeals board
    Student representatives elected by ward
    No grades restriction on student govnmt. participation
    Parents advise on curriculum & policy proposals
    Parents participate in task forces

Written performance objectives for courses

Innovations Checklist

(**New in 1959-64 period)

Code #	Curriculum	Have you ever adopted this?	If so, when?	Still in use?
	Science:			
111	**B.S.C.S.			
112	**C.B.A.			
113	**Chem study			
114	**P.S.S.C.			
115	**E.S.C.S.			
116	Electronics			
117	Electricity			
118	Mental Health			
	Mathematics:			
121	**S.M.S.G.			
122	**U.I.C.S.M.			
123	**Integration of plane and solid geometry			
124	**Probability & statistics			
125	**Industrial math			
	Languages:			
131	**Russian			
132	**Chinese			
133	**Japanese			
134	**Greek			
135	**Italian			
136	**English for foreign students			
137	**Introduction to modern languages (for freshmen)			
138	Four-year sequence in some foreign languages			
	Social Studies and History:			
141	Non-western civilization			
142	**Contemporary thought			
143	**Cultural history of the Western world			
144	**Russian history			
145	**Contributions of the Negro			
146	**Summer seminar on problems of the inner city			
147	**Political Science			
	Music, Theater and Art:			
151	Fine arts appreciation			
152	Art heritage or history			
153	Music history and appreciation			
154	Technical theater			
155	**Performing arts workshop			
156	Radio announcing			
157	**TV production			

(**New in 1959-64 period)

Code #	Curriculum	Have you ever adopted this?	If so, when?	Still in use?
	Business and Industrial Arts:			
161	**Data processing--punch card			
	--computer			
163	**Notehand			
164	Engineering industrial arts			
165	Pre-technical industrial arts			
166	Home design			
	Special Courses:			
171	Driver education			
172	Physical fitness			
173	Geography of Africa and Asia			

Teaching Methods

Code #				
211	Radio station			
212	Closed-circuit TV			
213	**Open-circuit TV			
214	Overhead or automatic-slide projectors			
215	Team teaching--English			
216	--social studies & history			
217	** --science			
218	**Programmed instruction			
219	Language lab			
220	Office practices lab			
221	Driver training lab			
222	**Audio-lingual approach to language instruction			
223	**Lay readers in English			
224	Listening facilities for library and reading lab			
225	**Film production by students			
226	Art libraries in all buildings			
227	Foreign exchange student teachers in languages			
228	Teacher-pupil feedback			
229	Class size limitations			
230	Classroom library in world history (vs. single text)			
231	Item analysis of tests			
232	Operation of Nursery school			
233	**Separate social science library			
234	English rental library			
235	School orchestra			

(**New in 1959-64 period)

Code #	Class Composition	Have you ever adopted this?	If so, when?	Still in use?
311	Multiple tracks--English			
312	--social studies & history			
313	--science			
314	--math			
315	--languages			
316	Advanced seminars--English			
317	--social studies & history			
318	** --science			
319	--math			
320	--languages			
321	** --art			
322	Advanced placement courses for college-bound			
323	Advanced placement for entering 8th grade			
324	Honors courses			
325	Individual Research projects			
326	EMH program--speech therapy			
327	--occupational training			
328	--instructions for homebound			
329	--instruction for hard of hearing			
330	--developmental reading			
331	--basic curriculum			
332	**Demonstration center for gifted children			
333	Science and social studies fairs			

Counseling

Code #				
411	College counseling			
412	Vocational counseling			
413	Distributive occupations			
414	Diversified occupations			
415	Psychologist on staff			
416	School social workers			
417	Appointment of a director of testing and research			
418	Group guidance			
419	Study of drop-out characteristics			
420	Entrance tests			
421	Follow-up study of graduates			
422	Reduced student/counselor ratio			
423	Honorariums for guest speakers on careers			
424	Discipline committee			
425	**Night adjustment school for drop-outs and problem students			

Innovations Checklist

Code #	Government	Have you ever adopted this?	If so, when?	Still in use?
511	NDEA--Title III			
512	--Title V			
513	--Title VIII			
514	Vocational rehabilitation (in co-operation with War on Poverty)			

Organizational

Staff Positions:

Code #				
611	Assistant superintendent			
612	Assistant to the superintendent			
613	Assistant principal			
614	Business manager			
615	Curriculum coordinator			
616	Director of Research			
617	Chairman of buidance & counseling department			
618	Audio-visual coordinator			
619	Director of Secretarial staff			
620	Nurse in each school			
621	Departmental clerks			
622	Class counselors			
623	Negro teachers on staff			

Salary and Benefit Plans:

631	Revised salary schedule to reward better teachers			
632	Extra pay for extra-curricular activities			
633	Medical insurance			
634	Sabbatical leave			

Teacher Training:

641	In-service training			
642	Summer workshops for curriculum improvement			
643	Teacher discussion groups during academic year			
644	Subsidized education for M.S. and Ph.D. degrees			
645	Participation in Master of Arts in teaching program			

Computer Applications:

651	Records, reports, payroll, etc.			
652	Class scheduling			
653	Test scoring			

Innovations Checklist

Code #	Organizational	Have you ever adopted this?	If so, when?	Still in use?
	Design of Facilities			
661	School-within-a-school			
662	Windowless school			
663	Separate buildings for freshmen/ sophomores and juniors/seniors (the two-two plan)			
664	Inner court design			
665	Movable partitions for flexible classrooms			
666	Center for instructional materials			
667	Intra-school phone system			
	Use of Consultants:			
671	Planning school expansion			
672	Evaluating innovations			
673	Evaluating performance of various departments			
674	Evaluating business operations			
675	Citizens Consulting Committee			
676	Physical plant safety survey			
	Community Educational Needs:			
681	Adult evening school			
682	Summer school			
683	Junior college			
684	Articulation of curriculum with elementary schools			
685	Double shifts			
686	Creation of scholarship fund for college-bound			
	Role Definition:			
691	Written policies of Board of Education			
692	Job description for administrative personnel			

APPENDIX C

RATING SCALES AND AVERAGE SCORES FOR INNOVATION

BENEFIT, COST AND CHANGE

Attached is a list of educational programs, courses, and
innovations which have been adopted in many schools over
the past several years.

Please rate each innovation on the five-point scale according
to whether college-bound or terminal students would tend to
utilize and benefit from its adoption. Advanced language
courses, for instance, would probably be most utilized by
college-bound students, while vocational courses would be
most utilized by terminal students. Other innovations, such
as team teaching in required English courses or organizational
changes may benefit all students equally.

We are asking your subjective evaluation for these ratings. It
is not necessary that you have first-hand experience with each
innovation. Just give your best estimate. In the event you
have absolutely no knowledge of a particular program and feel
you can't rate it, you may leave that line blank.

Please look over the entire list of programs before you start
in order to get a feel for the kinds of innovations involved.
Those innovations which tend to benefit only terminal students
should have the number "1" circled in the far left column. Those
that tend to benefit only college-bound students should have the
number "5" circled in the far right column. Other innovations
would be rated in between.

Teaching Techniques:	Tend to benefit only terminal students (Actual score)	Mostly benefit terminal students	Benefit terminal & college bound about equally	Mostly benefit college bound	Tend to benefit only college bound
Utilize computer in math	1 (3.88)	2	3	4	5
Mini or short courses	1 (3.11)	2	3	4	5
Suspend classes for 2-3 days and substitute diverse mini courses	1 (3.11)	2	3	4	5
For use in a course offering:					
Open-circuit TV	1 (2.78)	2	3	4	5
Closed-circuit TV	1 (3.00)	2	3	4	5
Team or cooperative teaching	1 (3.22)	2	3	4	5
Programmed instruction	1 (3.33)	2	3	4	5
Multiple tracks	1 (3.11)	2	3	4	5
Individualized progress	1 (2.89)	2	3	4	5
Let student contract to take a course on his own	1 (3.63)	2	3	4	5
Set up a resource center	1 (3.33)	2	3	4	5
Lay readers in English	1 (3.00)	2	3	4	5
Demonstration center for gifted children	1 (4.22)	2	3	4	5
Student tutors	1 (2.00)	2	3	4	5
Drivers ed simulators	1 (3.00)	2	3	4	5
Program to identify potential failures and give special attention	1 (2.11)	2	3	4	5
Dial access retrieval systems	1 (3.38)	2	3	4	5
Group meetings/counseling of parents of problem students	1 (2.44)	2	3	4	5
Separate facilities for problem students	1 (2.25)	2	3	4	5
Program for expelled students	1 (2.14)	2	3	4	5
Separate afternoon or evening classes for problem students	1 (2.22)	2	3	4	5
Language laboratory	1 (3.78)	2	3	4	5
Item analysis of tests	1 (3.00)	2	3	4	5
Volunteer talent pool (volunteer experts speak, tutor, or assist in schools	1 (3.00)	2	3	4	5

Coursework additions and curriculum changes:

	Tend to benefit only terminal students (Actual score)	Mostly benefit terminal students	Benefit terminal & college bound about equally	Mostly benefit college bound	Tend to benefit only college bound
Computer programming	1 (3.33)	2	3	4	5
Punch card data processing	1 (2.67)	2	3	4	5
Film production by students	1 (3.22)	2	3	4	5
TV production by students	1 (3.22)	2	3	4	5
Notehand	1 (4.00)	2	3	4	5
Theatre workshop	1 (3.33)	2	3	4	5
Transformational geometry	1 (4.50)	2	3	4	5
Cosmotology	1 (1.50)	2	3	4	5
Welding	1 (1.50)	2	3	4	5
Child Care	1 (2.33)	2	3	4	5
Home Ec for boys	1 (2.78)	2	3	4	5
Horticulture	1 (2.50)	2	3	4	5
Turf management	1 (2.13)	2	3	4	5
Power mechanics	1 (1.63)	2	3	4	5
Power mechanics for girls	1 (2.38)	2	3	4	5
Film study	1 (3.22)	2	3	4	5
Oceanography	1 (3.50)	2	3	4	5
Printing	1 (1.75)	2	3	4	5

	Tend to benefit only terminal students	Mostly benefit terminal students	Benefit terminal & college bound about equally	Mostly benefit college bound	Tend to benefit only college bound
Environment	1 (3.00)	2	3	4	5
Black History	1 (3.33)	2	3	4	5
Black Drama	1 (3.44)	2	3	4	5
Social Science practicum (students work in social agencies w/o pay)	1 (3.13)	2	3	4	5
Use photography in design (art)	1 (3.00)	2	3	4	5
Advanced photography	1 (3.38)	2	3	4	5
Integration of plane and solid geometry	1 (4.00)	2	3	4	5
Probability and statistics	1 (4.11)	2	3	4	5
Industrial math	1 (2.22)	2	3	4	5
English for foreign students	1 (2.88)	2	3	4	5
Introduction to foreign languages	1 (3.67)	2	3	4	5
Contemporary thought	1 (3.44)	2	3	4	5
Russian history	1 (3.89)	2	3	4	5
Cultural history of western world	1 (3.56)	2	3	4	5
Political science	1 (3.33)	2	3	4	5
Urban problems	1 (3.22)	2	3	4	5
Advanced seminar in a discipline	1 (4.22)	2	3	4	5
APEX (Appropriate Placement for excellence--Jr.-Sr. electives from broad range of English courses)	1 (3.89)	2	3	4	5
PSSC (Physical sciences study committee course)	1 (4.56)	2	3	4	5
BSCS (Biological sciences course)	1 (4.00)	2	3	4	5
CBA (Chem-bond approach in chemistry)	1 (4.22)	2	3	4	5
Chem study	1 (4.11)	2	3	4	5
ESCS (Earth sciences course)	1 (3.11)	2	3	4	5
Modern math: UICSM (U of Ill Committee on Secondary Math)	1 (3.75)	2	3	4	5
SMSG (School math study group)	1 (4.00)	2	3	4	5
Philosophy program (Carnegie)	1 (4.14)	2	3	4	5
Physics sequence for noncollegebound	1 (2.25)	2	3	4	5
Harvard project physics	1 (4.11)	2	3	4	5
Elective courses in Phys. Ed.	1 (3.00)	2	3	4	5
Foreign language not before offered	1 (4.22)	2	3	4	5

Organizational:

Management by objectives for administrators	1 (3.22)	2	3	4	5
PPBS (Program planning budgeting system)	1 (3.11)	2	3	4	5
Designated student smoking areas	1 (2.57)	2	3	4	5
Students appointed to sit with school board	1 (3.63)	2	3	4	5
Self-scheduling (students select section and time)	1 (2.63)	2	3	4	5
Modular scheduling	1 (3.00)	2	3	4	5
Block scheduling	1 (2.86)	2	3	4	5
Flexible scheduling	1 (3.00)	2	3	4	5
Management reorganization	1 (3.00)	2	3	4	5
Personnel: Director of Research	1 (3.00)	2	3	4	5
Professional for union negotiations	1 (3.00)	2	3	4	5
K-12 curriculum coordinator	1 (3.00)	2	3	4	5

	Tend to benefit only terminal students	Mostly benefit terminal students	Benefit terminal & college bound about equally	Mostly benefit college bound	Tend to benefit only college bound
High school credit courses at night	1 (2.67)	2	3	4	5
Paid teacher summer workshops	1 (2.67)	2	3	4	5
Written performance objectives for courses	1 (3.22)	2	3	4	5
Students advise on curriculum proposals	1 (3.00)	2	3	4	5
Tuition free summer school	1 (2.89)	2	3	4	5
Computer application to:					
Records, reports, payroll, etc.	1 (3.00)	2	3	4	5
Class scheduling	1 (3.00)	2	3	4	5
Test scoring	1 (3.00)	2	3	4	5
Staggered salary review	1 (3.00)	2	3	4	5

Other:

Fulltime psychologist	1 (2.67)	2	3	4	5
Fulltime learning disabilities teacher	1 (1.78)	2	3	4	5
Pass/fail option	1 (2.89)	2	3	4	5
Manpower development training program for community residents	1 (2.00)	2	3	4	5
Senior option program (seniors may do parttime work independent study or community service in lieu of 4th major)	1 (3.22)	2	3	4	5
Program to humanize education (in service training, rap session, emphasis on black-white relations and other interpersonal issues)	1 (3.00)	2	3	4	5
Open campus:					
Open lunch	1 (3.00)	2	3	4	5
Unassigned time within school	1 (3.00)	2	3	4	5
Students may enter or leave campus as they wish	1 (3.11)	2	3	4	5
Community resource program (increase use of community resources in educational process)	1 (3.00)	2	3	4	5

Attached is a list of educational programs, courses, and innovations which have been adopted in many schools over the past several years.

Please rate the innovations on the five-point scale according to their relative cost. Cost means the investment of dollars in salaries, books, and equipment that could have been used elsewhere had the program not been adopted.

Sometimes the cost of a new program or innovation will depend on particular circumstances, such as whether an additional teacher has to be hired, the availability of government funding, or how widely the program is used. In those cases rate the innovation according to the most probable dollar cost that would be incurred by your district for its initial adoption.

We are asking your subjective evaluation for these ratings. It is not necessary that you have first-hand experience with each program. Just give your best estimate. In the event you have absolutely no knowledge of a particular program and feel you can't rate it, you may leave that line blank.

Please look over the entire list of programs before you start in order to get a feel for the kinds of innovations involved. Those innovations which would involve almost no dollar cost should have the number "1" circled in the far left column. Those innovations that are very expensive should have the number "5" circled in the far right column. Other innovations should be rated in between.

Teaching Techniques:	Almost no financial cost to adopt		Some cost	Moderate Cost	Consider-able cost	Very ex-pensive to adopt
	(Actual score)					
Utilize computer in math	1	(4.44)	2	3	4	5
Mini or short courses	1	(1.70)	2	3	4	5
Suspend classes for 2-3 days and substitute diverse mini courses	1	(1.80)	2	3	4	5
For use in a course offering:						
Open-circuit TV	1	(3.38)	2	3	4	5
Closed-circuit TV	1	(4.33)	2	3	4	5
Team or cooperative teaching	1	(2.33)	2	3	4	5
Programmed instruction	1	(3.00)	2	3	4	5
Multiple tracks	1	(2.80)	2	3	4	5
Individualized progress	1	(3.33)	2	3	4	5
Let student contract to take a course on his own	1	(1.30)	2	3	4	5
Set up a resource center	1	(4.10)	2	3	4	5
Lay readers in English	1	(3.40)	2	3	4	5
Demonstration center for gifted children	1	(3.89)	2	3	4	5
Student tutors	1	(1.67)	2	3	4	5
Drivers ed simulators	1	(3.75)	2	3	4	5
Program to identify potential failures and give special attention	1	(2.90)	2	3	4	5
Dial access retrieval systems	1	(5.00)	2	3	4	5
Group meetings/counseling of parents of problem students	1	(2.60)	2	3	4	5
Separate facilities for problem students	1	(4.20)	2	3	4	5
Program for expelled students	1	(3.70)	2	3	4	5
Separate afternoon or evening classes for problem students	1	(3.80)	2	3	4	5
Language laboratory	1	(4.11)	2	3	4	5
Item analysis of tests	1	(2.56)	2	3	4	5
Volunteer talent pool (volunteer experts speak, tutor, or assist in schools	1	(1.40)	2	3	4	5

Coursework additions and curriculum changes:

Computer programming	1	(4.00)	2	3	4	5
Punch card data processing	1	(3.67)	2	3	4	5
Film production by students	1	(3.70)	2	3	4	5
TV production by students	1	(4.20)	2	3	4	5
Notehand	1	(1.60)	2	3	4	5
Theatre workshop	1	(2.10)	2	3	4	5
Transformational geometry	1	(1.70)	2	3	4	5
Cosmotology	1	(2.88)	2	3	4	5
Welding	1	(3.33)	2	3	4	5
Child Care	1	(2.80)	2	3	4	5
Home Ec for boys	1	(2.00)	2	3	4	5
Horticulture	1	(3.00)	2	3	4	5
Turf management	1	(3.13)	2	3	4	5
Power mechanics	1	(3.67)	2	3	4	5
Power mechanics for girls	1	(3.25)	2	3	4	5
Film study	1	(2.80)	2	3	4	5
Oceanography	1	(3.00)	2	3	4	5
Printing	1	(4.33)	2	3	4	5

	Almost no financial cost to adopt	Some cost	Moderate Cost	Considerable cost	Very expensive to adopt
Environment	1 (2.00)	2	3	4	5
Black History	1 (1.80)	2	3	4	5
Black Drama	1 (1.90)	2	3	4	5
Social Science practicum (students work in social agencies w/o pay)	1 (2.00)	2	3	4	5
Use photography in design (art)	1 (3.00)	2	3	4	5
Advanced photography	1 (3.38)	2	3	4	5
Integration of plane and solid geometry	1 (1.22)	2	3	4	5
Probability and statistics	1 (1.44)	2	3	4	5
Industrial math	1 (1.44)	2	3	4	5
English for foreign students	1 (2.44)	2	3	4	5
Introduction to foreign languages	1 (1.44)	2	3	4	5
Contemporary thought	1 (1.40)	2	3	4	5
Russian history	1 (1.75)	2	3	4	5
Cultural history of western world	1 (1.40)	2	3	4	5
Political science	1 (1.50)	2	3	4	5
Urban problems	1 (1.70)	2	3	4	5
Advanced seminar in a discipline	1 (2.22)	2	3	4	5
APEX (Appropriate Placement for excellence--Jr.-Sr. electives from broad range of English courses)	1 (2.60)	2	3	4	5
PSSC (Physical sciences study committee course)	1 (2.10)	2	3	4	5
BSCS (Biological sciences course)	1 (2.11)	2	3	4	5
CBA (Chem-bond approach in chemistry)	1 (2.10)	2	3	4	5
Chem study	1 (2.10)	2	3	4	5
ESCS (Earth sciences course)	1 (2.00)	2	3	4	5
Modern math: UICSM (U of Ill Committee on Secondary Math)	1 (2.22)	2	3	4	5
SMSG (School math study group)	1 (2.50)	2	3	4	5
Philosophy program (Carnegie)	1 (1.83)	2	3	4	5
Physics sequence for noncollegebound	1 (2.13)	2	3	4	5
Harvard project physics	1 (2.38)	2	3	4	5
Elective courses in Phys. Ed.	1 (2.10)	2	3	4	5
Foreign language not before offered	1 (2.67)	2	3	4	5

Organizational:

	Almost no financial cost to adopt	Some cost	Moderate Cost	Considerable cost	Very expensive to adopt
Management by objectives for administrators	1 (2.20)	2	3	4	5
PPBS (Program planning budgeting system)	1 (3.25)	2	3	4	5
Designated student smoking areas	1 (2.13)	2	3	4	5
Students appointed to sit with school board	1 (1.00)	2	3	4	5
Self-scheduling (students select section and time)	1 (2.11)	2	3	4	5
Modular scheduling	1 (3.67)	2	3	4	5
Block scheduling	1 (2.43)	2	3	4	5
Flexible scheduling	1 (3.22)	2	3	4	5
Management reorganization	1 (3.43)	2	3	4	5
Personnel: Director of Research	1 (4.11)	2	3	4	5
Professional for union negotiations	1 (3.50)	2	3	4	5
K-12 curriculum coordinator	1 (3.57)	2	3	4	5

	Almost no financial cost to adopt	Some cost	Moderate Cost	Considerable cost	Very expensive to adopt
High school credit courses at night	1 (2.70)	2	3	4	5
Paid teacher summer workshops	1 (3.10)	2	3	4	5
Written performance objectives for courses	1 (2.75)	2	3	4	5
Students advise on curriculum proposals	1 (1.20)	2	3	4	5
Tuition free summer school	1 (3.00)	2	3	4	5
Computer application to:					
Records, reports, payroll, etc.	1 (4.00)	2	3	4	5
Class scheduling	1 (4.00)	2	3	4	5
Test scoring	1 (3.67)	2	3	4	5
Staggered salary review	1 (2.00)	2	3	4	5

Other:

	Almost no financial cost to adopt	Some cost	Moderate Cost	Considerable cost	Very expensive to adopt
Fulltime psychologist	1 (4.00)	2	3	4	5
Fulltime learning disabilities teacher	1 (3.78)	2	3	4	5
Pass/fail option	1 (1.00)	2	3	4	5
Manpower development training program for community residents	1 (3.40)	2	3	4	5
Senior option program (seniors may do parttime work independent study or community service in lieu of 4th major)	1 (1.40)	2	3	4	5
Program to humanize education (in service training, rap session, emphasis on black-white relations and other interpersonal issues)	1 (2.60)	2	3	4	5
Open campus:					
Open lunch	1 (1.40)	2	3	4	5
Unassigned time within school	1 (1.60)	2	3	4	5
Students may enter or leave campus as they wish	1 (1.78)	2	3	4	5
Community resource program (increase use of community resources in educational process)	1 (1.78)	2	3	4	5

Attached is a list of educational programs, courses, and innovations
which have been adopted in many schools over the past several years.

Please rate each innovation on the five-point scale according to its
radicalness. <u>Radicalness</u> refers to the amount of change which has to
take place in the school as a result of adopting a new program. It
would probably be best to think of the number of people or jobs which
are affected by the change. For instance, adopting a new English
curriculum may involve reorientation for many teachers and students.
This would be more radical than the adoption of one additional English
course which may affect only one teacher and a few students. Usually,
the more radical the innovation, the more difficult and time-consuming
it is to get implemented.

Sometimes the radicalness of an innovation will depend on specific
conditions, such as how widely used it is. In those cases you may
rate the innovation according to the most likely way it would be
adopted in your district.

We are asking for your subjective evaluation for these ratings. It
is not necessary that you have first-hand experience with each
innovation. Just give your best estimate. In the event you have
absolutely no knowledge of a particular innovation and feel you can't
rate it, you may leave that line blank.

Please look over the entire list of innovations before you start in
order to get a feel for the kinds of innovations involved. Those
innovations which require little change in the school's way of doing
things, i.e., few people or positions affected, should have the number
"1" circled in the far left column. Those innovations which would
have widespread impact should have the number "5" circled in the far
right column. Other innovations should be rated in between.

Teaching Techniques:	Adoption requires little change. Very few people affected (Actual score)	Some change	Moderate change	Consid-erable change	Adoption requires a great deal of change. Many people affected
Utilize computer in math	1 (2.11)	2	3	4	5
Mini or short courses	1 (3.33)	2	3	4	5
Suspend classes for 2-3 days and substitute diverse mini courses	1 (4.11)	2	3	4	5
For use in a course offering:					
Open-circuit TV	1 (2.89)	2	3	4	5
Closed-circuit TV	1 (2.56)	2	3	4	5
Team or cooperative teaching	1 (3.11)	2	3	4	5
Programmed instruction	1 (3.11)	2	3	4	5
Multiple tracks	1 (4.00)	2	3	4	5
Individualized progress	1 (4.00)	2	3	4	5
Let student contract to take a course on his own	1 (2.78)	2	3	4	5
Set up a resource center	1 (3.50)	2	3	4	5
Lay readers in English	1 (2.25)	2	3	4	5
Demonstration center for gifted children	1 (2.71)	2	3	4	5
Student tutors	1 (2.00)	2	3	4	5
Drivers ed simulators	1 (2.22)	2	3	4	5
Program to identify potential failures and give special attention	1 (2.78)	2	3	4	5
Dial access retrieval systems	1 (3.67)	2	3	4	5
Group meetings/counseling of parents of problem students	1 (2.22)	2	3	4	5
Separate facilities for problem students	1 (3.44)	2	3	4	5
Program for expelled students	1 (3.00)	2	3	4	5
Separate afternoon or evening classes for problem students	1 (3.00)	2	3	4	5
Language laboratory	1 (2.44)	2	3	4	5
Item analysis of tests	1 (2.22)	2	3	4	5
Volunteer talent pool (volunteer experts speak, tutor, or assist in schools	1 (2.11)	2	3	4	5

Coursework additions and curriculum changes:

Computer programming	1 (2.33)	2	3	4	5
Punch card data processing	1 (1.89)	2	3	4	5
Film production by students	1 (2.67)	2	3	4	5
TV production by students	1 (2.22)	2	3	4	5
Notehand	1 (1.44)	2	3	4	5
Theatre workshop	1 (1.33)	2	3	4	5
Transformational geometry	1 (1.75)	2	3	4	5
Cosmotology	1 (2.00)	2	3	4	5
Welding	1 (1.56)	2	3	4	5
Child Care	1 (1.67)	2	3	4	5
Home Ec for boys	1 (1.78)	2	3	4	5
Horticulture	1 (1.89)	2	3	4	5
Turf management	1 (2.00)	2	3	4	5
Power mechanics	1 (2.11)	2	3	4	5
Power mechanics for girls	1 (2.33)	2	3	4	5
Film study	1 (1.56)	2	3	4	5
Oceanography	1 (1.38)	2	3	4	5
Printing	1 (2.22)	2	3	4	5

	Adoption requires little change. Very few people affected	Some change	Moderate change	Considerable change	Adoption requires a great deal of change. Many people affected
Environment	1 (1.78)	2	3	4	5
Black History	1 (1.56)	2	3	4	5
Black Drama	1 (1.56)	2	3	4	5
Social Science practicum (students work in social agencies w/o pay)	1 (3.00)	2	3	4	5
Use photography in design (art)	1 (2.00)	2	3	4	5
Advanced photography	1 (2.00)	2	3	4	5
Integration of plane and solid geometry	1 (2.11)	2	3	4	5
Probability and statistics	1 (1.56)	2	3	4	5
Industrial math	1 (2.13)	2	3	4	5
English for foreign students	1 (1.67)	2	3	4	5
Introduction to foreign languages	1 (1.33)	2	3	4	5
Contemporary thought	1 (1.33)	2	3	4	5
Russian history	1 (1.44)	2	3	4	5
Cultural history of western world	1 (1.33)	2	3	4	5
Political science	1 (1.33)	2	3	4	5
Urban problems	1 (1.44)	2	3	4	5
Advanced seminar in a discipline	1 (2.11)	2	3	4	5
APEX (Appropriate Placement for excellence--Jr.-Sr. electives from broad range of English courses)	1 (2.33)	2	3	4	5
PSSC (Physical sciences study committee course)	1 (2.11)	2	3	4	5
BSCS (Biological sciences course)	1 (1.89)	2	3	4	5
CBA (Chem-bond approach in chemistry)	1 (2.00)	2	3	4	5
Chem study	1 (2.00)	2	3	4	5
ESCS (Earth sciences course)	1 (1.89)	2	3	4	5
Modern math:					
UICSM (U of Ill Committee on Secondary Math)	1 (2.33)	2	3	4	5
SMSG (School math study group)	1 (1.75)	2	3	4	5
Philosophy program (Carnegie)	1 (2.00)	2	3	4	5
Physics sequence for noncollegebound	1 (2.13)	2	3	4	5
Harvard project physics	1 (1.89)	2	3	4	5
Elective courses in Phys. Ed.	1 (2.89)	2	3	4	5
Foreign language not before offered	1 (2.44)	2	3	4	5

Organizational:

	Adoption requires little change. Very few people affected	Some change	Moderate change	Considerable change	Adoption requires a great deal of change. Many people affected
Management by objectives for administrators	1 (3.56)	2	3	4	5
PPBS (Program planning budgeting system)	1 (4.56)	2	3	4	5
Designated student smoking areas	1 (3.67)	2	3	4	5
Students appointed to sit with school board	1 (3.33)	2	3	4	5
Self-scheduling (students select section and time)	1 (4.00)	2	3	4	5
Modular scheduling	1 (4.44)	2	3	4	5
Block scheduling	1 (3.89)	2	3	4	3
Flexible scheduling	1 (4.00)	2	3	4	5
Management reorganization	1 (4.00)	2	3	4	5
Personnel:					
Director of Research	1 (2.11)	2	3	4	5
Professional for union negotiations	1 (2.25)	2	3	4	5
K-12 curriculum coordinator	1 (2.63)	2	3	4	5

	Adoption requires little change. Very few people affected	Some change	Moderate change	Consid-erable change	Adoption requires a great deal of change. Many people affected
High school credit courses at night	1 (2.22) 2		3	4	5
Paid teacher summer workshops	1 (1.89) 2		3	4	5
Written performance objectives for courses	1 (2.89) 2		3	4	5
Students advise on curriculum proposals	1 (2.44) 2		3	4	5
Tuition free summer school	1 (2.67) 2		3	4	5
Computer application to:					
Records, reports, payroll, etc.	1 (2.22) 2		3	4	5
Class scheduling	1 (3.00) 2		3	4	5
Test scoring	1 (1.89) 2		3	4	5
Staggered salary review	1 (3.43) 2		3	4	5

Other:

	Little change	Some change	Moderate change	Consid-erable change	Great deal of change
Fulltime psychologist	1 (1.78) 2		3	4	5
Fulltime learning disabilities teacher	1 (1.56) 2		3	4	5
Pass/fail option	1 (3.11) 2		3	4	5
Manpower development training program for community residents	1 (2.43) 2		3	4	5
Senior option program (seniors may do parttime work independent study or community service in lieu of 4th major)	1 (2.75) 2		3	4	5
Program to humanize education (in service training, rap session, emphasis on black-white relations and other interpersonal issues)	1 (2.89) 2		3	4	5
Open campus:					
Open lunch	1 (3.33) 2		3	4	5
Unassigned time within school	1 (3.56) 2		3	4	5
Students may enter or leave campus as they wish	1 (4.44) 2		3	4	5
Community resource program (increase use of community resources in educational process)	1 (3.44) 2		3	4	5

APPENDIX D

MEANS, STANDARD DEVIATIONS AND

CORRELATION MATRICES

Variable Name	Number of Variable
Innovativeness, College Preparatory	01
Innovativeness, Terminal Education	02
Community Educational Level	03
Elite Attitude toward Innovation	04
Decentralization of Decision-Making	05
Certified Staff Ratio	06
Annual Growth Rate During Period	07
Teacher Professionalism	08
Total Educational Expenditures per Pupil .	09
Administrative Ratio	10
Percentage Vocational Teachers	11
Elite Quality Goals for District	12
Elite Perceived Slack Resources	13
Organizational Complexity	14
Organization Size	15
Number Vocational Teachers	16
Slack Resources	17
Teacher Free Time	18
Travel Expenditures per Teacher	19

TABLE 14

MEANS AND STANDARD DEVIATIONS

Variable	1968-72		1959-64	
	Mean	Std. Dev.	Mean	Std. Dev.
01	6.69	3.35	12.00	4.83
02	4.77	3.11	..	..
03	.67	.13	.55	.14
04	1.81	.18	1.69	.20
05	4.23	1.74	..	..
06	.090	.032	.081	.053
07	.034	.030	.10	.058
08	.56	.13	.59	.14
09	1369.00	281.00	745.00	130.00
10	.033	.011	.050	.024
11	.153	.044	.103	.050
12	3.80	.25	..	..
13	3.05	1.15	..	..
14	15.43	2.29	..	..
15	6076.00	2975.00	3322.00	1049.00
16	48.31	21.21	19.00	7.86
17	.307	.075	.25	.18
18	.34	.16	..	..
19	56.41	21.74	..	..

TABLE 15

MATRIX OF CORRELATIONS, 1968-72 PERIOD
(N = 13)

	01	02	03	04	05	06	07	08	09	10	11	12	13	14	15	16	17	18
01																		
02	.26																	
03	.62	.04																
04	.47	-.10	-.07															
05	.11	.33	-.19	-.32														
06	.54	.14	.16	.05	.15													
07	-.15	.64	.02	-.38	.33	-.39												
08	.65	-.31	.75	.09	-.07	.46	-.57											
09	.55	-.33	.57	.09	-.21	.64	-.68	.89										
10	-.13	.43	-.18	.08	-.33	.01	.29	-.46	-.21									
11	-.73	.08	-.74	-.30	.29	-.50	.42	-.84	-.78	.28								
12	.67	-.30	.28	.54	-.07	.52	-.65	.70	.71	-.35	-.66							
13	.07	-.05	.39	.08	-.13	-.26	-.13	.36	.20	-.04	-.29	.10						
14	.24	.27	.08	-.18	.31	.65	-.16	.29	.29	-.31	-.36	.18	.01					
15	.41	.54	.28	.13	.33	-.01	.36	.07	-.14	-.06	-.09	.03	.28	.40				
16	.07	.54	-.06	.01	.36	-.16	.45	-.28	-.40	-.12	.32	-.19	.16	.26	.90			
17	-.18	-.05	.42	-.50	-.28	-.07	-.02	.24	.11	-.01	-.10	-.29	.31	.08	-.13	-.14		
18	.23	-.28	.46	.33	-.57	-.07	-.32	.45	.41	-.17	-.72	.30	.38	-.11	-.27	-.57	.05	
19	-.30	-.12	-.15	.03	-.31	-.08	-.42	.02	.01	.21	.12	-.16	.42	.02	-.18	-.06	.60	-.02

TABLE 16

MATRIX OF CORRELATIONS, 1959-64 PERIOD
(N = 13)

	01	03	04	06	07	08	09	10	11[a]	15	17
01											
03	.77										
04	.60	.47									
06	.37	.19	.25								
07	-.26	.04	-.15	-.46							
08	.63	.37	.54	.44	-.67						
09	.72	.54	.43	.33	-.59	.75					
10	-.48	-.16	-.37	.14	.11	-.19	-.08				
11	-.74	-.79	-.20	-.06	-.25	-.22	-.41	.19			
15	.28	.06	.27	.19	-.10	.46	.51	-.07	-.32		
17	.05	.31	-.20	-.26	.61	-.46	.32	-.10	-.31	-.53	

Bibliography

Aiken, Michael, and Hage, Jerald. "The Organic Organization and Innovation", *Sociology 5 (1971)*.

———. *Social Change in Complex Organizations*. New York: Random House, 1970.

American Management Association. *Managing Advancing Technology*. Vol. 1 *Strategies and Tactics of Product Innovation*, edited by Staff of *Innovation* Magazine. New York: Amer. Management Assoc., 1972.

Argyris, Chris. *Organization and Innovation*. Homewood, Ill.: Irwin-Dorsey, 1965.

———. *The Applicability of Organizational Sociology*. Cambridge: Cambridge University Press, 1972.

Baldridge, J. Victor, and Burnham, Robert A. "Organizational Innovation: Individual, Organizational and Environmental Impacts", *Administrative Science Quarterly* 20 (June 1975).

Becker, Selwyn W., and Neuhauser, Duncan. *The Efficient Organization*. New York: Elsevier, 1975.

Becker, Selwyn W., and Stafford, Frank. "Some Determinants of Organizational Success", *Journal of Business* 40 (October 1967).

Becker, Selwyn W., and Whisler, Thomas L. "The Innovative Organization: A Selective View of Current Theory and Research," *Journal of Business* 40 (October 1967).

Bennis, W. *Changing Organizations*. New York: McGraw-Hill, 1966.

Bidwell, C.E., and J.D. Kasarda. "School District Organization and Student Achievement," *American Sociological Review* 40 (1975).

Blau, Peter M. *The Organization of Academic Work*. New York: Wiley, 1973.

Bradshaw, Patricia J. "The Process of Organizational Differentiation: A Study of New Departments in Ontario Universities." Bachelor of Commerce thesis, Queen's University, 1976.

Bredo, Anneke E., and Bredo, Eric R. "Effects of Environment and Structure on the Process of Innovation," in *Managing Change in Educational Or-*

ganizations, edited by J. V. Baldredge and T. E. Deal, Berekely, Calif.: McCutchan, 1975.

Campbell, Donald T., and Stanley, Julian C. *Experimental and Quasi-Experimental Designs for Research*. Chicago: Rand-McNally, 1963.

Carlson, Richard O. "Barriers to Change in Public Schools," in *Change Processes in Public Schools*. Eugene, Ore.: The Center for Advanced Study of Educational Administration, University of Oregon, 1965.

Carter, C.F., and Williams, B.R. *Industry and Technical Progress: Factors Governing the Speed of Application of Science*, London: Oxford University Press, 1957.

Child, John. "Organizational Structure, Environment and Performance: The Role of Strategic Choice," *Sociology* 6 (1972).

Christie, Samuel F., and Scribner, Jay D. "A Social System Analysis of Innovation in 16 School Districts." Paper presented at the Annual Meeting of the American Educational Research Association, Los Angeles, California, February, 1959.

Clark, Peter. "Organizational Design: A Review of Key Problems," *Administration and Society* 7 (August 1975).

————. *Organizational Design: Theory and Practice*. London: Tavistock. 1972.

Cohen, Michael D., and March, James G. *Leadership and Ambiguity: The American College President*. New York: McGraw-Hill, 1974.

Cohen, Michael D., March, James G., and Olsen, Johan P. "A Garbage Can Model of Organizational Choice," *Administrative Science Quarterly* 17 (March 1972).

Corwin, Ronald G. "Innovation in Organizations: The Case of Schools," *Sociology of Education* 48 (Winter 1975.

————. "Strategies for Organizational Innovation: An Empirical Comparison," *American Sociological Review* 37 (August 1972).

Cyert, Richard M., and March, James G. *A Behavioral Theory of the Firm*. Englewood Cliffs, N.J.: Prentice-Hall, 1963.

————. Dill, W.R., and March, J.G. "The Role of Expectations in Business Decision Making," *Administrative Science Quarterly* 3 (December 1958).

Daft, Richard L. "The Process of Organizational Innovation: An Empirical Study of Thirteen High School Districts." Ph.D. dissertation, University of Chicago, 1974.

————. "Research and Development in the Transportation Industry: A Case Study of Canadian National." Kingston, Ontario: Canadian Institute of Guided Ground Transport, Report No. 75-17, 1975.

————, and Becker, Selwyn W. "Organization Structure and Environment: A Theory and Longitudinal Test." Paper presented at the Academy of Management Meetings, Kissimmee, Florida, August 14–17, 1977.

————, and Becker, Selwyn W. "High School District Characteristics and Perceived District Quality." Working paper, University of Chicago, 1976.

————, and Bradshaw, Patricia J. "University Innovation: The Institutionalization of New Departments." Working paper, Queen's University, Kingston, Ontario, 1976.

Dalton, G.W. *The Distribution of Authority in Formal Organizations*. Boston: Harvard University Division of Research, 1968.

Davis, James A. *Elementary Survey Analysis*. Englewood Cliffs, N.J.: Prentice-Hall, 1971.

Einhorn, Hillel J. "Alchemy in the Behavioral Sciences," *The Public Opinion Quarterly* 36 (Fall 1972).

————, and Hogarth, Robin M. "Unit Weighting Schemes for Decision Making," *Organizational Behavior and Human Performance* 13 (1975).

Evan, William M. "Organizational Lag," *Human Organization*, 25 (Spring 1966).

————, and Black, Guy. "Innovation in Business Organizations: Some Factors Associated with Success or Failure of Staff Proposals," *Journal of Business* 40 (October 1967).

Fliegel, Frederick C., and Kivlan, Joseph E. "Attributes of Innovation as Factors in Diffusion," *American Journal of Sociology* 72 (1966).

Goodman, S.M. *The Assessment of School Quality*. Albany, New York: New York State Education Department, 1959.

Gordon, Gerald, Morse, Edward V., Gordon, S.M., de Kervasdone, J., Kimberly, J., Moch, Michael, and Schwartz, D.G. "Organizational Structure and Hospital Adaptation to Environmental Demands." Paper presented at University of North Carolina Health Services Research Center Symposium on Innovation in Health Care Organizations, Chapel Hill, N.C., May 18–19, 1972.

Griffiths, Daniel. "Administrative Theory and Change in Organizations," in *Innovation of Education*, edited by Matthew Miles. New York: Bureau of Publications, Teachers College, Columbia University, 1964.

Gross, Neal, Giacquinta, Joseph B., and Berstein, Marilyn. "Complex Organizations: The Implementation of Major Organizational Innovations." Paper presented at the annual meeting of the American Sociological Association, Boston, August 1968.

————, ————, ————. *Implementing Organizational Innovations: A Sociological Analysis of Planned Educational Change*. New York: Basic Books, 1971.

Grossman, Joel B. "The Supreme Court and Social Change," *American Behavioral Scientist*, 13 (1970).

Guetzkow, Harold. "The Creative Person in Organizations," *The Creative Organization*, edited by Gary A. Steiner. Chicago: The University of Chicago Press, 1965.

Hage, Jerald. "An Axiomatic Theory of Organizations," *Administrative Science Quarterly* 10 (December 1965).

————, and Aitken, Michael. "Program Change and Organizational Properties," *American Journal of Sociology* 72 (March 1967).

————, and Dewar, Robert. "Elite Values Versus Organizational Structure in Predicting Innovation," *Administrative Science Quarterly* 18 (September 1973).

Hall, Richard H. "Intraorganizational Structure Variations," *Administrative Science Quarterly* 7 (December 1962).

Hamberg, D. "Invention in the Industrial Research Laboratory," *Journal of Political Economy* 71 (April 1963).

Harvey, Edward, and Mills, Russell. "Patterns of Organizational Adaptation: A Political Perspective," in *Power in Organizations*, edited by Mayer N. Zald. Nashville, Tenn.: Vanderbilt University Press, 1970.

Havelock, Ronald G. *Planning for Innovation*. Ann Arbor: Institute for Social Research, University of Michigan, 1971.

Hayami, Y. "Elements of Induced Innovation," in *Explorations in Economic History* 8 (Summer 1971).

Heise, David R. "Causal Inference from Panel Data," in *Sociological Methodology 1970*, edited by Edgar F. Borgatta and George W. Bohrnstedt, San Francisco: Jossey-Bass, 1970.

Homans, George C. *The Nature of Social Science*. New York: Harcourt, Brace & World, 1967.

Hughes, Larry W. "A Study of Administrative Arrangements in Different Types of School Districts." Microfilm: Ohio State University, 1965.

Janowitz, M. *The Professional Soldier: A Social and Political Portrait*. New York: The Free Press, 1960.

Johnson, Homer M., and Marcum, R. Lavern. "Organizational Climate and the Adoption of Educational Innovations." Paper presented at the American Educational Research Association, Los Angeles, California, February 1969.

Kaluzny, Arnold D., Veney, James E., and Gentry, John T. "Innovation of Health Services: A Comparative Study of Hospitals and Health Departments," Paper presented at the University of North Carolina Health Services Research Symposium on Innovation in Health Care Organizations, Chapel Hill, N.C., May 18–19, 1972.

Katz, Daniel, and Kahn, Robert. *The Social Psychology of Organizations*. New York: John Wiley and Sons, 1966.

Knight, Kenneth E. "A Descriptive Model of the Intra-Firm Innovation Process," *Journal of Business* 40 (October 1967).

Laflant, James C. "School District Innovativeness and Expectations for the School Board Role." Paper presented to the American Educational Research Association, New York, February 1967.

Lawrence, Paul R. "How to Deal with Resistance to Change," *Harvard Business Review* 32 (May-June 1954).

————, and Lorsch, Jay W. *Organization and Environment*. Homewood, Ill.: Irwin, 1969.

Little, Arthur D., Inc. *A Model for Innovation Adoption in Public School Districts*. Cambridge, Mass., 1968.

Lorsch, Jay W., and Lawrence, Paul R. "Organizing for Product Innovation," Organizational Structure and Design, eds. Dalton, Gene W., Lawrence, Paul R. and Lorsch, Jay W., Homewood, Illinois: Irwin-Dorsey, 1970.

MacDonald, V.N., McLeod, G., and Nininger, J.R. *Organizational Change in Municipal Government*. Manuscript in progress, Queen's University, 1977.

Mansfield, Edwin. "Technical Change and the Rate of Innovation," *Econometrics*, 29 (October 1961).

———. "Size of Firm, Market Structure and Innovation," *Econometrics*, 29 (October 1961).

———. "Size of Firm, Market Structure and Innovation," *Journal of Political Economy* 41 (December 1973).

———. et al *Research and Innovation in the Modern Corporation*. New York: Norton and Co., 1971.

March, James G., and Simon, Herbert A., *Organizations*. New York: John Wiley and Sons, 1958.

Maslow, A.H. "A Holistic Approach to Creativity," *Climate for Creativity*, edited by Calvin Taylor. New York: Pergamon Press, 1972.

Miller, Roger. *Innovation, Organization and Environment*. Sherbrooke: Institut de Recherche et de Perfectionnement en Administration, Université de Sherbrooke, 1971.

Mintzberg, Henry. *The Nature of Managerial Work*. New York: Harper and Row, 1973.

Mohr, Lawrence. "Determinants of Innovation in Organizations," *American Political Science Review* 63 (March 1969).

Mort, Paul R. *Principles of School Administration*. New York: McGraw-Hill, 1946.

———, and Cornell, F.G. *American Schools in Transition*, New York: Bureau of Publications, Teachers College, Columbia University, 1941.

Mueller, W.F. "The Origins of the Basic Inventions Underlying Dupont's Major Product and Process Innovations, 1920–1950," in *The Rate and Direction of the Inventive Activity: Economic and Social Factors*, edited by R. Nelson, Princeton: Princeton University Press, 1962.

Myers, Sumner, and Marquis, Donald G. *Successful Industrial Innovations*. Washington: National Science Foundation, NSF 69-17 1969.

Mytinger, Robert E. "Innovation in Local Health Services." Washington, D.C.: Government Printing Office, Public Health Service Publication, 1968.

Nie, Norman H., Bent, Dale H., and Hull, Hadlai D. *SPSS: Statistical Package for the Social Sciences*. New York: McGraw-Hill, 1970.

Normann, R. "Organizational Innovativeness: Product Variation and Reorientation," *Administrative Science Quarterly*, 16 (June 1971).

Paulson, Steven K. "Causal Analysis of Interorganizational Relations: An Axiomatic Theory Revised," *Administrative Science Quarterly* 19 (September 1974).

Peck, M. "Inventions in the Post-War American Aluminum Industry," in *The Rate and Direction of Inventive Activity: Economic and Social Factors*, edited by R. Nelson. Princeton: Princeton University Press, 1962.

Pelz, Donald C., and Lew, Robert A. "Heise's Causal Model Applied," in Borgatta and Borhnstedt, *Sociological Methodology 1970*.

Peterson, Robert A., Rudeluis, William, and Wood, Glenn, L. "The Spread of Marketing Innovations in a Service Industy," *Journal of Business* 45 (1972).

Pierce, T.M. *Controllable Community Characteristics Related to the Quality of Education*. New York: Bureau of Publications, Teachers College, Columbia University, 1947.

Pincus, John. "Incentives for Innovation in the Public Schools." *Review of Educational Research* 44 (Winter 1974).

Pondy, Louis R. "Leadership is a Language Game," in *Leadership: Where Else Can We Go?*, edited by M. McCall and M. Lombardo, Greensboro, N.C.: Centre for Creative Leadership, 1976.

Preising, Paul P. "The Relationship of Staff Tenure and Administrative Succession to Structural Innovation." Paper presented at the Annual Meeting of the American Research Association, Los Angeles, California, February 1969.

Rogers, E.M. *Diffusion of Innovations*. New York: The Free Press, 1962.

————. "What Are Innovators Like?" in *Change Processes in Public Schools*. Eugene, Ore: The Center for Advanced Study of Educational Administration, University of Oregon, 1965.

Rosenberg, Morris. *The Logic of Survey Analysis*. New York: Basic Books, 1968.

Rosner, Martin M. "Administrative Controls and Innovation," *Behavioral Science* 12 (January 1968).

Ross, Donald H. *Administration For Adaptability*. New York: Metropolitan School Study Council, 1958.

Sapolsky, Harvey M. "Organizational Structure and Innovation," *Journal of Business* 41 (October 1967).

Science Policy Research Unit, University of Sussex. "Success and Failure in Industrial Innovation," Report on Project SAPPHO. London: Centre for the Study of Industrial Innovation, 1972.

Shephard, Herbert A. "Innovation-Resisting and Innovation-Producing Organizations," *Journal of Business* 40 (October 1967).

Strauss, George, and Sayles, Leonard R. *Personnel: The Human Problems of Management*. Englewood Cliffs, N.J.: Prentice-Hall, Inc., 1960.

Street, David, Vinter, Robert, and Perrow, Charles. *Organization for Treatment*. New York: The Free Press, 1966.

Terreberry, Shirley. "The Evolution of Organizational Environments," *Administrative Science Quarterly* 12 (March 1968).

Thompson, James D. *Organizations in Action*. New York: McGraw-Hill, 1967.

Thompson, Victor. "Bureaucracy and Innovation," *Administrative Science Quarterly* 10 (1965).

Utterback, James M. "The Process of Technological Innovation Within the Firm," *Academy of Management Journal* 14 (March 1971).

Walton, G.M. "Obstacles to Technical Diffusion in Ocean Shipping," in *Explorations in Economic History*, 8 No. 4. Summer 1971.

Watson, Goodwin. "Resistance to Change," in *Processes and Phenomena of Social Change*, edited by G. Zaltman, New York: Wiley Interscience, 1973.

Weber, Max. "The Essentials of Bureaucratic Organization: An Ideal-Type

Construction," in *Reader in Bureaucracy*, eds. Robert K. Merton, Alisa P. Gray, Barbara Hockey, Hanan C. Selvin. Glencoe, Ill.: Free Press, 1952.

Weick, Karl E. "Educational Organizations as Loosely Coupled Systems," *Administrative Science Quarterly*, 21 (March 1976).

Wilson, James Q. "Innovations in Organizations: Notes Toward a Theory," *Approaches to Organizational Design*, ed. James D. Thompson, Pittsburgh: University of Pittsburgh Press, 1966.

Zald, Mayer N., and Denton, Patricia. "From Evangelism to General Service: The Transformation of the YMCA," *Administrative Science Quarterly* 7 (September 1963).

———, ed. *Power in Organizations*. Nashville, Tenn.: Vanderbilt University Press, 1970.

Zaltman, Gerald, Duncan, Robert, and Holbeck, Johnny. *Innovations and Organizations*. New York: John Wiley and Sons, 1973.

———. *Processes and Phenomena of Social Change*. New York: Wiley Interscience Publishers, Inc., 1973.

Index

(Bold print indicates reference to a chart or table)

Principal. *See also* Administration; as buffer, 189; as innovation source, 102–103

Problem(s), identifying, 194

Problem-solving, 167; organizing for, 12; professionalism and frequency of innovations, correlation with, **116–117**

Problem teams, 208

Production, innovations for, 208

Professionalism (teachers'), 53, 135ff; administrative innovations and, 146, 172, 203; administrator(s)' role in upgrading, 190–191; awareness of problems and, 174; change over study period, 74, 79; collegebound innovations and, 58, 62–63, 80, 109, 118; defined, 32; educational innovations and, 105–106, 172; as enabler variable, 15, 144; impact on differentiation of decisions, 159; innovation, 20, 100, 102, 109–119, 172, 174; model district, 195–196; as motivation for change, 193–194; technical innovations and, 146; terminalbound innovations and, 89, 91, 95, **110**; training for, 191; upgrading of, 190ff

Profit organizations, 204; growth and, 23

Program, planning, and budgeting system (PPBS), as innovation, 130

Proposal(s): development of, 52ff; evaluation, 207

Proposal committees, 207

Radicalness, of proposals, 124–125

Radicalness continuum, innovation type and, 125

Rand Corporation, 152

Rational behavior, in organization, 9–10; defined, 18; as strategy for problem-solving, 127–136

Research: analysis procedure, 47; change during study, 74–75; cross-validation, for collegebound innovations, 70ff; hypotheses of, 17–24; innovation index, 42–46; longitudinal design, advantages of, 27ff; organization theory, implications for, 120ff; regression analysis for collegebound students, 54–61, 66–70; regression analysis for terminalbound students, 87–93; sample, 29–30; time span, 30; variables, 30ff

Resistance to change, 136, 145–149; from community, 190; idea champion and, 211; from organizational differentiation, 157ff; organizational goals, source of, 148–149; from teachers, 105

Resources. *See* Slack resources

Revenues. *See* Slack resources

Rewards, 198, 205ff; proposing innovations and, 12

Risk: of early innovation adoption, 14; organizational size and, 14, 15

Routine, innovation and, 149–152

Salaries: increase of for support staff, 154ff; increase of for professional teachers, 154

Scanlon plan. 207–208

Scheduling: innovation in, 98–99; modular concept of, 125

Schools. *See also* High schools; change during study, 73; elementary, 131; primary, 148; summer, 192

Search behavior, 11–12, 168

Simon, Herbert A., 6, 9, 131, 133

Slack resources (of schools), 21–22, 153–154; collegebound innovations and, 56, 60–61, 67, 82; defined, 21, 32; elite's perception of, 22; innovation process and, 175; lobbying for, 191–192; for personnel recruitment, 175; professionalism and, 154–155; terminalbound innovations, 91, 94

Solutions. *See* Innovation ideas

Specialists. *See* Coordinators

Specialization: coordinators and, 157; resistance to change and, 140; significance of, 137; as stimulus for alternatives, 204–205

Sponsorship, enlisting, 211

Sputnik era, education in, 42

Stability, desire for, 9

State Superintendent's Office, 31–32

Steel industry, 7–8, 152

Street, David, 188

Structural variables. *See also* Differentiation; Size; high risk innovations and, 15

Student(s): as innovation source, 102–103; involvement in education, 125

Superintendent(s), 29. *See also* Elite; attitude toward innovation, 24, 81, 89, 94, 200; awareness of innovation sources, 114–115; as change agent, 186; community standards for education and, 18; and innovation, 102–103, 185ff; goal(s), 86, 94, 187ff;